**The Essential
Arnold Lazarus**

PERLEY

The Whurr Counselling and Psychotherapy Series seeks to publish selected works of foremost experts in the field of counselling and psychotherapy. Each volume features the best of a key figure's work, bringing together papers that have been published widely in the professional literature. In this way the work of leading counsellors and psychotherapists is made accessible in single volumes.

Windy Dryden
Series Editor

Titles in the Counselling and Psychotherapy Series

Person-centred Counselling: Therapeutic and Spiritual Dimensions
Brian Thorne

Reason and Therapeutic Change
Windy Dryden

The Essential Arnold Lazarus
Edited by Windy Dryden

Breakthroughs and Integrations: Collected Papers in Psychology and Psychotherapy
John Rowan

From Medicine to Psychotherapy
Mark Aveline

Preface

Arnold Lazarus's contributions to psychotherapy have been immense. He has been at the forefront of developments in both behaviour therapy and cognitive-behaviour therapy and has pioneered a technically eclectic approach to clinical practice based on a thorough multimodal assessment of client problems.

Born in South Africa in 1932, Arnold Lazarus went to work in the United States of America in the early 1960s where he has remained ever since. He is Distinguished Professor at Rutgers - The State University of New Jersey, a position he has held since 1972.

Throughout his career, Lazarus has made an active contribution to professional psychology. He has been elected President of several professional associations, has served on the editorial boards of 20 scientific journals, has been a consultant to numerous agencies, both public and private, and has Fellowship status in several professional societies. He has received many honours for his contributions, most notably the 'Distinguished Service Award' from the American Board of Professional Psychology and the 'Distinguished Career Achievement Award' from the American Board of Medical Psychotherapists. He was also inducted into the National Academies of Practice in Psychology. He is listed in *Who's Who in America* as well as in *Who's Who in the World*. His 12 books and more than 150 journal articles and book chapters have led him to give invited addresses throughout the world. Several opinion polls have cited Arnold Lazarus as one of the most influential psychotherapists of the twentieth century.

It was a very difficult task for me to select 20 articles that represent the essence of Arnold Lazarus's work, such is the man's genius for combining quantity with quality of output. In making my choice (which has the full support of Lazarus himself), my main goal was to show the development of Lazarus's thought over the full period of his career to date, as a contributor to the professional literature. However, I also wanted to include as many clinical vignettes as possible showing Arnold Lazarus in action as a therapist because he is generally recognised as an innovative and talented clinician. Consequently, the articles I have selected (which I briefly introduce) reveal Lazarus both as an advocate of flexible and personalistic psychological treatments and as a master practitioner. In short, the selections reflect the 'Essential Arnold Lazarus'.

At present, Arnold Lazarus's main professional interests centre on multimodal marriage therapy, and on the limits of eclecticism and integration in psychotherapy.

Windy Dryden
April 1991

Contents

Preface   v

Chapter 1

A psychological approach to alcoholism (1956)   1

Chapter 2

New methods in psychotherapy (1958)   8

Chapter 3

Group therapy of phobic disorders by systematic
desensitization (1961)   17

Chapter 4

The use of 'emotive imagery' in the treatment of
children's phobias (1962)   30

Chapter 5

Behavior therapy, incomplete treatment and symptom
substitution (1965)   36

Chapter 6

Behavior rehearsal vs non-directive therapy vs advice
in effecting behavior change (1966)   44

Chapter 7

In support of technical eclecticism (1967)   50

Chapter 8

Learning theory and the treatment of depression (1968)   53

Chapter 9

Multimodal behavior therapy: Treating the 'BASIC ID' (1973)   62

Chapter 10

Desensitization and cognitive restructuring (1974)   73

Chapter 11   .

Has behavior therapy outlived its usefulness? (1977)   83

Chapter 12

Toward delineating some causes of change in
  psychotherapy (1980)   89

Chapter 13

Resistance or rationalization? (1982)   98

Chapter 14

The specificity factor in psychotherapy (1984)   114

Chapter 15

The multimodal approach with adult outpatients (1987)   120

Chapter 16

A multimodal perspective on problems of sexual
desire (1988)   159

Chapter 17

Why I am an eclectic (not an integrationist) (1989)   181

Chapter 18

The case of George (1989)   193

Chapter 19

Emotions: A multimodal therapy perspective (1990)   205

Chapter 20

Can psychotherapists transcend the shackles
of their training and superstitions? (1990)   218

Books by Arnold Lazarus   228

Author index   229

Subject index   233

Chapter 1
A Psychological Approach
to Alcoholism (1956)

Lazarus's first professional publication clearly shows the broad-based thinking that later exemplified his scientific and clinical outlook. He pointed to 'contradictory concepts' and the 'fragmentary nature of theory' as they pertain to the field of alcoholism. Subsequently, Lazarus found out that these shortcomings are by no means restricted to the study of substance abuse. As a result, he has often stressed the need to subscribe only to those theories that are capable of being verified or disproved, and he has consistently called for a wide-ranging therapeutic armamentarium. In 1956 he concluded that the rehabilitation of alcoholism seems to require a *synthesis* that would include active treatment strategies, educative procedures, socioeconomic interventions, and many adjunctive measures such as vitamin supplements and the use of medication. Thus, even as a graduate student, Arnold Lazarus emphasised what he later called a 'broad-spectrum' orientation, which then evolved into his 'multimodal' position. He addressed the subject of alcoholism again 9 years later ('Towards the understanding and effective treatment of alcoholism', *South African Medical Journal*, 1965, **39**, 736–741) in which he clearly delineated the need to (1) attend to the patient's physical problems, (2) employ active methods to break compulsive habits, (3) examine the interaction between the patient and his or her social network, (4) apply a wide range of psychotherapeutic strategies and techniques, and (5) where relevant, to elicit cooperation from the patient's spouse. In later writings, as will become apparent, the significance of 'treatment breadth' became a focal issue that was embellished and applied to many problem areas.

Enlightened medical and psychological knowledge has done little to lessen the prejudice and discrimination directed against the alcoholic. In South Africa, only the skilled and trained personnel who work in the field are familiar with the 'disease factor' in alcoholism and its implications; there is still an urgent need for enlightenment of the public. Even among pro-

This chapter was first published in 1956 as a summary of a thesis in partial fulfilment of a BA Hons degree in Psychology, University of the Witwatersrand, South Africa. It is reproduced, with the permission of the Medical Association of South Africa, from Lazarus, A.A. (1956). A psychological approach to alcoholism. *South African Medical Journal*, **30**, 707–710.

fessional groups prejudices still exist. In the southern Transvaal, for instance, the majority of hospital boards do not admit alcoholics as such for treatment. 'Hospitals', they say, 'are designed for sick people and not for drunkards.' Consequently, where medical supervision is indicated the alcoholic is usually hospitalized for 'acute anxiety' or a 'liver complaint'. Alcoholism is still viewed in the light of 'bad character' and 'weak will-power', and the majority of alcoholics must still ensure the pull-yourself-together doctrine with its concomitant emotional appeals, morality lectures, threats, promises and the like.

The study of alcoholism has mainly developed under the interests represented by psychology, psychiatry, sociology, religion and economics. These diverse influences have visibly contributed to the contradictory concepts and the fragmentary nature of theory in this field. Moreover, the general urgency of the problem and the desire for rapid progress lend acceptance to technically faulty work that would not pass muster in other fields. While semantic difficulties seem almost inherent in the social sciences, the study of alcoholism has added to this confusion by introducing a myriad of terms – 'chronic alcoholism', 'acute alcoholism', 'alcohol addiction', 'pathologic alcoholism', 'primary alcoholism', 'secondary alcoholism', 'toxic alcoholism', to mention only a few – all varyingly defined and applied with neither consistency nor uniformity. An attempt to define these conditions operationally is the one measure that will reduce the amount of confusion and controversy which abounds in this field.

Discussion of a Definition of Alcoholism

The term 'alcoholism' is itself a matter of dispute. In some circles the term 'problem drinking' is preferred, but the point is that we are told little about 'alcoholics' or 'problem drinkers' other than the descriptive facts that they are addicted to alcohol, that they drink excessively, that they crave for alcohol, and that they cannot control their drinking. We venture therefore to submit the following definition:

> *Alcoholism is a psychobiological malfunction which manifests itself in a compulsive and progressive craving for alcohol, as the result of a pattern of conditioning, habit formation, and a biological inability to cope with alcohol.*

Let us discuss this definition. We term 'alcoholism' a 'psychobiological malfunction' because neither the pure psychological explanations of the condition nor the biological theories on their own are very illuminating.

The psychological explanations range from various Freudian theories, which include an emphasis on the oral erotic aspects, repressed homosexuality and unconscious guilt feelings brought about by thwarted aggressiveness in the erotic field, to a behavioristic emphasis on 'habit systems', 'memory-traces' and the like. However, some theorists consider alcoholism to be solely a product of such physical factors as cerebral lesions, liver deficiencies and endocrine imbalance. Whilst there is evidence to suggest that the root-cause of alcoholism is not to be found in the psychological make-up or social environment of the individual, but in his or her physiological interior (it would appear that some individuals, because of inherent physiological 'defects', are unable to digest or assimilate alcohol in the 'normal' manner), it is the psychological factors that finally determine whether or not the individual becomes an alcoholic. Conversely, the role of the biological factors in accounting for alcoholism must not be underestimated, for the evidence indicates that an actual *tissue need* for alcohol, as a result of certain physiological and biochemical changes, in fact underlies the inordinate craving for drink (Kolle, 1939).

While no one has conclusively demonstrated that these obvious physio-pathological factors are not in fact entirely secondary to prolonged over-indulgence, the majority of writers regard the alcoholic's characteristic 'craving for and sensitivity to alcohol' as a hereditary predisposition which usually comes to the fore after many years of progressive but controlled drinking. It must be noted, however, that this does not mean that 'alcoholism is hereditary'. Many individuals may have this 'physiological sensitivity', but because of an ability to cope with environmental stress, they never become 'alcoholics'. Thus, ultimately, 'personality' furnishes the terrain on which alcohol addiction may or may not grow. But to ask, 'what is more important in accounting for alcoholism, the psychological or the physiological factors?' is as meaningless and as futile as the age-worn 'nature–nurture' controversy.

Referring to our definition again, the psychology of alcoholism embraces *a pattern of conditioning (and) habit formation.* The sequence may be as follows:

> The individual in stress situations makes a number of different responses, one of which might be the consumption of alcohol, which affords him temporary relief. Repetition of this behavior pattern eventually leads to a conditioned response between *stress* and *consumption of alcohol*. In terms of 'stimulus generalization', an endless variety of stimuli are later perceived as 'stress situations'. The consequent increase in drinking behaviour may cause financial difficulties, domestic problems etc. This may soon occasion feelings of guilt and perhaps a deterioration in health, which in turn add to the already mounting stress. This 'self-perpetuated stress' precipitates further drinking (in terms of the already established conditioned response) which affords the individual the usual short-lived relief. When this wears off the individual is again faced with his difficulties and problems and, in this manner, a circular pattern of causation is pre-eminently the psychological mechanism maintaining the phenomena of alcoholism.

There are, of course, many variations of the pattern but the vicious circle is apparent in all cases. This, as we shall outline, has far-reaching implications for therapy. It may be indicated at this stage that the vicious circle must be broken at several strategic points, not at one alone, if a cure is to be established.

The underlying dynamics of this vicious circle are best understood in terms of the effect of alcohol on the human brain. The active substance in any alcoholic beverage is ethyl alcohol, which, contrary to popular opinion, is an *anesthetic drug* and acts as a *depressant* and not as a stimulant. The deceptive appearance of stimulation arises from the release of the lower nervous centers from the control of the higher by the narcotization of the latter. In other words, the first effect of alcohol on the brain is the deadening or anesthesia of the higher centers (which determine the functions of self-criticism and judgment, the power of inhibition etc.) thus causing a temporary depression of the drinker's tensions, inhibitions, anxieties and general inadequacies. Hence the individual appears stimulated.

Before turning to the therapeutic considerations of alcoholism, we should like to cite some typical examples of the loose thinking and vague generalizations so prevalent in this field. One writer, with no experimental backing, states categorically that 'the pre-alcoholic personality is always distinctly inhibitory' (Salter, 1952). Elsewhere, we read that 'at least 90% of all abnormal drinkers are predominantly of the introverted type' (Strecker and Chambers, 1939). Further, we hear much about the 'typical alcoholic'. It is important to verify whether we are in fact entitled to describe anyone as a 'typical alcoholic' and it is equally important to know whether there is any justification for terms such as 'the pre-alcoholic personality' or 'the alcoholic personality'.

The results of a *preliminary investigation* conducted by the present writer provide no justification for the use of these terms. The central questions of the inquiry were phrased as follows:

1. Is there a personality type with a relatively constant combination of psychological traits which renders the individual especially susceptible to the intemperate use of alcohol?
2. If there is no unitary personality type among alcoholics, is there perhaps a variety of different but well-defined personality types?*

The results indicated that alcoholics are not a homogeneous group as far as temperament or personality make-up is concerned. They could be distinguished from the non-alcoholic controls only roughly and with many exceptions. We therefore concluded that we cannot speak of a personality structure which is typical of the alcoholic, and that compulsive drinking seems to depend upon the total effect of environmental stress upon a par-

*The definition of the word 'personality' as used here is: Personality is the dynamic organization within the individual of those psychophysical systems that determine his unique adjustment to his environment. Allport, G.W. (1951). *Personality: A Psychological Interpretation*, p. 48. London: Constable.

ticular individual who has a biological inability to cope with alcohol.

Therapy

Turning now to the therapeutic procedures for combating alcoholism in South Africa, we must note that the reported percentages of 'cures' are at best disappointing. This is not surprising when we recall that the usual approach to the alcoholic in this country is to hospitalize him for a short time, during which he is kept off alcohol and given vitamin injections. While this is a useful means of preparing the patient for further treatment, all too often it is administered as a cure in itself. There are, however, several sanatoria, homes and clinics which provide far more extensive means of treatment for the alcoholic. But even the measures adopted there, when viewed in the light of the vicious circle previously outlined, are inadequate. The mere regimen of physical rehabilitation coupled with occupational therapy and 'healthy living' (as provided by some of these specialized homes and clinics) is insufficient. Unfortunately, the expectation of a possible 'panacea approach' is still prevalent among many clinicians, so that the problem is generally tackled within a unitary, or at best a 'bimodal', frame of reference.

Each of the following curatives and therapies has made energetic attempts to hold the center of the stage as *prima donna* but, unhappily, each in turn has been relegated to the chorus. They include: relaxation therapy, psychoanalysis, conditioned reflex therapy, vitamin therapy, hypnotherapy and the various drug therapies. The fault lies not with the methods, but with the failure to combine the advantages offered by each. For instance, it is estimated that psychotherapies, as they are applied at present without many selective criteria, may have an average success of 25–30 per cent in terms of 2–4 years of total abstinence (Jellinek, 1942), whereas when combined with conditioned-reflex therapy, Cotlier lists cures ranging from 50 to 75 per cent (Hampton, 1947).

On the basis of 32 alcoholic case studies and Thematic Apperception Test interpretations (TAT), we submit that the consequences of alcoholism usually require a series of active steps in order to break the compulsion, as well as substitutive treatment (the fostering of hobbies and other recreational and occupational pursuits) and other forms of environmental manipulation, which all form part of a wide and all-embracing re-educative programme. The final and complete dissolution of the aforementioned vicious circle can usually be achieved by applying the following four-fold plan.

Active measures to break the compulsion

The gradual weaning process is supplemented by large doses of vitamin preparations administered intramuscularly. When the patient has regained his physical well-being, certain steps are recommended to ensure his total abstinence from drink while undergoing psychotherapy. This is best achieved by either administering a course of conditioned-reflex therapy or else tetraethylthiuram disulfide (Antabuse).

1. The former procedure consists of repeated sessions in which the individual is given a dose of emetine or apomorphine and shortly after sees, smells or drinks various alcoholic beverages. The emetine or apomorphine induces nausea and vomiting and, because this becomes associated with the alcohol, the patient develops an aversion to it. The unconditioned stimulus is concerned with the elicitation of nausea or vomiting, and various alcoholic beverages represent the conditioned stimulus. This, it must be stressed again, is not intended as 'a cure for alcoholism'. Experience has indicated that, in many cases, this conditioned aversion to alcohol breaks down after a few months, even when the response is 'reinforced' (Voegtlin, Lemere and Broz, 1940). But if the individual can be made to avoid the apparently inevitable 'slips' during therapy, a positive prognosis is greatly facilitated.

2. The use of tetraethylthiuram disulfide is less involved than the conditioned-reflex therapy. The patient takes the drug orally in tablet form every day (any attempt to administer it without the patient's knowledge is contraindicated) and it creates a sensitivity to alcohol, so that the patient cannot take alcohol without experiencing disagreeable and often violent reactions. This, unless medically inadvisable, is a valuable aid in rendering the alcoholic more amenable to psychotherapy.

Educative procedures

By attending group or individual discussions, the alcoholic must learn the nature of his condition. He must be led to realize that he is suffering from an incurable disease (in the sense that he can never drink socially again) and that complete abstinence from any alcoholic beverage whatsoever is his only salvation.

Psychotherapeutic procedures

Individual psychotherapy should consist of (1) diagnostic interviews, i.e. a psychological and social diagnosis – an evaluation of the interaction of the patient and his environment; and (2) treatment, which is designed to help the patient to gain 'insight'. Insight into, say, the relation between A and B in the life situation is a function of an intellectual and an affective bond between the two. It is a matter of *knowing* and *feeling* into the situation. The ultimate aim of psychotherapy is to ensure that the alcoholic remains abstinent by way of favorable readjustments in his personality. This implies the use of techniques that are designed to uncover the true motives behind the addiction and to provide the patient with a basis for readjustment through insight into his motives.

Socioeconomic procedures

A specially trained social worker should visit the home of the alcoholic with the primary purpose of explaining to his or her family the 'disease factor' in alcoholism. Furthermore, the alcoholic should receive advice and help in securing employment, the correction of faulty home-environment, associates etc., and aid in smoothing out domestic and other incompatibilities.

We are not suggesting that this four-fold plan is *the* cure for alcoholism. Nor are we under the impression that it constitutes anything novel. What we are attempting to convey is simply that, all too often, therapists are prone to overlook the importance of each of these steps in turn, and unless this wider therapeutic approach is widely adopted, few of the alleged 90 000 European alcoholics in South Africa will escape the searing effects of their terrible affliction.

A most useful adjunct to psychotherapy is progressive relaxation, because repeated practice of relaxation inhibits the tensions which may lead to drink. In some circles, injections of adrenal cortical extract are lauded. The successes claimed by Alcoholics Anonymous range from 50 to 70 per cent. We submit that their successes are due largely to an effective mobilization of emotional relationships and, hence, participation in this movement should be encouraged where the patient's personality is considered amenable to their teachings.

Finally, we should like to emphasize again that since alcoholics form a heterogeneous population embracing different and even antagonistic personality types, no one treatment or approach can prove beneficial to all abnormal drinkers.

References

HAMPTON, P.J. (1947). *J. Soc. Psychol.* **25**, 162.

JELLINEK, E.M. (1942). *Alcohol Addiction and Chronic Alcoholism*, p. 79. New Haven: Yale University Press.

KOLLE, K. (1939). *Allg. Z. Psychiat.* **112**, 397.

SALTER, A. (1952). *Conditioned Reflex Therapy*, p. 1. London: George Allen & Unwin Ltd.

STRECKER, E.A. and CHAMBERS, F.T. JR (1939). *Alcohol: One Man's Meat*, pp. 46–47. New York: Macmillan.

VOEGTLIN, W.L., LEMERE, F. AND BROZ, W. (1940). *Q. J. Stud. Alcohol.* **1**, 501.

Chapter 2
New Methods In
Psychotherapy (1958)

Certain facets of this article may be outdated, but its overall tenor and the specific clinical procedures employed are remarkably current. Whilst Lazarus disavowed anything 'spectacular' or especially 'dramatic' about the case history that comprises most of the paper, it is in fact one of the very first cases in which a wide-ranging battery of behavioural procedures was employed, and it was perhaps the first published instance of the systematic use of *aversive imagery*. Moreover, this was the article that first introduced the terms 'behaviour therapy' and 'behaviour therapist' into the scientific literature.

Cure comes through learning healthy personal relationships *now*, and not by stewing over past emotional frustrations (Salter, 1953).

The general medical practitioner is frequently quoted as saying that more than half the patients he encounters in his daily rounds are 'just plain neurotic'. Since the general practitioner cannot spend hours treating his neurotic cases, a large number of them receive no therapy other than tonics and sedation. Others, less fortunate, succumb to the exhortations of swamis, mystics and a host of pseudo-scientific practitioners. This is an alarming situation. The initial responsibility for the psychological welfare of his patients usually rests with the family doctor, but the field of psychotherapy is itself so confusing that many doctors have expressed undisguised skepticism about its value. Most medical men do not have time to venture into the complicated polemics of orthodox Freudian psychoanalysis, or the claims of Jungian analysts, or the counterclaims of any other deviant psychoanalytic school. Similarly, the average doctor is not concerned with the differences between the various eclectic therapists or any other of the numerous controversies which characterize the field. It is therefore confusing, even for the average professional person, to view the

First published in 1958. Reproduced, with the permission of the Medical Association of South Africa, from Lazarus, A. A. (1958). New methods in psychotherapy: A case study. *South African Medical Journal*, 32, 660-664.

many methods of treatment that are employed for emotional illness. But even more confusing is the fact that 'roughly 2/3rds of a group of neurotic patients will recover or improve to a marked extent within about 2 years of the onset of their illness, whether they are treated by means of psychotherapy or not' (Eysenck, 1952).

The last decade, however, has seen the growth of a new behaviorist psychotherapy built on the firm scientific bedrock of neurophysiology. Its concepts stem from carefully controlled laboratory experiments and its therapeutic tools are derived from the laws of learning. The *South African Medical Journal* has already printed several articles dealing with the experimental and theoretical background, methodology, therapeutic efficacy and clinical advantages of behavior therapy (Wolpe, 1950, 1952; Lazarus and Rachman, 1957; Rachman, 1958). The present chapter is intended to provide the general practitioner with a broad working knowledge of this approach. We firmly believe that more intimate team-work between doctor and psychotherapist will, in the long run, prove most beneficial. We also hope to disprove the myth that psychotherapy, by its very nature, must always be difficult, time-consuming and inefficient.

Where necessary, the behaviorist or objective psychotherapist employs all the usual psychotherapeutic techniques, such as support, guidance, insight, catharsis, interpretation, environmental manipulation etc., but in addition to these more 'orthodox' procedures, the behavior therapist applies objective techniques that are designed to inhibit specific neurotic patterns. His orientation is away from the analysis of hypothetical 'minds-within-minds', and his or her focus of attention is placed instead on his or her patient's behavior. Patients learn to behave in a maladaptive fashion, and if the patient is to be cured these ways of behaving must be eliminated. Wolpe's (Wolpe, 1948, 1954) experimental evidence and clinical research have revealed that neuroses are acquired in anxiety-generating situations and that successful therapy of the neuroses therefore depends on the reciprocal inhibition of neurotic anxiety responses. His methods have yielded a 90 per cent level of 'apparently cured or much improved' cases (Wolpe, 1954). It is probably safe to say that regardless of differences in theory or technique, the 'cures' that occur are accompanied by kinds of changes in personality that can be interpreted as involving learning (Bugelski, 1956). Recognizing that neuroses are learned within a social milieu, much emphasis is placed on the fact that the patient is not a clinical label but a human member of society and therefore all specific procedures are applied within the very broad context of social adaptation. This broad social and cultural emphasis by no means precludes the application of detailed or specific procedures where indicated. Behavior science is concerned with the entire range of activity from the most complex aspects of human interaction right down to the firing of a single neuron. Thus behavior therapists do not limit themselves to a specific technique – their repertoire of therapeutic methods is sufficiently large and flexible to fit the needs of the individual patient. Therefore the objective therapist is able to swing the focus of attention back and forth from the individual and his or her parts, to the individual in his or her social setting. Another difference between the behavior therapist and most other psychotherapists is the fact that the behaviorist is not bound by any fixed ritual to delve into the remote history of *all* his or her patients. As Rachman (1958) has shown, many impressive cures have been effected without any attention being given to the causative factors involved. In our view, 'the emphasis in psychological rehabilitation must be on a *synthesis* which would embrace a diverse range of effective therapeutic techniques, as well as innumerable adjunctive measures, to form part of a wide and all-embracing re-educative program' (see Chapter 1).

The presentation of a treatment project should clarify many of these issues and enable the doctor to appreciate more fully the advantages of modern behaviorist psychotherapy. The following case was selected for several reasons: (1) a variety of techniques was employed; (2) many of our general statements are clearly illustrated; and (3) the didactic elements of the case are not obscured by its complexities. We propose to present a fairly detailed account of each session from the initial diagnostic interviews until the termination of therapy.

The Case of LHR

Extract from GP's letter of referral

This is to introduce Mr LHR, aged 36 years....He appears to be suffering from anxiety and tension....tranquillizers have not helped and his condition seems to have deteriorated in recent weeks....

Initial interview* (time 75 minutes)

After putting the patient at ease a detailed life history was taken. Here are the relevant points: youngest of five children; unhappy home life (inadequate father, stern and over-solicitous mother); poor sibling relationships; childhood terrors retained until early puberty (fear of the dark, nightmares and kidnappers); extreme masturbatory guilts during adolescence; volunteered for active service but was rejected owing to high blood pressure and 'black-outs' (no 'black-outs' for last 12 years); work situation unsatisfactory (employed as a draughtsman although he has an architectural diploma); poor social and interpersonal relationships ('I have a few friends but most people try to ride me'); principal interests 'painting, sketching and science fiction'; present adjustment towards sex satisfactory ('We

---

*Unless otherwise stated, the patient was seen twice weekly.

hope to get married if I can get a better job'); his three brothers were killed on active service; his father died shortly after the war from 'heart failure'; his sister is married and lives in Canada; patient shares a two-roomed flat with his mother.

Asked to express his problems in his own words, Mr LHR replied: 'I've always been jittery and too particular about things. I suppose I expect too much of myself. Anyhow most of the time I just feel....miserable. I sometimes get stupid thoughts like doing away with myself....I'm already 36 and what have I got to show for it?....My worst trouble is that I'm always checking and re-checking everything. You know, even when I know for sure that the door's locked I've always got to go back and make sure again and again. It's like that with everything. At work, for instance, I'll check the scales again and again and even though I know that the detail is correctly mapped, I go over the figure about ten times before I do the next one. Sometimes it nearly drives me mad but I've just got to go on and on....'

General impressions

Well-groomed, pleasant looking, slender build, active, tense and agitated, timid and reserved. He appears to have little (if any) insight. At this stage, he could be summed up as an anxious, compulsive and inhibited individual.

Second interview (time 40 minutes)

This session was largely an extension and elaboration of the previous interview. Certain areas of the patient's history were discussed and checked. Additional information emerged, such as the fact that he was still being dominated by his mother and that his compulsive acts (which started in early puberty) became more severe after the death of his father. 'In the last few months things have really been worse than ever – quite unbearably so. I don't know why this is, but I suppose that it has to do a lot with the way my mother has been carrying on....She's been going at me pretty solid....She says that it's a pity that I wasn't killed up North instead of the others. Of course she doesn't mean anything by it, but it's upsetting....Also my girlfriend and her don't get on so well and my mother said that if I marry her, she'll cut me out of her will.'

The discussion then turned to the more detailed and intimate aspects of his home background. The Willoughby Neurotic Tendency Inventory (Willoughby, 1934) was applied and the score (63) indicated a high level of neurotic disturbance. The qualitative conclusions were: 'This person shows obvious insecurity mingled with feelings of hypersensitivity and guilt.'

Third interview (time 2 hours)

This session (apart from a brief discussion on relaxation) was devoted solely to diagnostic psychological testing. The patient was shown to have 'superior' Mental Alertness as measured by the NIPR Test A/1/1 (National Institute for Personnel Research – Mental Alertness A/1/A – test for matriculated persons) and his corrected IQ was 120 on the South African Individual Scale. Selected items on the Thematic Apperception Test (Murray, 1943) together with the Holsopple–Miale Sentence Completion Blank (Holsopple and Miale, 1954) revealed significant clinical trends. Apart from obvious compulsive features, these records indicated underlying trends of unexpressed hostility towards parental figures (especially towards the maternal figure), coupled with generalized anxiety. There was also evidence that he avoided personal challenge presented by others and offered little himself. Although aggressive responses were prevalent throughout, more often than not these impulses were intrapunitive (i.e. 'self-punishing').

Readers who are at all familiar with Freudian writings will find this case rife with analytic material. From the behavioristic viewpoint, however, the important etiological factors are briefly the faulty habits which were generated in the home situation and then reinforced by subsequent stress situations. It follows, therefore, that the therapy program was designed to eliminate or reduce the frequency and intensity of these non-adaptive responses.

Fourth interview (time 1 hour)

Approximately 30 minutes of this session were devoted to further discussion about the patient's early homelife. The patient was allowed free rein and dwelt mainly on the 'injustices of his upbringing'. Certain of his statements suggested paranoid elements but most of his remarks had the ring of helplessness and self-pity. After about 20 minutes, the interpretation was suggested that the patient's remarks seemed to indicate feelings of hostility towards the individual members of his family. He immediately countered with vehement over-protestations about their 'underlying good intentions'. The therapist's non-commital 'uh-huh' precipitated a severe reaction: the patient immediately covered his face and wept. After a while he looked up and said, 'You're right, I hate the ... lot of them!' This significant admission led to further uncontrolled weeping which gradually subsided when the therapist finally managed to impart his acceptance, approval and sympathy together with the fact that the patient's feelings and reactions were 'normal and quite justifiable'. The remainder of the session consisted of training in progressive relaxation (Jacobson, 1938).

Fifth interview (time 1 hour)

Mr LHR stated that he was generally feeling much better, but that 'my mother is now getting me down more than ever before....Let's face it, I'm financially dependent on my mother....and my work has been slower than ever because of that....checking and re-checking'. The patient then switched the emphasis to his early sexual difficulties and a frank discussion followed which was designed to dissipate residual guilt-feelings by sanctioning his conduct and by imparting non-moralistic insight into all matters pertaining to sex. The patient was then given preliminary training in 'assertive responses' (Salter, 1952; Wolpe, 1954) (i.e. he was provided with specific instructions on handling all interpersonal relationships adequately and spontaneously 'standing up for his own rights').

Sixth interview (time 1 hour)

After a short discussion about Mr LHR's girlfriend, further training in assertive responses was given. The patient was urged to be assertive in all situations. He complained that the mere thought of being assertive made him feel afraid, but he was told that, with practice, these techniques would soon come to him automatically. Training in progressive relaxation completed the remainder of this session.

Seventh interview (time 1 hour)

The patient spoke at length about his father and about his present attitude towards his mother ('If I ever want to live, I've got to break away from her'). His compulsive behavior was then discussed and the patient summarized the situation as follows: 'If I could only stop myself from this business of re-checking everything ten times then I'd have a chance. I know I'm good at my work but I'll never get senior posts until I manage to work faster....These compulsions are the things that mess up my whole life.'

Eighth interview (time 40 minutes)

Approximately 20 minutes were devoted to additional training in assertive responses by means of 'psychodrama' (i.e. the therapist assumed the role of various 'threatening figures' and the patient was required to oppose them). The rest of the session consisted of relaxation therapy with preliminary hypnotic suggestions. He responded well to the hypnotic procedures and a catalepsy of his right arm was easily induced.

Ninth interview (time 40 minutes)

The patient seemed unusually excited. 'It's working,' he announced as soon as he walked in, 'yesterday for the first time, I stood up to my mother and she got such a shock that she just said nothing....I even asked my boss for a raise. I didn't get it, but at least I asked...'. The therapist expressed his approval and delight at his progress and encouraged him to continue practicing this new habit of assertive responses. (One obviously has to use one's discretion in advising assertive behavior as the aim is definitely not to make people become objectionably aggressive. In this instance, Mr LHR was so very inhibited that there was never any risk of making him permanently aggressive and at best, by acquiring assertive habits, he would be able to achieve a better balance in his assertiveness–submissiveness ratio and not serve as a perpetual doormat for the rest of his life. Hypnotic relaxation was then administered for 15 minutes and a glove anesthesia was induced without difficulty.

Tenth interview (time 30 minutes)

The patient was hypnotized and given more or less the following instructions while in a deep hypnotic trance: 'You feel calm and relaxed, deeply relaxed and peaceful. Now I want you to imagine yourself at work. You still feel calm and relaxed. Now imagine yourself drawing a plan and checking as you go along. You're quite relaxed. You check it once. Everything is correct. You make sure and go over it again. You are still calm and relaxed. You begin to check it a third time, but now suddenly you feel anxious. You feel uneasy and tense. Rapidly the tension mounts. [The patient was writhing and breathing very heavily at this stage.] You leave the plan. You do not check it again. Now you start a new drawing. Picture the new situation. As soon as you start the new activity you are once again calm and relaxed. You feel calm and peaceful...When I count up to five you will open your eyes.' When asked to recall what had transpired under hypnosis, the patient at first appeared to be completely amnesic, but after a while he was able to recollect the entire session and reported that he had visualized the situation 'just as though I was there at the time'.

Eleventh to nineteenth interviews (time of each 30 minutes)

The hypnotic procedure employed in the previous interview was applied, with slight modifications, until the end of the nineteenth interview, when the patient reported that his compulsions no longer troubled him in the work situation. 'I'm turning out five times more work than before....Sometimes I still tend to fuss over things more than I ought to, but that doesn't worry me.' Specific instructions in assertive behavior were also given prominence throughout these interviews. On the twelfth interview, the therapist was about 20 minutes behind time and Mr LHR politely reprimanded him by saying, 'You should have told me that you were running late and I would have slipped down for a haircut meanwhile.' This was indeed an impressive improvement from his previously inhibited and almost obsequious behavior. The therapist apologized for the delay and later expressed his strong approval of Mr LHR's assertive behavior.

Twentieth interview (time 30 minutes)

The patient was not seen for nearly 5 weeks. He had had an emergency appendicetomy and had developed certain complications after the operation. 'I've been back at work now for two days...I've been doing a lot of thinking this past month and you'll be surprised to hear what I've done...I've asked Betty (his same girlfriend) to marry me...I've accepted a job in Cape Town...My aunt recently lost her husband and she is coming to live with my mother...We plan to leave town as man and wife before the 16th (less than 3 weeks)...Do you approve of all this?' The therapist expressed his strong approval of all Mr LHR's decisions. The need to continue practicing assertive behavior was again impressed upon him.

Twenty-first interview (time 1 hour)

This interview took place 15 days after the previous one. Mr LHR was accompanied by his fiancée. She was interviewed privately and seemed a sensible person with considerable understanding and insight. At the end of the interview she said. 'Now that L. has learnt to stand on his own two feet, I'm sure we will make out just fine.' Mr LHR was then asked to come in, and the conversation terminated with a general discussion about their future plans.

Periodically he communicated with the therapist by letter. Eight months after therapy, en route to Rhodesia, Mr LHR telephoned the therapist and reported that he had maintained a satisfactory adjustment. 'I have conquered the compulsions for good and everything is better than I ever expected.'

Discussion

This case was not presented for its dramatic interest, because it is by no means spectacular and it is certainly not intended as a 'model case'.

The first four interviews employ the usual diagnostic and psychotherapeutic procedures but, after that, the more objective techniques are brought into clearer focus. It is soon apparent that the patient's principal problems are 'inhibitions and compulsions', and from the sixth interview onwards, the therapist is obviously of the opinion that if these two factors are eliminated, the rest will automatically fall into place. By the eighth interview, the emphasis is present-and-future oriented and, contrary to analytic preachings, little time is devoted to 'digging up the past'. The reader will have observed the fact that the compulsive features were adequately reduced without any attention being given to the causative factors involved.

We should like to give a brief theoretical explanation of our hypnotic procedure as applied to the patient's compulsive acts. It is generally agreed that obsessional or compulsive symptoms have the effect of allaying or inhibiting anxiety. We know, for instance, that if a patient is prevented from satisfying his compulsive urges he displays acute anxiety until he finally carries out his ritual. Now if we reverse this process (i.e. the patient becomes anxious when performing his compulsive act and feels complacent when avoiding compulsive behavior) the compulsive acts should automatically fall away. This, at least, is the theory behind the hypnotic procedure employed. Wolpe (1958) however, reports more sophisticated objective techniques, with wider applicability, for handling compulsive and obsessional neurotics. 'Orthodox' practitioners would argue that symptom removal without the elimination of the 'underlying cause' does not constitute a 'cure'. Rachman (1954), however, has shown that 'too great a concern with "underlying causes" may under certain circumstances even impede therapeutic progress.' Eysenck (1957) expertly summarizes the situation as follows: 'According to Freud there is a "disease" which produces symptoms: cure the disease and the symptom will vanish. According to the alternative view, there is no "disease", there are merely wrong habits which have been learned and must be unlearned.' The bulk of the treatment (i.e. 19 interviews) extended over 10 weeks and the total time spent with the patient amounted to less than 16 hours. He was considered 'much improved' in terms of Knight's five criteria – symptom improvement, increased productiveness, improved adjustment and pleasure in sex, improved interpersonal relationships and increased stress-tolerance.

References

BUGELSKI, B.R. (1956). *The Psychology of Learning*. New York: Henry Holt.

EYSENCK, H.J. (1952). *The Scientific Study of Personality*. London: Routledge & Kegan Paul.

EYSENCK, H.J. (1957). *The Dynamics of Anxiety and Hysteria*. London: Routledge & Kegan Paul.

HOLSOPPLE, J.Q. and MIALE, F.R. (1954). *Sentence Completion: A Projective Method for the Study of Personality*. Illinois: Charles C. Thomas.

JACOBSON, E. (1938). *Progressive Relaxation*. Chicago: University of Chicago Press.

KNIGHT, R.P. (1941). *Am. J. Psychiatr.* **98**, 434.

LAZARUS, A.A. and RACHMAN, S. (1957). *S. Afr. Med. J.* **31**, 934.

RACHMAN, S. (1958). *S. Afr. Med. J.* **32**, 19.

SALTER, A. (1952). *Conditioned Reflex Therapy*. London: George Allen & Unwin.

MURRAY, H.A. (1943). *Thematic Apperception Test Manual*. Boston, MA: Harvard University Press.

SALTER, A. (1953). *The Case against Psychoanalysis*. New York: Medical Publications.

WILLOUGHBY, R. (1934). *J. Soc. Psychol.* **5**, 91.

WOLPE, J. (1948). *An approach to the problem of neurosis based on the conditioned response*. MD thesis, University of Witwatersrand, Johannesburg.

WOLPE, J. (1950). *S. Afr. Med. J.* **24**, 613.

WOLPE, J. (1952). *S. Afr. Med. J.* **26**, 825.

WOLPE, J. (1952). *S. Arch. Neurol. Psychiatr.* **72**, 205.

Chapter 3
Group Therapy of Phobic Disorders by Systematic Desensitization (1961)

Based on Lazarus's doctoral dissertation, this paper again contains a number of 'firsts'. It is the first published report of group desensitisation, and it is the first account of quantitative and objective pre- and post-treatment assessments of phobic avoidance. Although the major design flaw is that Lazarus was the sole experimenter and assessor of treatment outcomes, it is nevertheless interesting that whilst desensitisation proved far superior to the use of interpretation, the latter was nonetheless shown to have had some positive effects. In this paper, the power of the therapeutic relationship is mentioned. It was many years later that the role and importance of relationship factors were recognised by other 'behaviourists'. It was this article that caught the attention of Professor Albert Bandura who invited Lazarus to visit Stanford University in 1963. Lazarus subsequently expanded his use of behavioural (and then multimodal) methods in groups – he introduced group assertiveness training, treated couples in marital groups, and addressed the group treatment of (what was called) impotence and frigidity.

The increasing demands for psychological and psychiatric services dictate the need for effective short-term therapeutic techniques and the extension of the existing services. Consequently, group techniques have grown in clinical stature, and the past decade has witnessed the development of numerous divergent procedures. A most promising variety of short-term therapy is Wolpe's (1958) system of 'reciprocal inhibition', by which he achieved the recovery of 188 out of 210 neurotic cases in an average of 34.8 sessions.

A double economy can be achieved by combining the advantages of Wolpe's (1958) expedient clinical procedures with the additional time- and effort-saving properties of group therapy. This paper describes the

First published in 1961. Reproduced from Lazarus, A. A. (1961). Group therapy of phobic disorder by systematic desensitization. *Journal of Abnormal and Social Psychology*, **63**, 505–510.
The paper is an outline of the experimental session of a thesis entitled 'New group techniques in the treatment of phobic conditions' which was accepted by the University of Witwatersrand in December 1960, for the degree of Doctor of Philosophy.

adaptation of Wolpe's most important therapeutic procedure – the technique of systematic desensitization based on relaxation – to the group treatment of phobic disorders. In addition, the therapeutic effects of group desensitization were compared with more conventional forms of interpretive group psychotherapy on matched pairs of phobic subjects.

Method

General procedure

The sample consisted of 35 middle-class urban white South Africans who were handicapped by phobic disorders.* Social class membership was defined in terms of education, vocation, and income. There were 7 university graduates, 16 matriculants, and 12 patients with at least 3 years of secondary schooling. Apart from 3 professional women, the majority of female patients were housewives whose husbands' average earnings were the equivalent of $550 a month. The mean income for the rest of the group was approximately $600 a month. In all, there were 12 men and 23 women, the mean age being 33.2 years with a standard deviation of 9.87.

The entire group included 11 acrophobics, 15 claustrophobics, 5 impotent men (treated as suffering from sexual phobia), and a mixed group of 4 phobic patients. The latter comprised a girl with a fear of sharp objects, a man with a fear of physical violence, a woman who was afraid to be a passenger in a moving vehicle and a woman with a phobia for dogs.

The basic experimental design was to compare group desensitization therapy with more conventional methods of group treatment (or therapy based on 'group dynamics'). The group desensitization technique consisted of systematically counterposing by relaxation graded lists of anxiety evoking stimuli which the separate groups of patients were asked to imagine.

The efficacy of group desensitization was first compared with group interpretation. The same therapist (the investigator) conducted all the therapeutic groups.

The initial comparison was made on a group of five acrophobic patients, two of whom received desensitization therapy, and three who were treated by interpretive group procedures.

Throughout the experiment, pairs of phobic patients were matched in terms of sex, age (within a 4-year range), and the nature and objective severity of the phobic disorders. A coin was tossed to decide whether a

---

*The sample was not drawn from psychiatric hospitals or institutions as it was felt that extraneous variables would be introduced. Since the rules of the South African Psychological Association forbid registered psychologists to advertise in the press, the patients were obtained with the generous aid of friends and colleagues who made announcements at lectures and contacted their own associates.

given member of each matched pair would be treated by desensitization therapy or by group interpretation. Extra (unmatched) individuals were always placed in the interpretive groups because it is generally agreed that these groups require a minimum of three members (Corsini, 1957).

When, after six sessions, treatment with the acrophobic groups was well under way, the next group (five impotent men) was selected and similarly subdivided into two additional groups, treated by desensitization and interpretation, respectively.

Three months later, the group of six claustrophobic patients was selected and equally subdivided to form a third separate desensitization–interpretation comparison.

Thus, at the end of 6 months, a total of seven patients had received group desensitization and nine had been treated by group interpretation.

Seven months later, additional acrophobic and claustrophobic patients were obtained in order to investigate the effects of relaxation per se. It was hypothesized that individuals who received training in relaxation at the end of each interpretive session would show a greater diminution of phobic reactions than those patients who had been treated solely by group interpretation. The suggestion that interpretation plus relaxation might be more effective than desensitization was also tested.

Accordingly, an additional six acrophobic patients were equally divided into two matched groups, the one receiving desensitization therapy and the other receiving interpretation plus relaxation. The latter group was trained in an accelerated version of Jacobson's (1938) progressive relaxation for about 15 minutes at the end of each interpretive therapeutic discussion.

A few weeks later, an additional nine claustrophobic patients were similarly subdivided. Group desensitization was administered to four patients and group interpretation plus relaxation was applied to five.

Finally, the mixed phobic group was treated by desensitization in order to determine whether desensitization could be successfully applied to a heterogeneous phobic group.

Thus, group desensitization was applied to 18 patients, group interpretation was applied to 9 patients, and 8 patients were treated by group interpretation plus relaxation.

Selection of phobic patients

Although there were numerous volunteers for inclusion in the investigation, only those people whose phobias imposed a severe limitation on their social mobility, jeopardized their interpersonal relationships or hindered their constructive abilities were admitted to the therapeutic groups.

Several people who were greatly handicapped by phobic disorders were excluded because they had received previous psychiatric treatment, ranging from psychoanalysis to electroconvulsive therapy. These people were given individual treatment in order to avoid ambiguity concerning the effects of the therapeutic groups.

The character and severity of the phobias were assessed in the following manner: patients reporting acrophobic symptoms were privately and individually required to climb a metal fire escape. The experimenter climbed the stairs directly behind the patients and urged them to see how high they could climb. Few of the patients were able to proceed higher than the first landing (approximately 15–20 feet from ground level). The patients who were admitted to the acrophobic groups were all able to achieve a pre-therapeutic height of between 15 and 25 feet.

Similarly, patients with claustrophobic traits were admitted individually into a well-ventilated cubicle with large French windows which opened onto a balcony. The patient sat facing the open windows. To the left of the patient was a movable screen which could be pushed as far as the center of the cubicle, thus creating a sensation of space constriction. The patients were told that the experimeter would first shut the French windows and then proceed to push the screen towards the center of the room. They were urged to remain in the cubicle for as long as possible and to reopen the windows only when they felt that the need for air had become unbearable. Most of the patients showed visible signs of discomfort as soon as the windows were shut, and no one was able to tolerate the screen at a distance of less than 20 inches.

Detailed information regarding the purpose of the investigation was withheld from the patients to avoid possible prejudice to the results. They were merely informed that the experimenter was conducting research into the alleviation of phobic disorders by group methods.

Apart from the initial screening procedures, individual contact with the patients was avoided in order to exclude the influence of any additional therapeutic factors. It is thought, for instance, that history taking and psychometric investigations may in themselves be therapeutic. In order to determine the value of group therapy per se, it was considered necessary to eliminate as many of these extraneous variables as possible. Attention was deliberately focused, therefore, on the specific techniques under investigation, avoiding the use of any supplementary measures which might facilitate therapeutic progress. For instance, in clinical practice it is customary to precede the application of systematic desensitization by a brief outline of the theoretical rationale behind the technique. Since it could be argued that this practice has a direct bearing on the results, the patients were directly desensitized without any preliminary explanation.

Group desensitization

Anxiety hierarchies (graded lists of stimuli to which the patients reacted with unadaptive anxiety) were constructed (Wolpe, 1958). In preparing these hierarchies, the experimenter extracted common elements from remarks which individual patients wrote on the questionnaires they filled out, and a group hierarchy was constructed. It must be emphasized that the hierarchical situations were imaginary ones, listed on paper and presented only symbolically to the patients.

The acrophobic group hierarchy, for example, consisted of the following situations: looking down from a very high building, seeing films taken from an airplane, looking down from a height of 80–100 feet, looking down a well, sitting high up on a grandstand during a football game, looking down from a 60-foot balcony, sitting on a narrow ledge at a height of 60 feet with a safety net a few feet away, looking down from a height of about 55 feet, seeing someone jump from a 50-foot diving board, sitting on a wide ledge about 35 feet from the ground, looking down from a height of approximately 20 feet, looking down from a height of about 10 feet.

The claustrophobic group hierarchy consisted of 16 situations ranging from 'sitting in a large and airy room with all the windows open', to 'sitting in front of an open fire in a small room with the doors and windows shut'. The group hierarchy applied to the impotent men contained 10 items referring progressively to intimate sexual situations requiring increasing amounts of initiative.

The first therapeutic session was devoted entirely to training the patients in intensive muscular relaxation. At the end of the session, the patients were instructed to practice specific relaxation exercises for about 15 minutes morning and night.

The second session was held 3 days later, when further training in relaxation was provided. Towards the end of this session, desensitization commenced with the presentation (in imagination) of the two weakest items of the relevant anxiety hierarchy. The acrophobic patients, for example, were first told to picture themselves looking out of a window about 10 feet from the level of the street. It was impressed upon them that if any scene proved upsetting or disturbing, they were to indicate this by raising their left hand. When any patient signaled in this manner, the scene was 'withdrawn' immediately.

When the two least disturbing items in the relevant anxiety hierarchy had been presented, each of the patients was asked to report on the clarity of the imagined scenes and their accompanying levels of disturbance. The second session ended after the patients had been told to practice relaxation twice daily for periods of about 10 minutes.

The subsequent desensitization sessions followed a set pattern. The therapist named the various muscle groups to be relaxed. When a deep level of relaxation was reached, the patients were presented with successive items from the hierarchical series. The desensitization procedure was conducted at the pace of the 'slowest' (i.e. most anxious) subject.

The third session was terminated only when all the patients were able to tolerate an exposure of about 10 seconds to the first three items on the hierarchy without signaling anxiety. Thereafter, new items were introduced only when a 10-second tolerance to the preceding item had been achieved. It took several sessions before the entire group was able to visualize a given item for as long as 10 seconds without one or another member's signaling some disturbance.

Apart from occasional restlessness in those who were ready for more 'difficult' anxiety items but who were constantly re-exposed to stimuli which they had long since mastered, no harm seemed to ensue from proceeding at a pace that was obviously too slow for part of the group. However, experience has shown that too rapid a pace can prove extremely antitherapeutic and lead to increased levels of anxiety.

Therapy in the desensitization groups was terminated when the final item on the hierarchy was tolerated by the patients for 10 seconds without signaling. Patients often reported a marked amelioration of their phobic responses when the anxiety hierarchies were only half completed. It was insisted that each member would nevertheless have to undergo desensitization of the entire hierarchy in order to consolidate and reinforce their therapeutic gains.

The treatment of the claustrophobic groups was conducted out of doors. The patients in the mixed phobic groups were handed the items of their relevant anxiety hierarchies on slips of paper. Here, the relaxation procedure adopted was as previously outlined, but instead of describing the items, the therapist handed a typewritten anxiety scene to each group member and instructed him or her to read the description of the scene, to close his or her eyes and to try to imagine the situation with tranquility. The patients were instructed to signal in the usual manner when a given situation became disturbing, and then immediately to stop imagining the scene and to continue relaxing. After about 10 seconds, all the patients were told to stop picturing the scene and remain relaxed. Those who had successfully imagined their item without undue disturbance were then handed a new anxiety situation. In this manner, each group member was able to proceed at his or her own pace. No more than two successive items were presented at any one session.

Group interpretation

The approach used in the interpretive groups was a form of insight therapy with re-educative goals (Wolberg, 1954). Leadership was basically democratic, and the therapist's primary role was that of a participant observer. The groups passed through two phases: first, there was an introductory period during which the group situation was structured with the emphasis on a free and permissive emotional atmosphere. Feelings of initial tension and reticence were dealt with by open discussion, emphasizing group tolerance and acceptance and clarifying numerous misconceptions. Secondly, descriptions of phobic symptoms preceded intensive discussions which focused attention on emotions and on current interpersonal relationships. The emphasis shifted from a situational to a personal exploration. A considerable amount of historical data emerged and frequently provided abreactive and cathartic responses. The recall of forgotten memories was often accompanied by violent emotional reactions.

The group of impotent men displayed a high degree of empathy for one another, and frequently expressed feelings of hostility and resentment towards the therapist. These feelings were accepted by him and clarified for the patients; they were followed by discussions of the effects of frustration.

At the end of each session, the therapist provided a summary of the proceedings. He attempted not only to recapitulate the remarks of the subjects and to reflect back to the group the emotional significance of their statements but also to suggest possible connections between their symptoms and their feelings. Interpretive remarks dealt mainly with possible motives behind the facade of manifest behavior. Premature interpretations were vigilantly avoided. Obvious rationalizations, as well as statements of overprotestation, were challenged by the therapist only when he sensed a readiness on the part of the group.

Both the interpretive groups and the desensitization sessions were usually conducted three times a week. The desensitization groups were disbanded when all the patients were able to tolerate the most severe anxiety producing stimulus in the hierarchy without undue disturbance.

Members of the interpretive groups were given the same number of sessions as the corresponding desensitization groups. Since very few patients recovered from their phobias by means of the interpretive procedures, the ones whose phobic symptoms persisted were provided with an opportunity of undergoing group desensitization. (There were too few desensitization failures to satisfy the minimum numerical requirements for comparable interpretive groups.) Although the main response was an immediate willingness to introduce the 'different group technique', the group of impotent men decided to continue employing interpretive procedures a while longer. Group desensitization was then administered to those patients who were not rendered symptom-free by the interpretive methods.

Results

Assessment of recovery

One month after therapy had terminated, the acrophobic and claustrophobic patients who claimed to have recovered from their phobias were required to undergo additional stress tolerance tests.

The acrophobic subjects were required to climb to the third landing of a fire escape (a height of about 50 feet). From the third story, they were required to go by elevator with the experimenter to the roof garden, eight stories above street level, and then to count the number of passing cars for 2 minutes.

The claustrophobic subjects were required to remain in the cubicle with the French windows shut and the movable screen a few inches away. Those who were able to endure the situation with no apparent distress for 5 minutes were regarded as recoveries, provided that they were also able to present satisfactory evidence that they were no longer handicapped in their life situations. The tests were conducted individually in the presence of a witness.

With two exceptions, all the patients who stated that they had recovered from their phobias were able to face the tolerance tests with outward tranquility, although some of the acrophobic patients later admitted that they had felt 'a trifle anxious' when looking down from the edge of the roof garden.

Neither the impotent men nor the members of the mixed phobic group were objectively tested.

The most rigorous criteria were used in assessing therapeutic results. For instance, only those patients who displayed an unambiguous post-therapeutic freedom from their respective phobic disorders were classified as recoveries. These criteria were, of course, essentially symptomatic. If a claustrophobic patient, for instance, was still unable after therapy to visit the cinema for fear of suffocation, his treatment was considered a failure, regardless of any ex parte testimony to the contrary. Merely to enable a patient to 'accept his neurosis' or to achieve a so-called 'personality reintegration' without symptomatic relief was considered not good enough. Recovery from a phobic condition implies total neutrality or indifference to the formerly anxiety-generating stimulus constellation. The present study made no provision for moderate or slight improvements. The latter were all classified as failures.

Statistical analysis of the results

Results are summarized in Table 3.1. As shown, there were 13 recoveries and 5 failures for desensitization, 2 recoveries and 15 failures for other forms of treatment. The resulting χ^2 value is 10.69, which is highly significant ($P<0.01$).

Additional statistical comparisons were computed for the matched pairs of acrophobic and claustrophobic patients who received group desensitization or group interpretation, respectively. There was a total of five matched pairs in these groups. Both members remained unimproved in one pair; in four, the desensitization patients recovered but the interpreta-

Table 3.1. Number of patients assigned to each condition and the therapeutic outcome

Patients	Treated by desen-sitization	Re-covered	Treated by in-terpretation	Re-covered	Treated by in-terpretation and relaxa-tion	Re-covered
Acrophobics	5	4	3	0	3	1
Claustrophobics	7	4	3	0	5	1
Impotence	2	2	3	0	–	–
Mixed group	4	3	–	–	–	–
Total	18	13	9	0	8	2

tion cases failed. There were no pairs in which both recovered or in which only interpretive methods succeeded. By applying the null hypothesis that the two methods are equally effective, the probability of obtaining this result is 0.0625.

In the case of the impotent men, no matching was carried out. Fisher's (1946, p. 97) exact test, which gave a probability of 0.1, was employed for testing significance. When the two probabilities, 0.0625 and 0.1, were combined (Fisher, 1946, p. 99), the resulting level of significance was 0.03, favoring desensitization.

It is interesting to note that when comparisons were made between the matched pairs of acrophobic and claustrophobic patients who received group desensitization as opposed to group interpretation plus relaxation, the level of significance in favor of desensitization was only 12.5 per cent. There were three matched pairs in which desensitization proved successful and interpretation plus relaxation failed. There were no cases where group interpretation plus relaxation succeeded while group desensitization failed. Both methods failed with three matched pairs and both methods succeeded with one matched pair.

Since a significance level of 12.5 per cent falls outside the conventional limits, the obvious conclusion is that there is no evidence of differences between the desensitization and interpretation plus relaxation conditions. Of course, seven matched pairs provides one with little leverage and the statistical analysis of such a small number cannot be conclusive. It is worth noting, however, that of the six individuals who were initially unsuccessfully treated by interpretation plus relaxation, four later recovered from their phobias after a mean of 9.8 group desensitization sessions.

Of the total of 15 patients who had derived no apparent benefit from the interpretive procedures, 10 recovered from their phobias after a mean of 10.1 group desensitization sessions, as compared with the mean of 20.4 sessions which were necessary for effective group desensitization when only this procedure was employed.

Follow-up studies

Follow-up studies were conducted by means of the following questionnaire:

1. Has your original phobic disorder returned?
2. If you have had a relapse, is it slight, moderate, or severe?
3. Since receiving treatment have you developed any new symptoms? (If so, please elaborate.)
4. Please underline all the following complaints which apply to you:
   Tension   Depression   Anxiety   Palpitations   Dizziness   Insomnia   Nightmares   Headaches   Tremors   Sexual problems   Fatigue   Stomach trouble   Other symptoms (specify)
5. Please indicate whether any of the above complaints commenced *after* your participation in the therapeutic groups.
6. Are you still handicapped in any area of your daily living? (Specify.)
7. Have you consulted another therapist?

The duration of after-study history varied from group to group, and ranged from 15 months to 1.5 months with a mean of 9.05 months. All those subjects whose follow-up reports revealed even slight phobic recurrences were considered to have relapsed. Particular attention was devoted to the question of possible symptom substitution, but no evidence of this phenomenon was encountered.

When the follow-up evaluations were taken into account, 10 of the 13 patients who had recovered by means of group desensitization still maintained their freedom from phobic symptoms. Thus, 3 patients were regarded as having relapsed.

Of the two patients who had recovered after undergoing group interpretation plus relaxation, one maintained his recovery.

Eight of the ten patients who recovered after undergoing postinterpretive group desensitization maintained recovery.

Summary of findings

Group desensitization was applied to 18 patients of whom 13 initially recovered and 3 subsequently relapsed.

Group interpretation was applied to nine patients. There were no recoveries in this group.

Group interpretation plus relaxation was applied to eight patients of whom two recovered and one subsequently relapsed.

The 15 patients who had not benefited from the interpretive procedures were then treated by group desensitization. There were 10 recoveries of whom 2 subsequently relapsed.

Discussion

Wolpe (1958) has expressed the basis of his 'reciprocal inhibition' therapy as follows:

> If a response incompatible with anxiety can be made to occur in the presence of anxiety-evoking stimuli so that it is accompanied by a complete or partial suppression of the anxiety-responses, the bond between these stimuli and the anxiety-responses will be weakened.

His method of systematic desensitization based on relaxation incorporates Jacobson's (1938) finding that muscular relaxation inhibits anxiety and that their concurrent expression is physiologically impossible.

The deliberate use of the parasympathetic accompaniments of skeletal muscular relaxation to inhibit neurotic anxieties reciprocally may be termed 'specific reciprocal inhibition'. There is, however, a broad range of stimuli which have *non-specific* properties for inhibiting neurotic responses reciprocally. The more usual clinical medium of verbal interchange, for instance, may in itself bring about the incidental or non-specific reciprocal inhibition of neurotic responses. In other words, it is postulated that *interview situations* can sometimes evoke autonomic responses similar to those of deep muscle relaxation.

The fact that far fewer sessions were required to desensitize those subjects in the present sample who had previously received interpretive therapy may be explicable by the notion that interpretive group situations evoked appropriate emotional responses in most of the subjects to inhibit some of their anxieties. In other words, it is probable that some of the anxiety responses evoked by the group discussions underwent a measure of non-specific reciprocal inhibition. Furthermore, those patients who received postinterpretive group desensitization had the advantage of having established a therapeutic relationship with the experimenter. It is postulated that 'the therapeutic atmosphere of empathy and acceptance may in itself reciprocally inhibit neurotic anxieties' (Lazarus, 1959).

It should be mentioned that the interpretive groups apparently enabled many of the patients to achieve a constructive modification of their self-evaluation, often clarified their evaluation of others, and enhanced their potentialities of interpersonal integration. These gains, however, appeared to have little bearing on their phobic symptoms, which usually persisted until desensitization procedures were administered.

The comparatively high relapse rate in the present series is probably related to the fact that the treatment was rather narrowly confined to a single range of stimuli which could in some cases have been a small part of a broad constellation, other elements of which may have afforded additional and possibly more useful bases for desensitization. In a proper clinical setting, the group desensitization procedures would have been preceded by individual history taking and the compilation of detailed clinical information for use either individually or in the group situations. Consequently, the conditions for the application of desensitization therapy were far less than optimum, a point which suggests that the experimental outcomes are only minimally indicative of the utility of this therapeutic approach to phobic symptoms.

The concept of 'experimenter bias' is a relevant consideration in any study of this kind. It is difficult to determine the extent to which the present results were influenced by the therapist's theoretical affiliations. In terms of subjective interest, however, it should be noted that the experimenter's preferences were decidedly in favor of the interpretive methods. Fortunately, the ennui which is generated while applying desensitization procedures is adequately offset by the gratifying results.

If another therapist had treated the interpretive groups, a significant difference in the results might merely have reflected the superiority of the individual therapist rather than the methods employed. The treatment of phobias by interpretive methods, however, is well known to be difficult. Curran and Partridge (1955), for instance, state that 'phobic symptoms are notoriously resistant to treatment, and their complete removal is rarely achieved'. Similar views are expressed by Maslow and Mittelmann (1951), Henderson and Gillespie (1955), and Mayer-Gross, Slater and Roth (1955). By contrast, phobias respond to desensitization exceedingly well (Lazarus and Rachman, 1957; Wolpe, 1958; Eysenck, 1960). It is contended, therefore, that the superior results achieved by group desensitization are not a function of the therapist's disproportionate skills (or unconscious prejudices) but a reflection of the intrinsic value of desensitization per se in the treatment of phobic disorders.

The point may legitimately be raised as to whether desensitization achieves any result other than the elimination of the phobic symptom. Comments on the general repercussions of desensitization are not possible in the context of the present study. No attempt was made to study changes in personality or general adaptation. Many patients, however, made remarks which suggested that the elimination of a phobic symptom is not an isolated process, but has many diverse and positive implications. As Eysenck (1959) states:

> The disappearance of the very annoying symptom promotes peace in the home, allays anxiety, and leads to an all-round improvement in character and behavior.

The extent to which desensitization is a method of *general* applicability (i.e. whether this method would benefit any neurotic patients other than those suffering from phobic disorders) is also worthy of mention. The value of desensitization is limited to those conditions wherein appropriate hierarchies can be constructed and where specific rather than pervasive anxiety is present. In other words, it is only where reasonably well-defined stimulus configurations can be identified that desensitization techniques should be applied. For example, patients whose interpersonal relationships are clouded by specific fears of rejection, hypersensitivity to criticism, clear-cut areas of self-consciousness or similar specific anxiety evoking stimuli often derive benefit from desensitization procedures. By contrast, desensitization cannot readily be applied in such cases as character neuroses, hysterical disorders and chronic inadequacy. A further prerequisite for the effective application of desensitization is the ability to conjure up reasonably vivid visual images which elicit emotional reactions comparable to the feelings evoked in the real situation.

While dealing with the limitations of desensitization procedures, we should not lose sight of the fact that systematic desensitization appears to be a most valuable technique in the alleviation of phobic disorders. The fact that this method can be effectively administered in *groups* suggests greater availability with little loss in economy or effectiveness for phobic sufferers.

References

CORSINI, R.J. (1957). *Methods of Group Psychotherapy*. New York: McGraw-Hill.

CURRAN, D. and PARTRIDGE, M. (1955). *Psychological Medicine*. Edinburgh: Livingstone.

EYSENCK, H.J. (1959). Learning theory and behavior therapy. *J. Ment. Sci.* **106**, 61-75.

EYSENCK, H.J. (Ed.) (1960). *Behaviour Therapy and the Neuroses*. Oxford: Pergamon.

FISHER, R.A. (1946). *Statistical Methods for Research Workers*. Edinburgh: Oliver & Boyd.

HENDERSON, D. and GILLESPIE, R.D. (1955). *A Text-book of Psychiatry*. London: Oxford University Press.

JACOBSON, E. (1938). *Progressive Relaxation*. Chicago: University of Chicago Press.

LAZARUS, A.A. (1959). The elimination of children's phobias by deconditioning. *S. Afr. Med. Proc.* **5**, 261-265.

LAZARUS, A.A. and RACHMAN, S. (1957). The use of systematic desensitization in psychotherapy. *S. Afr. Med. J.* **31**, 934-937.

MASLOW, A.H. and MITTELMANN, B. (1951). *Principles of Abnormal Psychology*. New York: Harper.

MAYER-GROSS, W., SLATER, E. and ROTH, M. (1955). *Clinical Psychiatry*. London: Cassel.

WOLBERG, L.R. (1954). *The Technique of Psychotherapy*. New York: Grune & Stratton.

WOLPE, J. (1958). *Psychotherapy by Reciprocal Inhibition*. Stanford: Stanford University Press.

Chapter 4
The Use of 'Emotive Imagery' in the Treatment of Children's Phobias (1962)

This ingenious article is the forerunner of the many imagery techniques and their uses that Lazarus subsequently developed and elaborated upon, e.g. his 1984 book *In the Mind's Eye*, and his 1987 *Mind Power* (co-authored with Dr Bernie Zilbergeld). Abramovitz, a graduate student at the time, who later became the Head of the Psychology Department at the University of Cape Town, suggested they co-author this interesting paper after observing Lazarus's clinical applications of mental imagery. It vividly shows how to apply the power of mental imagery in overcoming children's fears and phobias. The main strategy weaves cleverly targeted, evocative mental pictures into stories that are tailored to children's own fantasies and hero-images. The clinical procedures described herein are no less compelling today than they were back in the early sixties.

Some of the earliest objective approaches to the removal of specific anxieties and fears in children were based on the fact that neurotic (learned, unadaptive) responses can be eliminated by the repeated and simultaneous evocation of stronger incompatible responses. An early and well-known example of this approach was the experiment of Jones (1924) in which a child's fear of rabbits was gradually eliminated by introducing a 'pleasant stimulus', i.e. *food* (thus evoking the anxiety-inhibiting response of eating) in the presence of the rabbit. The general method of 'gradual habituation' was advocated by Jersild and Holmes (1935) as being superior to all others in the elimination of children's fears. This rationale was crystallized in Wolpe's (1958) formulation of the reciprocal inhibition principle, which deserves the closest possible study:

> If a response antagonistic to anxiety can be made to occur in the presence of anxiety-evoking stimuli so that it is accompanied by a complete or partial suppression of the anxiety responses, the bond between these stimuli and the anxiety responses will be weakened.

Written with Arnold Abramovitz and first published in 1962. Reproduced, with permission of the Royal College of Psychiatrists, from Lazarus, A. A. and Abramovitz, A. (1962). The use of 'emotive imagery' in the treatment of children's phobias. *Journal of Mental Science*, **108**, 191–195.

A crucial issue in the application of this principle is the choice of a clinically suitable anxiety-inhibiting response. The most widely used method has been that of 'systematic desensitization' (Wolpe, 1961) which may be described as gradual habituation to the imagined stimulus through the anxiety-inhibiting response of *relaxation*. Lazarus (1960) reported several successful pediatric applications of this procedure, using both feeding and relaxation. It was subsequently found, however, that neither feeding nor relaxation was feasible in certain cases. Feeding has obvious disadvantages in routine therapy, while training in relaxation is often time-consuming and difficult or impossible to achieve with certain children. The possibility of inducing anxiety-inhibiting *emotive* images, without specific training in relaxation, was then explored, and the results of our preliminary investigation form the subject of this paper.

Our use of the term 'emotive imagery' requires clarification. In the present clinical context, it refers to those classes of imagery that are assumed to arouse feelings of self-assertion, pride, affection, mirth and similar anxiety-inhibiting responses.

The technique which was finally evolved can be described in the following steps:

1. As in the usual method of systematic desensitization, the range, intensity and circumstances of the patient's fears are ascertained, and a graduated hierarchy is drawn up, from the most feared to the least feared situation.
2. By sympathetic conversation and inquiry, the clinician establishes the nature of the child's hero-images – usually derived from radio, cinema, fiction or his or her own imagination – and the wish-fulfilments and identifications which accompany them.
3. The child is then asked to close his or her eyes and told to imagine a sequence of events that is close enough to his or her everyday life to be credible, but within which is woven a story concerning his or her favorite hero or alter ego.
4. If this is done with reasonable skill and empathy, it is possible to arouse to the necessary pitch the child's affective reactions. (In some cases this may be recognized by small changes in facial expression, breathing, muscle tension etc.).
5. When the clinician judges that these emotions have been maximally aroused, he introduces, as a natural part of the narrative, the lowest item in the hierarchy. Immediately afterwards he says: 'if you feel afraid (or unhappy, or uncomfortable) just raise your finger'. If anxiety is indicated, the phobic stimulus is 'withdrawn' from the narrative and the child's anxiety-inhibiting emotions are again aroused. The procedure is then repeated as in ordinary systematic desensitization, until the highest item in the hierarchy is tolerated without distress.

The use of this procedure is illustrated in the following cases.

Case 1

Stanley M., aged 14, suffered from an intense fear of dogs, of 2½–3 years' duration. He would take two buses on a roundabout route to school rather than risk exposure to dogs on a direct 300-yard walk. He was a rather dull (IQ 93), sluggish person, very large for his age, trying to be cooperative, but sadly unresponsive – especially to attempts at training in relaxation. In his desire to please, he would state that he had been perfectly relaxed even though he had betrayed himself by his intense fidgetiness. Training in relaxation was eventually abandoned, and an attempt was made to establish the nature of his aspirations and goals. By dint of much questioning and after following many false trails due to his inarticulateness, a topic was eventually tracked down that was absorbing enough to form the subject of his fantasies, namely racing motor-cars. He had a burning ambition to own a certain Alfa Romeo sports car and race it at the Indianapolis '500' event. Emotive imagery was induced as follows: 'Close your eyes. I want you to imagine, clearly and vividly, that your wish has come true. The Alfa Romeo is now in your possession. It is your car. It is standing in the street outside your block. You are looking at it now. Notice the beautiful, sleek lines. You decide to go for a drive with some friends of yours. You sit down at the wheel, and you feel a thrill of pride as you realize that you own this magnificent machine. You start up and listen to the wonderful roar of the exhaust. You let the clutch in and the car streaks off....You are out in a clear open road now; the car is performing like a pedigree; the speedometer is climbing into the nineties; you have a wonderful feeling of being in perfect control; you look at the trees whizzing by and you see a little dog standing next to one of them – if you feel any anxiety, just raise your finger etc., etc.' An item fairly high up on the hierarchy: 'You stop at a café in a little town and dozens of people crowd around to look enviously at this magnificent car and its lucky owner; you swell with pride; and at this moment a large boxer comes up and sniffs at your heels – If you feel any anxiety etc., etc.'

After three sessions using this method he reported a marked improvement in his reaction to dogs. He was given a few field assignments during the next two sessions, after which therapy was terminated. Twelve months later, reports both from the patient and his relatives indicated that there was no longer any trace of his former phobia.

Case 2

A 10-year-old boy was referred to treatment because his excessive fear of the dark exposed him to ridicule from his 12-year-old brother and imposed severe restrictions on his parents' social activities. The lad became acutely anxious whenever his parents went visiting at night and even when they remained at home he refused to enter any darkened room unaccompanied. He insisted on sharing a room with his brother and made constant use of a night light next to his bed. He was especially afraid of remaining alone in the bathroom and only used it if a member of the household stayed there with him. On questioning, the child stated that he was not anxious during the day but that he invariably became tense and afraid towards sunset.

His fears seemed to have originated a year or so previously when he saw a frightening film, and shortly thereafter was warned by his maternal grandmother (who lived with the family) to keep away from all doors and windows at night as burglars and kidnappers were on the prowl.

A previous therapist had embarked on a program of counseling with the parents and play-therapy with the child. Whilst some important areas of interpersonal friction were apparently ameliorated, the child's phobic responses remained unchanged. Training in 'emotive imagery' eliminated his repertoire of fears in three sessions.

The initial interview (90 minutes) was devoted to psychometric testing and the development of rapport. The test revealed a superior level of intelligence (IQ 135) with definite evidence of anxiety and insecurity. He responded well to praise and encouragement throughout the test situation. Approximately 30 minutes were devoted to a general discussion of the child's interests and activities, which was also calculated to win his confidence. Towards the end of this interview, the child's passion for two radio serials, 'Superman' and 'Captain Silver', had emerged.

A week later, the child was seen again. In addition to his usual fears he had been troubled by nightmares. Also, a quarterly school report had commented on a deterioration in his schoolwork. Emotive imagery was then introduced. The child was asked to imagine that Superman and Captain Silver had joined forces and had appointed him their agent. After a brief discussion concerning the topography of his house he was given his first assignment. The therapist said, 'Now I want you to close your eyes and imagine that you are sitting in the dining-room with your mother and father. It is night time. Suddenly, you receive a signal on the wrist radio that Superman has given you. You quickly run into the lounge because your mission must be kept a secret. There is only a little light coming into the lounge from the passage. Now pretend that you are all alone in the lounge waiting for Superman and Captain Silver to visit you. Think about this very clearly. If the idea makes you feel afraid, lift up your right hand.'

An ongoing scene was terminated as soon as any anxiety was indicated. When an image aroused anxiety, it would either be represented in a more challengingly assertive manner, or it would be altered slightly so as to prove less objectively threatening.

At the end of the third session, the child was able to picture himself alone in his bathroom with all the lights turned off, awaiting a communication from Superman.

Apart from ridding the child of his specific phobia, the effect of this treatment appeared to have diverse and positive implications on many facets of his personality. His schoolwork improved immeasurably and many former manifestations of insecurity were no longer apparent. A follow-up after 11 months revealed that he had maintained his gains and was, to quote his mother, 'a completely different child'.

Case 3

An 8-year-old girl was referred for treatment because of persistent nocturnal enuresis and a fear of going to school. Her fear of the school situation was apparently engendered by a series of emotional upsets in class. In order to avoid going to school, the child resorted to a variety of devices including temper tantrums, alleged pains and illnesses, and on one occasion she was caught playing truant and intemperately upbraided by her father. Professional assistance was finally sought when it was found that her younger sister was evincing the same behavior.

When the routine psychological investigations had been completed, emotive imagery was introduced with the aid of an Enid Blyton character, Noddy, who provided a hierarchy of assertive challenges centered around the school situation. The essence of this procedure was to create imagined situations where Noddy played the role of a truant and responded fearfully to the school setting. The patient would then protect him, either by active reassurance or by 'setting a good example'.

Only four sessions were required to eliminate her school-going phobia. Her enuresis, which had received no specific therapeutic attention, was far less frequent and disappeared entirely within 2 months. The child has continued to improve despite some additional upsets at the hands of an unsympathetic teacher.

Discussion

The technique of 'emotive imagery' has been applied to nine phobic children whose ages ranged from 7 to 14 years. Seven children recovered in a mean of only 3.3 sessions. The method failed with one child who refused to cooperate and later revealed widespread areas of disturbance, which required broader therapeutic handling. The other failure was a phobic child with a history of encephalitis. He was unable to concentrate on the emotive images and could not enter into the spirit of the 'game'.

Of the seven patients who recovered, two had previously undergone treatment at the hands of different therapists. Two others had been treated by the same therapist (AAL) using reassurance, relaxation and 'environmental manipulation'. In none of these four cases was there any appreciable remission of the phobic symptoms until the present methods were applied. In every instance where the method was used, improvement occurred contemporaneously with treatment.

Follow-up inquiries were usually conducted by means of home-visits, interviews and telephone conversations both with the child and his immediate associates. These revealed that in no case was there symptom substitution of any obvious kind and that in fact, favorable response generalization had occurred in some instances.

It has been suggested that these results may be due to the therapist's enthusiasm for the method. (Does this imply that other therapists are unenthusiastic about *their* methods?) Certainly, the nature of the procedure is such that it cannot be coldly and dispassionately applied. A warm rapport with the child and a close understanding of his or her wish-fulfilments and identifications are essential. But our claim is that, although warmth and acceptance are necessary in any psychotherapeutic undertaking, they are usually not *sufficient*. Over and above such non-specific anxiety-inhibiting factors, this technique, in common with other reciprocal inhibition methods, provides a clearly defined therapeutic tool which is claimed to have *specific* effects.

Encouraging as these preliminary experiences have been, it is not claimed that they are, as yet, anything more than suggestive evidence of the efficacy of the method. Until properly controlled studies are performed, no general inference can be drawn. It is evident, too, that our loose ad hoc term 'emotive imagery' reflects a basic lack of theoretical systematization in the field of the emotions. In her review of experimental data on autonomic functions, Martin (1960) deplores the paucity of replicated studies, the unreliability of the measures used, and the lack of operational definitions of qualitatively labeled emotions. The varieties of emotion we have included under the blanket term 'emotive imagery' and our simple conjecture of anxiety-inhibiting properties for all of them is an example of the a priori assumptions we are forced to make in view of the absence of firm empirical data and adequately formulated theory. It is hoped that our demonstration of the clinical value of these techniques will help to focus attention on an unaccountably neglected area of study, but one which lies at the core of experimental clinical psychology.

References

JERSILD, A.T. and HOLMES, F. B. (1935). Methods of overcoming children's fears. *J. Psychol.* 1, 75-104.

JONES, M.C. (1924). Elimination of children's fears. *J. Exp. Psychol.* 7, 382-390.

LAZARUS, A.A. (1960). The elimination of children's phobias by deconditioning. In: Eysenck, H.J. (Ed.). *Behaviour Therapy and the Neuroses.* Oxford: Pergamon.

MARTIN, I. (1960). Somatic reactivity. In: Eysenck, H.J. (Ed.), *Handbook of Abnormal Psychology.* London: Pitman Medical.

WOLPE, J. (1958). *Psychotherapy by Reciprocal Inhibition.* Stanford, CA: Stanford University Press.

WOLPE, J. (1961). The systematic desensitization treatment of neuroses. *J. Nerv. Mental Dis.* 132, 189-203.

Chapter 5
Behavior Therapy, Incomplete Treatment and Symptom Substitution (1965)

We find many issues in this article that still remain current and perhaps passionate topics of debate - problems of relapse, symptom substitution and the perennial issue of thorough vs superficial treatment procedures. Lazarus argues for a broad-based treatment regimen and discusses a specific uncomplicated case in order to illustrate his point. His 'technical eclecticism' stands out. He then discusses the treatment of a young woman with obsessive-compulsive problems. It is interesting to note how Lazarus struggled to find a means whereby the client's compulsive washing could be eliminated. In retrospect, he finally administered a form of 'response prevention', which is now considered an indispensable condition in the amelioration of most compulsive habits. It is noteworthy that Lazarus, although an ardent 'behaviour therapist' when he wrote this paper, emphasised the significance of empathy and the social influence of the patient-therapist relationship.

The clinical application of principles and methods consistent with experimental data on learning and conditioning has been termed 'behavior therapy' (Lazarus, 1958; Eysenck, 1959; Rachman, 1963a). Wolpe (1958), the leading exponent in the field, has devised several specific techniques which have proved highly effective in ameliorating a wide range of neurotic disorders. Although the literature in this rapidly developing field attests to the overall economy and effectiveness of these methods (when properly applied), substantial numbers of practitioners have nonetheless remained impervious to or suspicious of them. One of the main objections to behavior therapy appears to be the persistent contention that deconditioning procedures result in rapid relapse or in the development of new problems, sometimes more debilitating than the original complaints. Friedman (1959), in his discussion of phobic disorders, typifies this particular viewpoint: 'As long as the underlying conflicts remain untouched

First published in 1965. Reproduced, with the permission of Williams & Wilkins, Baltimore, from Lazarus, A.A. Behavior therapy, incomplete treatment, and symptom substitution. *Journal of Nervous and Mental Disease*, **140**, 80-86.

and unconscious, the patient is prone to develop a new phobic symptom in place of the one removed.'

An opposing point of view, exemplified by Yates (1958), is an outright dismissal of 'symptom substitution' as a spurious outgrowth of the psychodynamic model and its putative repressed complexes. Eysenck (Eysenck, 1959, 1963) has argued, however, that learning theory would predict a high relapse probability for certain disorders (e.g. hysteria, fetishism, homosexuality, alcoholism). The social learning theory espoused by Bandura and Walters (1963) makes explicit the concept of 'symptom substitution':

> If the patient has learned relatively few prosocial means of obtaining the rewards or relief which his deviant behavior was aimed at securing, it is always possible that following elimination of one deviant pattern, another set of deviant responses will occur.

It would seem far more profitable to examine the conditions under which 'symptom substitution' is likely to occur, instead of adopting either the unsubstantiated dogma that 'conditioning therapies result in substitute symptoms' or the equally frenetic counter that 'symptom substitution is a myth'.

The crux of the matter may be summarized as follows: when treatment is incomplete, patients are likely to relapse (i.e. to be troubled again by the same problems that originally motivated them to seek help) and/or acquire new aberrant response patterns ('symptom substitution'). It is essential to cite concrete examples of what is meant by 'complete' and 'incomplete' methods of treatment. First, it should be emphasized that theorists who equate conditioning therapies with techniques of hypnotic suppression or simple suggestion (Bookbinder, 1962) labor under a serious misapprehension. A recent attempt (Lazarus, 1964a) has been made to illustrate that, in behavior therapy, even so-called simple monosymptomatic phobias sometimes require therapeutic attention to areas beyond the presenting complaints. Broadly speaking, few experienced behavior therapists would disagree with the notion that treatment which leaves the neurotic roots untouched is likely to be short-lived and unreliable. The issue at point, however, is the precise nature of these 'neurotic roots'. Whereas dynamic theorists of varying persuasions debate the relative merits or demerits of id impulses, Oedipal irresolution, primordial images and parataxic distortions, behavior theory is inclined to draw upon a different set of postulates:

> On the basis of such a theory, the behavioral disturbance described as neurotic may be analysed into two types of response; (i) the CAD ('conditioned avoidance drive') or anxiety response itself which will have visceral, skeletal and nervous components, and (ii) various instrumental responses by which the conditioned stimuli are removed and hence the CAD reduced. Both are learned behavioral responses and, as such, are symptoms of the neurosis: their division may parallel the Freudian distinction between the underlying neurosis and its symptoms. (Jones, 1960)

Despite many obvious similarities between psychodynamic and learning-theory formulations (Dollard and Miller, 1950) the 'repressed material that is at root of patients' difficulties' (Coleman, 1960) is a very different conception from the CAD, 'both from the point of view of its origins, as well as from the point of view of the appropriate method of extinction' (Eysenck, 1959).

The following case history provides a clear example of behavior therapeutic strategy:

> A 32-year-old insurance clerk requested hypnotherapy for frequent attacks of abdominal spasm which his physicians had assured him were 'purely functional'. Life history data and psychometric testing revealed a tense and anxious individual whose servile attitude towards his father had generalized to most authority figures. Strong but covert resentment towards many facets of his work situation were evident. He also reported considerable reticence in his general dealings with people.
>
> The first six therapeutic sessions were devoted to training him in progressive (non-hypnotic) relaxation (Jacobson, 1938; Wolpe, 1958) and to an intellectual examination of the negative consequences which ensued from his timidity and inhibitions. The next eight sessions centered around 'behavior rehearsal' procedures. In this method patient and therapist role-played various scenes which posed assertive problems for the patient – expressing disagreement with a friend's social arrangements, asking a favor, upbraiding a subordinate at work, contradicting a fellow employee, refusing to accede to an unreasonable request, complaining to his employer about the inferior office fixtures, requesting an increment in salary, criticizing his father's attire, questioning his father's values, and so forth. Commencing with the less demanding situations, each scene was systematically rehearsed until the most troublesome encounters had been enacted to the satisfaction of patient and therapist.* A situation was regarded as 'satisfactorily covered' (1) when the patient was able to enact it without feeling anxious (if he became tense or anxious while rehearsing a scene, deep relaxation was applied until he felt calm again); (2) when his general demeanor, posture, facial expression, inflection in tone, and the like, lent substance to his words (repeated play-backs from a tape recorder helped to remove a querulous pitch from his voice); and (3) when agreement was reached that his words and actions would seem fair and fitting to an objective onlooker.
>
> In order to expedite the transfer from consulting room to actual life, the patient was initially encouraged to apply his newly acquired assertive skills only when negative consequences were highly improbable. Although he soon grew proficient at handling most situations that called for uninhibited and forthright behavior, he continued to be intimidated by his father. Consequently, while deeply relaxed, he was asked to imagine progressively more exacting altercations with his father. After 15 sessions of this systematic desensitization therapy (Wolpe, 1961a) he stated that he was no longer afraid of his father and attributed this to 'a better understanding of the old man's limitations'.

---

*The therapist usually role-played the significant persons in the patient's life according to descriptions provided by the latter. The patient's behavior was shaped by means of constructive criticism as well as modeling procedures (Bandura, 1961, 1964) in which the therapist assumed the patient's role and demonstrated the desirable responses.

On three occasions single full-capacity inhalations of 70% CO_2 and 30% O_2 were used. Wolpe (1958) has reported good results with this method in treating pervasive anxiety. In the present instance, very mild but essentially transient benefits could be attributed to the use of this procedure.

The patient was seen approximately twice-weekly for almost 4 months. His presenting complaint, abdominal spasm, disappeared as soon as he became fairly adept at relaxation (less than a month after commencing therapy). A follow-up examination after 13 months revealed that he had been promoted to a senior executive position and appeared to be coping extremely well; neither relapse nor symptom substitution had occurred.

This relatively uncomplex case would be regarded as a therapeutic oasis by most practitioners who have treated those hopelessly arid personalities which comprise a significant portion of the patient population. It should not be inferred that behavior therapy is of value only for 'simple' neuroses (Wolpe, 1964). Nevertheless, the abovementioned case affords an excellent opportunity to examine the heuristic virtues of several therapeutic strategies.

The administration of spasmolytics would clearly have been of limited effectiveness. Similarly, hypnotic suggestion would most probably have had ephemeral effects resulting in renewed abdominal pain or further stress-induced symptoms as described by Seitz (1953). Relaxation therapy as the sole treatment procedure might have reduced the patient's general anxiety (Wolpe, 1958; Lazarus, 1963a), but the necessary modification of his interpersonal inadequacies would have been left to fortuitous circumstances.

The actual treatment program served a dual purpose – it not only eliminated the patient's maladaptive anxieties but also provided specific training in the acquisition of adaptive responses. In short, treatment consisted of ferreting out the stimulus antecedents of the patient's neurotic reactions with special reference to basic anxiety-generating cues. The anxiety-response habits were then systematically eliminated whilst effective instrumental responses were simultaneously provided. Instead of dwelling on the reconstruction of past relationships and the gradual infiltration of information designed to yield insight, there is an obvious economy in treatment programs which attempt to modify maladaptive responses immediately by promoting, at the outset of therapy, the kinds of reactions necessary for coping behavior. Although the methods themselves are not new, they are certainly used quite differently from the manner advocated by their originators. Jacobson's (1938) pioneering work on the anxiety-inhibiting effects of relaxation, for instance, did not envisage the use of relaxation responses within the highly specific and systematic context of desensitization therapy (Wolpe, 1958, 1961a, 1962). Similarly, the 'behavior rehearsal' procedures described above may bear some resemblance to Moreno's 'psychodrama', but unlike the latter, they are directed solely at the patient's current interpersonal difficulties.

Some psychoanalysts would probably be inclined to go at least one step further and postulate a castration complex underlying the patient's symptomatology. Theoreticians are obviously at liberty to assume whatever they please, but the onus is on them to prove that their constructs are not only valid but also necessary. Assuming, however, that castration anxieties were at the root of the patient's problems, several considerations immediately become apparent. Did the abovementioned treatment inadvertently succeed in resolving the patient's intrapsychic conflicts? If so, precisely how was this accomplished?* If not, what will be the short-term, as well as long-term, consequences of this unresolved complex? Suffice it to say that the usefulness and accuracy of this type of theorizing is in serious dispute (Wohlgemuth, 1923; Johnson, 1948; Eysenck, 1953; Salter, 1953; Wolpe and Bandura, 1960; Wolpe, 1961b; Bandura and Walters, 1963; Levy, 1963; Rachman, 1963b; Wells, 1963).

Thus far, the emphasis has been on the necessity to extinguish the basic neurotic anxieties so that therapeutic outcomes may be positive and enduring. In certain obsessive–compulsive disorders, however, it is insufficient to eliminate the basic drive tendencies without treating the instrumental acts as well. Walton and Mather (1963) have provided evidence to support the contention that long-standing or *chronic* cases require 'the extinction of both the initial autonomic conditioned responses and the motor reactions'. The following case adds further support to this contention.

A 19-year-old girl had suffered for 3½ years from an urge to wash her hands excessively whenever she accidentally or deliberately touched any part of her own body. She dated the onset of her problem to a turbulent period of her life when she was 15 years old. At that time, she felt guilty about the fact that she was having sexual relations with her cousin, and was understandably concerned over a bout of amenorrhea which lasted for more than 2 months. At the same time, she was perturbed by the moralistic attitude adopted by a girlfriend in whom she had confided.

The therapist's accepting and non-judgmental attitude appeared to play a major role in reducing much of her overall anxiety. Since sexual participation had acquired aversive properties for her, she was desensitized to a variety of sexual stimuli which ranged from 'admiring glances from male friends' to 'asking a boyfriend for manual stimulation before or after sexual intercourse'. (For a more detailed account of the value of systematic desensitization in the treatment of frigidity, see Lazarus (1963b).)

More than 30 desensitization sessions were necessary before she was able to enjoy coitus to full orgastic capacity. Although she claimed to be feeling 'so much better and happier all round', and stated that she could fondle and caress her boyfriend with unambiguous enjoyment, her compulsion to wash was as pronounced as ever when she touched any part of her own body.

---

*During a recent discussion with a psychoanalyst, the opinion ventured was that the patient had introjected the therapist and now possessed a non-punitive father. Further discussion seemed to point to the inescapable conclusion that behavior therapy is the most efficient and effective form of psychoanalysis!

The following procedure was then adopted: deep relaxation was induced and thin sheets of paper were placed across her knees. She was asked to rest her hands on this paper and instructed to relax even further. Thinner and thinner sheets of paper were applied, until only a single sheet of porous tissue paper was used. Finally, deep relaxation was applied following actual contact between her hands and knees. Although this method enabled her to increase the latency between self-contact and washing, it decreased neither the frequency nor the intensity of her compulsive behavior. Utilizing a procedure described by Lazarus (1958), she was hypnotized and asked to imagine extreme feelings of discomfort while engaging in compulsive handwashing, followed by imagining marked relief when resisting the compulsive act. This also proved unsuccessful.

She was then provided with a portable faradic shock unit, instructed to attach the electrodes to her upper arms, and told to switch the current onto 'continuous shock' whenever she engaged in compulsive handwashing. It was impressed upon her that she was not to switch off the apparatus until she actually stopped washing her hands. She was asked to note the number of times she used the apparatus each day. During the first week, her frequency dropped from 16 times on the first day to 3 on the seventh day. By the end of the second week, she rarely engaged in compulsive handwashing more than once a day. It was then discovered that she was merely avoiding any contact with her own body, and that the urge to wash was only slightly weaker when contact did occur. Aversion therapy on a daily basis in the consulting room was then added to her regime. She was instructed to touch various parts of her body and invited to wash her hands when she so desired whilst the therapist administered unpleasant electric shocks (on an intermittent schedule) to her forearms from a larger faradic unit. After four sessions she pronounced herself 'cured', but overlearning was administered during an additional period of 6 days. (It is hoped that the methods of aversion therapy described in this paper stand in marked contrast to certain attacks on human dignity by means of violent emetic drugs which also go under the guise of 'behavior therapy'.)

Follow-up inquiries were conducted 3 months and 7 months after terminating treatment. During the first inquiry, she stated that she had not relapsed in any respect, but reported that she had been sleeping poorly for the past few weeks. This was regarded as possible evidence of 'symptom substitution', but during the second follow-up interview (4 months later), she stated that her former sound sleep pattern had soon returned. On this occasion, no evidence of relapse or symptom substitution could be found. She casually mentioned that she was even able to masturbate without afterwards engaging in compulsive washing.

Wolpe (1964) has also drawn attention to the existence of seemingly autonomous obsessive–compulsive habits which may persist even when there is no longer any apparent basis for them in terms of anxiety. The widespread notion that cases like the latter are notoriously resistant to treatment is probably due to the fact that maladaptive acts may persist even when 'intrapsychic conflicts' have been resolved. When compulsive behavior has been present over several years, 'treatment of the original CAD would not be expected to remove the motor compulsions, because the original stimuli, said to be associated with the CAD would be different from those now evoking the motor habits' (Walton and Mather, 1963). Conversely, if only the patient's instrumental acts were removed, her basic drive tendencies would probably have resulted in the acquisition of new compulsive reactions, or her previous handwashing pattern would once more have become manifest. According to this theory, effective treatment in these cases requires both the elimination of the primary anxieties and deliberate removal of the secondary instrumental acts. A correctly executed treatment program along these lines should not result in relapse or in 'symptom substitution'.

Wolpe (1963) has drawn timely attention to the fact that the misapplication of behavior therapy by certain individuals should not be permitted to discredit the entire system. Many individuals seem attracted to, or repelled by, behavior therapy for mistaken reasons. Those who find the apparent simplicity of the methods alluring and who venture to apply them without the benefits of a preliminary 'apprenticeship', often violate even elementary procedural steps. Moreover, 'interpersonal' and 'subjective' factors should not be minimized as they are still important to therapeutic success-and-failure. When confronted with the task of alleviating the suffering of a fellow human being, the competent behavior therapist can draw comfort from his 10 or 20 specific therapeutic techniques derived from 'modern learning theory', but his own empathetic, influencing characteristics cannot yet be ruled out of the final picture (Lazarus, 1961, 1963a). Hopefully, these vital 'non-specifics' can be explicated and set within a proper theoretical framework, but until this point is reached, hard-headed pseudotheoretical rigidity can only prove deleterious to the patient's ultimate welfare.

Acknowledgments

The writer wishes to express his appreciation to Dr Michael B. Conant and Dr Jon R. Davidson for their constructive criticisms.

References

BANDURA, A. (1961). Psychotherapy as a learning process. *Psychol. Bull.* **58**, 143–157.

BANDURA, A. (1964). Behavioral modification through modeling procedures. In: Krasner, L. and Ullmann, L.P. (Eds), *Research in Behavior Modification*. New York: Holt, Rinehart & Winston.

BANDURA, A. and WALTERS, R.H. (1963). *Social Learning and Personality Development*. New York: Holt, Rinehart & Winston.

BOOKBINDER, L.J. (1962). Simple conditioning vs. the dynamic approach to symptoms and symptom substitution: A reply to Yates. *Psychol. Rep.* **10**, 71–77.

COLEMAN, J. (1960). *Personality Dynamics and Effective Behavior*. Chicago: Scott, Foresman.

DOLLARD, J. and MILLER, N.E. (1950). *Personality and Psychotherapy*. New York: McGraw-Hill.

EYSENCK, H.J. (1953). *The Uses and Abuses of Psychology*. London: Penguin Books.

EYSENCK, H.J. (1959). Learning theory and behavior therapy. *J. Ment. Sci.* **105**, 61–75.

EYSENCK, H.J. (1963). Behavior therapy, extinction and relapse in neurosis. *Br. J. Psychiatr.* **109**, 12-18.

FRIEDMAN, P. (1959). The phobias. In: Arieti. S. (Ed.), *American Handbook of Psychiatry*, Vol. 1, pp. 293-306. New York: Basic Books.

JACOBSON, E. (1938). *Progressive Relaxation.* Chicago: University of Chicago Press.

JOHNSON, H.K. (1948). Psychoanalysis: A critique. *Psychiatr. Q.* **22**, 321-338.

JONES, H.G. (1960). Learning and abnormal behavior. In: Eysenck, H.J. (Ed.), *Handbook of Abnormal Psychology*, pp. 488-528. London: Pitman.

LAZARUS, A.A. (1958). New methods in psychotherapy: A case study. *S. Afr. Med. J.* **33**, 660-663.

LAZARUS, A.A. (1961). Group therapy of phobic disorders by systematic desensitization. *J. Abnorm. Soc. Psychol.* **63**, 504-510.

LAZARUS, A.A. (1963a). The results of behavior therapy in 126 cases of severe neurosis. *Behav. Res. Ther.* **1**, 69-79.

LAZARUS, A.A. (1963b). The treatment of chronic frigidity by systematic desensitization. *J. Nerv. Ment. Dis.* **136**, 272-278.

LAZARUS, A.A. (1964a). Behavior therapy with identical twins. *Behav. Res. Ther.* **1**, 313-319.

LAZARUS, A.A. (1964b). Crucial procedural factors in desensitization therapy. *Behav. Res. Ther.* **2**, 65-70.

LEVY, L.H. (1963). *Psychological Interpretation.* New York: Holt, Rinehart & Winston.

RACHMAN, S. (1963a). Introduction to behavior therapy. *Behav. Res. Ther.* **1**, 3-15.

RACHMAN, S. (Ed.) (1963b). *Critical Essays on Psychoanalysis.* Oxford: Pergamon Press.

SALTER, A. (1953). *The Case Against Psychoanalysis.* New York: Holt.

SEITZ, P.F.D. (1953). Experiments in the substitution of symptoms by hypnosis: II. *Psychosom. Med.* **15**, 405-422.

WALTON, D. and MATHER, M.D. (1963). The application of learning principles to the treatment of obsessive-compulsive states in the acute and chronic phases of illness. *Behav. Res. Ther.* **1**, 163-171.

WELLS, H.K. (1963). *The Failure of Psychoanalysis.* New York: International Publishers.

WOHLGEMUTH, A. (1923). *Critical Examination of Psychoanalysis.* London: Allen & Unwin.

WOLPE, J. (1958). *Psychotherapy by Reciprocal Inhibition.* Stanford: Stanford University Press.

WOLPE, J. (1961a). The systematic desensitization treatment of neuroses. *J. Nerv. Ment. Dis.* **132**, 189-203.

WOLPE, J. (1961b). The prognosis in unpsychoanalysed recovery from neurosis. *Am. J. Psychiatr.* **118**, 35-39.

WOLPE, J. (1962). Isolation of a conditioning procedure as the crucial psychotherapeutic factor: A case study. *J. Nerv. Ment. Dis.* **134**, 316-329.

WOLPE, J. (1963). Behavior therapy. *Lancet* i, 886.

WOLPE, J. (1964). Behavior therapy in complex neurotic states. *Br. J. Psychiatr.* **110**, 28-34.

WOLPE, J. and RACHMAN, S. (1960). Psychoanalytic 'evidence': A critique based on Freud's case of little Hans. *J. Nerv. Ment. Dis.* **131**, 135-148.

YATES, A.J. (1958). Symptoms and symptom substitution. *Psychol. Rev.* **65**, 371-374.

Chapter 6
Behavior Rehearsal vs Non-directive Therapy vs Advice in Effecting Behavior Change (1966)

In 1963, Lazarus introduced the term 'behaviour rehearsal' to describe active role-playing and role-reversal procedures primarily intended to enable clients to develop social and assertive skills. In this chapter, Lazarus reports a clinical experiment in which he found behaviour rehearsal to be significantly more effective than interpretation and/or advice. These clinical impressions are in keeping with the observatiaon that active performance-based methods are usually superior to purely verbal processes and procedures.

Introduction and Procedure

To date, the only behavior therapy techniques to have been experimentally tested are systematic desensitization and aversion therapy (Lazovik and Lang, 1960; Lazarus, 1961; Lang and Lazovik, 1963; Feldman and McCulloch, 1965; Paul, 1966). The present paper offers the first objective clinical appraisal of *behavior rehearsal* (Lazarus, 1963, 1964; see Chapter 5), which has also been called 'behavioristic psychodrama' (Wolpe, 1958; Sturm, 1965), role-playing, and play-acting. The appellation 'behavior rehearsal' seems preferable because it indicates both the content and intent of the actual procedure. Behavior rehearsal is a specific procedure which aims to replace deficient or inadequate social or interpersonal responses by efficient and effective behavior patterns. The patient achieves this by practicing the desired forms of behavior under the direction and supervision of the therapist.

Behavior rehearsal is most commonly employed with patients lacking in assertive behavior. The therapist plays the role of someone to whom the patient usually reacts with excessive anxiety, while the patient is directed

First published in 1966. Reproduced, with the permission of Pergamon Press, from Lazarus, A.A. (1966). Behaviour rehearsal vs nondirective therapy vs advice in effecting behaviour change. *Behaviour Research and Therapy*, 4, 209–212.

to respond in an uninhibited, forthright and even aggressive manner. Repeated rehearsals usually diminish the patient's anxieties so that he or she is eventually able to extend his or her gains beyond the confines of the consulting room. Role reversal (where the therapist plays the patient's role and models the desirable responses) is often employed and affords a useful means of learning by imitation (Bandura, 1961, 1965).

The following is a characteristic account of a training procedure designed for the development of assertive responses by means of behavior rehearsal (Chapter 5):

> In this method patient and therapist role-played various scenes which posed assertive problems for the patient...expressing disagreement with a friend's social arrangements, asking a favor, upbraiding a subordinate at work, contradicting a fellow employee, refusing to accede to an unreasonable request, complaining to his employer about the inferior office fixtures, requesting an increment in salary, criticizing his father's attire, questioning his father's values, and so forth. Commencing with the less demanding situations, each scene was systematically rehearsed until the most troublesome encounters had been enacted to the satisfaction of patient and therapist. The therapist usually role-played the significant persons in the patient's life according to descriptions provided by the latter. The patient's behavior was shaped by means of constructive criticism as well as modeling procedures in which the therapist assumed the patient's role and demonstrated the desirable responses. A situation was regarded as 'satisfactorily covered' (1) when the patient was able to enact it without feeling anxious (if he became tense or anxious while rehearsing a scene, deep relaxation was applied until he felt calm again); (2) when his general demeanor, posture, facial expression, inflection in tone, and the like, lent substance to his words (repeated play-backs from a tape recorder helped to remove a querulous pitch from his voice); and (3) when agreement was reached that his words and actions would seem fair and fitting to an objective onlooker. In order to expedite the transfer from consulting room to actual life, the patient was initially encouraged to apply his newly acquired assertive skills only when negative consequences were highly improbable...he soon grew proficient at handling most situations that called for uninhibited and forthright behavior...

In addition to their use in the acquisition of assertive responses, behavior rehearsal procedures can be applied to a variety of behavior patterns. Here are some typical complaints to which their application would be relevant:

1. 'I'm being interviewed for a job next week and I just don't know how to get across the fact that I really know my work although my qualifications are not as high as they should be.'
2. 'I keep putting off 'phoning Mary for a date because I don't know what to say to her.'
3. 'I'm completely useless at starting conversations with strangers.'
4. 'How can I get my husband to realize that if I take a morning job, the house and the children will not be neglected?'
5. 'In two weeks' time I'm having an oral test on counseling techniques. I wonder what sort of questions they can put to me?'

6. 'I never know what to say when people ask me questions about my
   daughter who is in a mental hospital.'

People seldom enter therapy solely for help with isolated problems of this
kind, but they frequently raise them during therapy. Traditional psychotherapists usually handle these individual difficulties by reflection or
interpretation; and some of those who are more directive may offer
advice. It is obviously important to compare the relative effectiveness of
reflection–interpretation, advice and behavior rehearsal in meeting these
situations.

The present study was stimulated about a year ago when a 19-year-old
girl consulted the writer primarily for the alleviation of tension headaches
and dysmenorrhea. She felt that her symptoms were largely a reaction to
the stresses at home (her widowed mother had remarried some 2 years
previously and the patient had become progressively more antagonistic to
the fact that her stepfather was inclined to over-assert his authority over
her). She considered it necessary to live away from home but hesitated to
make a move as she felt that this would hurt her mother. A previous therapist, after exploring the dynamics of the situation, was in agreement that
a break from home was indicated. The patient had derived comfort and
reassurance from this therapy but she lacked the instrumental responses
for putting her insights into action. 'I don't know how to put it to my
Mom ... My stepfather is very good to her and I don't want to breed any
ill-will between them.' The writer advised her to stop procrastinating and
to discuss the matter with her parents, deflecting the emphasis away from
her negative attitude towards her stepfather, but stressing instead that two
therapists considered it necessary for her to live away from home so as to
develop self-sufficiency and independence (which was in fact a subsidiary
goal). A week later, she stated that she had still not 'plucked up enough
courage' to confront her parents, and bolstered her passive attitude with
elaborate rationalizations. Behavior rehearsal was then employed. The
therapist commenced the procedure by playing the patient's role while
she in turn played the part of her mother. The roles were then reversed
and the patient finally succeeded in acting her own part in a rational, persuasive and tactful manner. She telephoned the following day to inform
the therapist that she had discussed the matter with her parents and that,
after minor objections, they had agreed to accede to her wishes. It might
be mentioned in passing that her tension headaches soon disappeared and
her bouts of dysmenorrhea, although still troublesome, became less debilitating.

Cases like the one above have repeatedly suggested the superior effectiveness of behavior rehearsal in teaching people to meet and cope with
specific interpersonal problems, but as in the foregoing instance, there
was no clear indication that behavior rehearsal alone deserved credit for

the final execution of the desired response. To what extent had the previous therapist's dynamic exploration and reassurance paved the way? What role was played by the writer's explicit advice which he proferred before employing behavior rehearsal? In order to assess the value of behavior rehearsal per se, the following plan was adopted.

Each patient who had received no previous treatment and who brought specific social and/or interpersonal difficulties to the attention of the therapist (regardless of their overall problems and primary reasons for seeking therapy) was treated for these specific problems by reflection–interpretation, by direct advice or by behavior rehearsal. Patients were arbitrarily assigned to one of the three procedures. When patients presented more than one specific problem area, the most pressing difficulty was selected for treatment. (It might be noted that at the completion of the experiment, two patients who each raised three specific interpersonal problems received a reflective-interpretative treatment for one of their difficulties; advice was dispensed in the hope of overcoming a second problem; and behavior rehearsal was employed with the remaining problem. In each instance, the problem area which received behavior rehearsal was soon resolved, but the difficulties which were treated by advice and by means of interpretation remained unresolved until they too received behavior rehearsal.)

A maximum of four 30-min sessions was devoted to each treatment condition. If there was no evidence of change or learning within one month the treatment was regarded as having failed. The criterion of change or learning was objective evidence that the patient was indeed behaving adaptively in the area which had previously constituted a problem – the reticent and socially awkward young girl was going out on regular 'dates'; the company executive was effecting a promising merger with a rival concern; the secretary had received her much desired salary increment; the timid suitor had successfully proposed marriage to his girlfriend; the considerate husband had persuaded his wife that it would be to their ultimate advantage to move out of her parents' house into a home of their own; and so forth. The experiment was terminated when 75 patients had been evenly covered by the three treatment procedures. The therapeutic results are shown in Table 6.1. Of the 31 patients who did not benefit either from reflection-interpretation or from advice, 27 were then treated by means

Table 6.1. Outcome of treatment

Treatment procedure	No.	Evidence of learning	Percentage
Reflection–interpretation	25	8	32
Advice	25	11	44
Behavior rehearsal	25	23	92

of behavior rehearsal. There was evidence of learning in 22 (81 per cent). Thus, the overall effectiveness of behavior rehearsal in 52 cases was 86.5 per cent.

Discussion

These results suggest that behavior rehearsal is significantly more effective in resolving specific social and interpersonal problems than direct advice or non-directive therapy. Since all three therapeutic procedures were administered by the writer, however, the possibility of experimenter bias has not been excluded. Nevertheless on theoretical grounds the superior effectiveness of behavior rehearsal may be predicted. This technique is a crucial and versatile learning device which places exclusive emphasis on *active participation*. Sturm (1965) has indicated that techniques such as behavior rehearsal would reveal an advantage over traditional psychotherapy in that they have 'a far greater potential to (1) generate vivid, life-like behavior and cues, thereby maximizing the utility of response and stimulus generalization; (2) condition a *total* behavioral response – physiological, motoric and ideational – rather than one merely verbal; and (3) dispense the powerful reinforcements of enacted models and other characters, who in real life or in fantasy have already dispensed reinforcements.' Sturm also notes that the skilful application of flexible techniques such as behavior rehearsal helps to create near-veridical behavior while focusing on the problem at hand, thereby facilitating the patient's ease and efficiency in participating and learning. In short, it may be argued that behavior rehearsal deserves a more prominent place in the repertoire of therapists of diverse theoretical persuasions.

Acknowledgment

Special thanks are due to Professor Joseph Wolpe for his constructive criticisms.

References

BANDURA, A. (1961). Psychotherapy as a learning process. *Psychol. Bull.* **58**, 143–157.

BANDURA, A. (1965). Behavioral modification through modelling procedures. In: Krasner L. and Ullmann, L.P. (Eds), *Research in Behavior Modification*, pp. 310–340. New York: Holt, Rinehart & Winston.

FELDMAN, P. and McCULLOCH, M. (1965). The application of avoidance learning to the treatment of homosexuality. *Behav. Res. Ther.* **2**, 165–172.

LANG, P.J. and LAZOVIK, A.D. (1963). The experimental desensitization of a phobia. *J. Abnorm. Soc. Psychol.* **66**, 519–525.

LAZARUS, A.A. (1961). Group therapy of phobic disorders by systematic desensitization. *J. Abnorm. Soc. Psychol.* **63**, 504–510.

LAZARUS, A.A. (1963). The results of behaviour therapy in 126 cases of severe neurosis. *Behav. Res. Ther.* **1**, 69–79.

LAZARUS, A.A. (1964). Behaviour therapy with identical twins. *Behav. Res. Ther.* **1**, 313-319.

LAZOVIK, A.D. and LANG, P.J. (1960). A laboratory demonstration of systematic desensitization psychotherapy. *J. Psychol. Stud.* **11**, 238-247.

PAUL, G.L. (1966). *Insight Vs. Desensitization in Psychotherapy: An Experiment in Anxiety Reduction.* Stanford: Stanford University Press.

STURM, I.E. (1965). The behavioristic aspect of psychodrama. *Group Psychother.* **18**, 50-64.

WOLPE, J. (1958). *Psychotherapy by Reciprocal Inhibition.* Stanford: Stanford University Press.

WOLPE, J. and LAZARUS, A.A. (1966). *Behaviour Therapy Techniques.* Oxford: Pergamon Press.

Chapter 7
In Support of Technical Eclecticism (1967)

Today, the field of psychotherapy is characterised by a diversity of eclectic and integrationist viewpoints. There are now national and international societies and professional journals devoted to the study of systematic (technical) eclecticism. Lazarus is recognised as the first therapist to emphasise the differences between theoretical and technical eclecticism, and he is also described as the most pro-lific, eloquent and influential spokesperson for a technically eclectic position. This short report back in 1967 succinctly underscored the major essentials of a view that has become one of the main streams within the present-day psycho-therapeutic community. Lazarus has written many thorough and sophisticated accounts of technical eclecticism, but this, his very first statement on the subject, remains eminently cogent.

The plethora of psychological theories is exceeded only by the dearth of testable deductions emanating therefrom. Harper (1959), for instance, described 36 separate systems of psychotherapy which he regarded as 'the main types of psychological treatment'. There are, in fact, many other clearly identifiable 'systems' which can be added to Harper's list. These would include: transactional analysis, psychosynthesis, reality therapy, reparative psychotherapy, integrity therapy, implosive psychotherapy and Morita therapy, to mention a few.

Faced with this complex, contradictory and often confusing array of psychological theories and systems, most practitioners seek refuge in those notions which best satisfy their own subjective needs. Yet one may legitimately inquire whether the consequence of adhering to a particular school of thought is to exclude from one's armamentarium a significant range of effective procedures. Who, even in a life-time of endeavor, can hope to encompass such a diverse and multifarious range of thought and theory? Indeed, an attempt to imbibe and digest this overwhelming mass

First published in 1967. Reprinted with permission of publisher from: Lazarus, A.A. In support of technical eclecticism. *Psychological Reports*, 1967, **21**, 415–416.

of information (and misinformation) may be no more rewarding than gluttony at any other level. Is there a way out of this morass?

To luxuriate in a metaphor, we might conceivably wield Occam's razor the way Alexander the Great used his sword, to cut *through* the Gordian knot instead of becoming involved in its intricacies. Occam taught that explanatory principles should not be needlessly multiplied. In keeping with this, the general principle of scientific thinking is that given two equally tenable hypotheses the simpler of the two is to be preferred. Add to this London's (1964) profound observation that: 'However interesting, plausible, and appealing a theory may be, it is techniques, not theories, that are actually used on people. Study of the effects of psychotherapy, therefore, is always the study of the effectiveness of techniques.'

Can a practicing psychotherapist afford to ignore any effective technique, regardless of its theoretical origins? Obviously, a technique derived from a source or system which is at variance with one's own theoretical beliefs may nevertheless possess healing properties – not necessarily for reasons which attach to the theories of its originator. Consider the case of a highly anxious patient who received relaxation therapy (Jacobson, 1964) to diminish his or her overall tensions, while receiving systematic desensitization (Wolpe, 1961; Wolpe and Lazarus, 1966) to various subjectively threatening situations and also being trained to be 'excitatory' (Salter, 1949) by assertively standing up for his or her rights and by giving vent to his or her feelings. This was extended to embrace self-disclosure (rather than a life of concealment and camouflage) as a means of achieving social harmony (Jourard, 1964). The patient's irrational ideas were handled along lines advocated by Ellis (1962).

Now, the theoretical notions espoused by Jacobson, Wolpe, Salter, Jourard and Ellis are very much at odds with one another. The eclectic theorist who borrows bits and pieces from divergent theories in the hope of building a composite system must inevitably embrace contradictory notions and thus is likely to find him- or herself in a state of confusion worse confounded. But it is not necessary to accept or reconcile divergent theoretical systems in order to utilize their techniques.

And so it is with Harper's (1959) three-dozen systems and the dozens of others we could add to his original list. To attempt a theoretical *rapprochement* is as futile as seriously trying to picture the edge of the universe. But to read through the vast mass of literature on psychotherapy, *in search of techniques*, can be clinically enriching and therapeutically rewarding.

However, this should not presuppose a random melange of techniques taken eclectically out of the air. While the basic point of this paper is a plea for psychotherapists to try several effective techniques (even those not necessarily prompted by the logic of their own theories), it is nevertheless assumed that any selected maneuver will at least have the benefit of empirical support. Complete unity between a systematic theory of personality and an effective method of treatment derived therefrom remains a cherished ideal. Meanwhile, it is well for the practicing psychotherapist to be content in the role of a technician rather than that of a scientist and to observe that those who impugn technical proficiency are often able to explain everything but to accomplish almost nothing.

References

ELLIS, A. (1962). *Reason and Emotion in Psychotherapy*. New York: Lyle Stuart.

HARPER, R.A. (1959). *Psychoanalysis and Psychotherapy: 36 Systems.* Englewood Cliffs, NJ: Prentice-Hall.

JACOBSON, E. (1964). *Anxiety and Tension Control*. Philadelphia: Lippincott.

JOURARD, S.M. (1964). *The Transparent Self*. New Jersey: Van Nostrand.

LONDON, P. (1964). *The Modes and Morals of Psychotherapy*. New York: Holt, Rinehart & Winston.

SALTER, A. (1949). *Conditioned Reflex Therapy*. New York: Creative Age Press.

WOLPE, J. (1961). The systematic desensitization of neuroses. *J. Nerv. Ment. Dis.* **132**, 189–203.

WOLPE, J. and LAZARUS, A.A. (1966). *Behaviour Therapy Techniques*. Oxford: Pergamon Press.

Chapter 8
Learning Theory and the Treatment of Depression (1968)

Whilst the understanding and treatment of depression have come a long way since 1968, when the following article appeared, it is nevertheless interesting to note how Lazarus drew upon a learning theory model to provide specific tactics for distinguishing between biological and psychological dysphoria. Viewing so-called psychogenic depression 'as a function of inadequate or insufficient reinforcers' (a position that was later echoed and adopted by other researchers and clinicians), Lazarus emphasised the need for thorough assessment and offered three novel methods for overcoming depression – time projection, affective expression, and behavioural deprivation and retraining. Again, Lazarus's ingenuity and inventiveness shine through.

Depression, according to Hathaway and McKinley (1951) 'is the most ubiquitous of the patterns seen in psychological abnormality'. Yet apart from exploratory studies on conditionability (e.g. Ban et al., 1966), behavior therapists have tended to ignore the subject or have dealt with it mainly en passant. Psychoanalysts, by contrast, have invested much energy in attempting to unravel the putative unconscious dynamics involved. The general psychiatric literature on the topic of depression, although extremely vast, is disappointingly inconsistent. For instance, there does not seem to be an acceptable system of classification or a standard nomenclature. Even the broadest nosological divisions are open to criticism. The validity of the numerous subdivisions such as 'involutional melancholia', in contrast to the 'manic–depressive reaction', as distinct from 'schizoaffective disorders' as opposed to 'agitated depressions' etc. certainly does not hold up well under statistical scrutiny (e.g. Stenstedt, 1959). The main difficulty, as Blinder (1966) points out, is that the current nosology and taxonomy of depression is based upon the old Kraepelinian classification of mental disorders as definite disease entities.

First published in 1968. Reproduced, with the permission of Pergamon Press, from Lazarus, A.A. (1968). Learning theory and the treatment of depression. *Behaviour Research and Therapy*, 6, 83–89.

Despite the perennial dispute which centers around the distinction between endogenous and exogenous (reactive) depressions, there is little doubt, as Maddison and Duncan (1965) point out, that many depressions are based entirely on *physiological* factors (i.e. some genetic, enzymatic, metabolic, endocrine or other biochemical disturbance). The picture is further complicated by 'mixed depressions' and so-called 'masked depressions' (in which the patient initially complains only of atypical somatic symptoms). Faced with these diagnostic difficulties it is well worth inquiring whether learning theory can bring the field into clearer focus.

In general, where a therapist finds himself unable to account for a persistent response pattern in terms of contiguous associations, drive reduction, stimulus generalization, positive or negative reinforcement, or any other principle of learning, he is best advised to consider the likelihood of organic pathology. This is by no means a cut-and-dried matter, but response patterns which have no logical antecedents cannot be ascribed to learning. Learned responses do not mysteriously well up from unconscious depths. They have a discernible history and, for this reason, a careful stimulus–response (S-R) analysis is considered indispensible for adequate diagnosis and therapy.

The main purpose of this chapter is to present some of the many and complex variables involved in understanding, assessing, and treating 'psychogenic' or 'reactive' depressions. It is perhaps necessary first to try and define the subject matter under discussion.

Problems of Definition

Depression is exceedingly difficult to define (let alone measure!) and it is clear that many diverse phenomena have been lumped together under this term. It is difficult to evoke 'depression' in experimental subjects, and even more difficult to isolate and maintain this response in a 'pure' state. Yet, the temptation to deny depression status as a subject matter for scientific consideration must be resisted – if for no reason other than the fact that clinicians are consulted daily by thousands of people who say they feel depressed. Literature, art, drama and psychiatric reports are replete with descriptions of depression which are often at variance with each other.

Shall we define depression as a subjective experience involving inner dejection, despair, misery, despondency, futility or perhaps in such terms as nuclear unworthiness or implosive aggression? Or should we avoid the snares of subjectivity and, like Skinner (1953), simply define depression as a general weakening of our behavioral repertoire? But as Ferster (1965) points out: 'Whether a man who moves and acts slowly is "depressed" or merely moving slowly is not easily or reliably determined by observing his behavior alone.'

If we compile a catalogue of operant responses, we might establish a base rate of frequent weeping, decreased food intake, frequent statements of dejection and self-reproach, psychomotor retardation, difficulties with memory and concentration, insomnia or a fitful sleep pattern, and general apathy and withdrawal. Descriptively, depressed patients primarily express a pool of gloomy feelings and pessimistic thoughts, and are relatively refractory to various kinds of stimulation, while displaying one or more of the abovementioned operant responses.

Some theorists separate depression from what Freud (1925) termed 'the normal emotion of grief' which he felt one would never regard as a morbid condition in need of therapeutic intervention. In fact, he stated that 'we look upon any interference with it as inadvisable or even harmful'. From a behavioral point of view, this separation seems to have no therapeutic usefulness. What criteria can be utilized to differentiate 'normal grief' from intense or protracted grief, which is indistinguishable from 'depression'?

Dengrove (1966) has in fact successfully treated grief reactions, whether due to the death of a loved one, separation or desertion, by systematic desensitization. He commences by having the patient visualize the person or the 'lost object' in a series of formerly happy and pleasant contexts. Then, under conditions of deep muscle relaxation, he slowly moves forward in time gradually progressing to the events of the funeral. He adds that, if fear of death or reactions of guilt are present, these are included in the hierarchy.

Depression and Anxiety

It is sometimes difficult to separate depression from 'anxiety'. While it is true that depression is often a consequence of 'anxiety that is unusually intense or prolonged' (Wolpe and Lazarus, 1966, p. 162), it is important to separate anxiety from depression and to stress that they usually have different antecedents.

Fundamentally, anxiety may be viewed as a response to noxious or threatening stimuli, and depression may be regarded as a function of inadequate or insufficient reinforcers. In Skinnerian terms, this would probably result in a weakened behavioral repertoire. A depressed person is virtually on an extinction trial. Some significant reinforcer has been withdrawn. There is loss and deprivation – loss of money or love, status or prestige, recognition or security etc. More subtle factors are sometimes involved, e.g. loss of youth or a particular loss of body functioning. Clinicians are sometimes puzzled by depressions which have their onset when an individual finally attains a pinnacle of success. One reason for these depressive patterns is perhaps the loss of striving.

Ferster (1965) describes how diverse factors, such as (1) sudden environmental changes, (2) punishment and aversive control and (3) shifts in reinforcement contingencies, give rise to depression. For him, the essential characteristic of a depressed person is 'a reduced frequency of emission of positively reinforced behavior'.

The essence of therapy in overcoming anxiety is to remove the noxious elements and/or change the patient's responses towards them. Depressed patients require a different schedule of reinforcement and/or need to learn a way of recognizing and utilizing certain reinforcers at their disposal.

Where depression is secondary to anxiety, it may prove helpful to deal with the anxiety component (e.g. by means of relaxation, desensitization, assertive training, aversion-relief, feeding responses, galvanic stimulation etc.). In this chapter, the section on therapy will consider the treatment of those cases in whom the depressive component is uppermost and in whom the removal of attendant anxieties is unlikely to dislodge the debilitating depressive reaction.

Clinical Assessment

One pragmatic rule is that, when the depressive verbalizations, such as nihilistic statements and complaints of helplessness and hopelessness, do not center around stressful or other provoking emotional experiences, endogenous (i.e. physiological) factors must receive diagnostic priority. The treatment of depressions which are primarily physiological in nature usually calls for drugs and/or electroconvulsive treatment (ECT) (Maddison and Duncan, 1965), possibly in a supportive psychotherapeutic setting. The converse is true when treating depressions in which psychological features predominate. Here, intensive psychological techniques are called for, and the use of medication (if any) is mainly palliative.

An adequate life history remains an indispensable aid towards a valid and reliable assessment of the patient's condition. Consider the following case: Miss BD, a 29-year-old unmarried female developed persistent feelings of depression following a prolonged bout of viral influenza. She felt most depressed in the early morning hours but was seldom depressed in the evenings. She fell asleep readily but kept waking up intermittently, and would usually fail to go back to sleep after 3 a.m. at which time she experienced perseverating morbid thoughts. She ate poorly since her illness, had lost weight and was constipated. She accused herself of indolence and had lost her joie de vivre. A family history revealed that the patient's mother had been treated for a 'puerperal depression'.

To the author's surprise, several clinicians ventured to make differential diagnoses based on the scanty material outlined above. Learning theory demands a detailed and precise description of S-R patterns before problem identification can be attempted. Presented with the syndrome described in the case of Miss BD (a physiological precipitant, diurnal variation, characteristic sleep pattern, weight loss, statements of self-recrimination and a family history of depression), too many clinicians might be inclined to label the problem 'endogenous' without further inquiry. A more detailed behavior analysis revealed that the patient had been unhappy for some time with her work situation, that her fiancé had been acting in an inconsistent manner, that her mother had become increasingly demanding, and that she was concerned about some financial reversals her family had suffered in recent months. Furthermore, her depressive content and her perseverating thoughts were always focused on her specific problem areas. A program of assertive training resulted in a new work situation, a new boyfriend, a contrite mother and an efficient accountant. Not surprisingly, she no longer complained of depression and has withstood a 3-year follow-up inquiry.

Specific Methods of Treatment

The generic conception of depression as a consequence of inadequate or insufficient reinforcement requires elaboration. The obvious withdrawal of a reinforcer (such as loss of money, work, or friendship) followed by a pattern of misery and gloom, calls for very little diagnostic ingenuity. The clinician is taxed most by those patients who show no obvious loss to account for their depression. Some very subtle features are sometimes operative. For instance, an expected loss or any anticipation of a non-reinforcing state of affairs may precipitate various intensities of depression. These cases are sometimes too hastily classified as 'endogenous depressions'. Furthermore, depression, which may have had physiological origins and/or obvious history of reinforcement–deprivation, may be maintained by operant consequences. The patient when 'blue' finds people who cheer-him-up and they thus reinforce his depressive behavior. Therapy must take cognizance of both antecedent factors and the consequences of behavior.

Most therapists, when confronted by depressed patients, prescribe antidepressant medication and a combination of reassurance and supportive therapy. Let us turn to some more specific therapeutic strategies.

Environmental manipulation has an obvious place in those cases where depression appears to be a consequence of inimical life situations – an unsatisfactory job, an unhappy marriage, social isolation etc. These non-rewarding circumstances are often altered by a touch of assertiveness and by some therapeutic ingenuity in fostering recreational pursuits, meaningful friendships, hobbies and other constructive activities. As already mentioned, when depression is secondary to anxiety, the elimination of the latter (by means of the usual behavioral techniques) is often enough of a rewarding contingency to break through the depressive condition. Three specific antidepressive behavioral techniques will now be outlined for those cases in whom 'reactive' depression is the primary complaint.

Time projection with positive reinforcement

The truism 'time heals' ignores the fact that the passage of time per se is not therapeutic, but that psychological healing occurs because time permits new or competing responses to emerge. Generally, an event which causes intense annoyance or distress can be viewed with indifference or detachment after, say, a lapse of 6 months or a year. The therapeutic utility and application of this observation is illustrated by the following case history.

> Miss CH, a 23-year-old student, became acutely depressed when her boyfriend informed her that he intended marrying one of her classmates. She became sleepless, anorexic, restless and weepy. Previously she had been a most talented and enthusiastic student; now she was unable to concentrate on her work, had stopped attending classes, and had become apathetic and listless. After 10 days, her parents persuaded her to consult a psychiatrist who prescribed amphetamines and barbiturates, whereupon she made a suicidal attempt by swallowing all her pills. Fortunately, the dose was not lethal. She refused to seek further psychiatric help, but her family physician nevertheless requested the writer to conduct a home visit.
>
> It was difficult to establish rapport but the patient was finally responsive to emphatic statements of sympathy and reassurance. She agreed to see the writer at his consulting room on the following day. A behavioral inquiry revealed that, prior to her unrequited love relationship, she had enjoyed painting, sculpting and practicing the guitar. She also went horse-riding and displayed some interest in symphony concerts. During the 10 months of her love affair, she had exchanged all of these activities for 'stock-car racing, amateur dramatics and a few wild parties'.
>
> As the patient proved highly susceptible to hypnotic techniques, a trance state was induced and the following time projection sequence was applied:

'It is almost 3:15 p.m. on Wednesday, April 14, 1965. (This was the date of the actual consultation.) Apart from sleeping, eating etc., how could you have occupied these 24 hours? You could have gone horse-riding for a change, or taken your guitar out of mothballs... (5-second pause) ... Let's push time forward another 24 hours. You are now 48 hours ahead in time. Enough time has elapsed to have started a painting and done some sculpting. You may even have enjoyed a ride in the country and attended a concert. Think about these activities; picture them in your mind; let them bring a good feeling of pleasant associations, of good times ... (5-second pause) ... Let's advance even further in time. A whole week has gone by, and another, and yet another. Now these past three weeks into which you have advanced have been busy and active. Reflect back for a moment on three weeks of enjoyable activity ... (10-second pause) ... Now you move further forward in time. Days are flying past; time advances; days become weeks; time passes; weeks become months. It is now 6 months later. It's the 14th of October, 1965. Look back on the past 6 months, from April to October. Think about the months that separate April from October. What have you done during May, June, July, August and September? (Pause of 5 seconds) ... Now 6 months ago, going back to April, you were very upset. In retrospect, how do you feel? Think back; reflect over an incident now more than 6 months old. If it still bothers you, signal to me by raising your left index finger.'

> As the patient did not raise her finger, she was told that she would recall the entire time projection sequence and return back in time to April 14, feeling as she did during October. She was then dehypnotized and asked to recount her feelings.

(If she had signaled, the time projection sequence would have been continued, up to 2 years ahead.) She stated: 'How can I put it in words? Let me just explain it in three ways. First, I feel kind of foolish; second, there are lots of pebbles on the beach; and number three, there's something inside that really wants to find an outlet on canvass. Does that make sense?'

Miss CH was interviewed a week later. She reported having enjoyed many productive hours, had regained her appetite and had been sleeping soundly. There were some minor episodes of 'gloom' which responded to self-induced imagery, similar to the therapeutic time-projection sequence. She cancelled her subsequent appointments, stating she had completely overcome her depression. This impression was confirmed by her parents and the referring physician. A follow-up after a year revealed that she had been exposed to a series of disappointments which often led to temporary bouts of depression (none, however, as severe as that which had led her to therapy).

Some patients have responded well to this technique when neither hypnosis nor relaxation were employed. All successful cases, however, were able to picture vivid images. Although depressed patients are usually deaf to advice and guidance, the cognitive effects of this procedure are similar to the old 'pull-yourself-together-sufficiently-to-do-something-creative-and-then-you-will-feel-better' doctrine. Once the patient can imagine him- or herself sufficiently freed from his or her oppressive inertia to engage in some enjoyable (or formerly enjoyable) activity, a lifting of depressive affect is often apparent. This may be sustained by ensuring that the patient thereupon experiences actual rewarding activities.

The time projection sequence has been used with 11 patients. Six cases responded excellently, two improved moderately and three were unimproved. These results refer to one-session trials.

Affective expression

Reference has already been made to the notion that depressed patients are relatively refractory to most forms of stimulation. Yet almost any stimulus which shatters this web of inertia may also vanquish their depression – temporarily at least. The writer recalls witnessing a severely depressed patient evince an extreme startle reaction followed by panic at a false fire alarm. Both his subjective report and his overt behavior revealed the absence of depression for many hours thereafter. It is hypothesized that when an individual feels or expresses anger, depressive affect is often undermined. This idea was bolstered when a patient who grew angry at the writer for asking too many personal questions remarked: 'I was feeling very depressed when I walked in here, but now I feel fine.' *In general, the writer submits that anger (or the deliberate stimulation of feelings of amusement, affection, sexual excitement or anxiety) tends to break the depressive cycle.* The clinical utility of this principle is suggested by a patient who was exceedingly depressed about the end of a love affair. He became furious when he discovered that his ex-girlfriend had spread false rumors about him, whereupon his depression immediately (and lastingly) disappeared. The writer has several cases on record in which the development of 'righteous indignation' rather than 'self-blame' appeared to coincide with the elimination of depression and suicidal feelings.

Behavioral deprivation and re-training

The schema of depression elaborated in the previous sections is that a chronic and/or acute non-reinforcing state of affairs can result in a condition where the person becomes relatively refractory to most stimuli and enters a state of 'depression'. A period of deliberate or enforced 'sensory deprivation' and inertia, may, however, make the depressed patient more susceptible to incoming stimuli, so that positive reinforcement may take effect. This is in keeping with the practices of 'Morita therapy' (Kora, 1965) where the patient is subjected to a 5- to 7-day period of absolute bed rest, without access to any external stimuli (i.e. no reading, writing, smoking, visitors or other distractions are permitted). At the end of this period, most people find positive reinforcement value in almost *any* external stimulus. After leaving bed, patients are gradually exposed to a graduated series of tasks commencing with 'light work' for 1 week (a form of occupational therapy) and eventually progress from 'heavy work' to 'complicated work'.

Although Morita therapy is not advocated by its practitioners specifically for the treatment of depression (they have applied it with success to cases of so-called neurasthenia, anxiety states and obsessional disorders), the author has had some encouraging preliminary results when applying it to depressed patients in a less stringent manner.

The well-known methods of narcosis or sleep therapy (e.g. Andreev, 1960; Loucas and Stafford-Clark, 1965) might also have a place in this schema. It must be emphasized again that, from the behavioral viewpoint, the rationale for these methods is that they render persons more amenable to a wider range of positive reinforcers.

To recapitulate, therapy for psychological depressions requires the introduction of sufficiently powerful reinforcers to disrupt the 'emotional inhibitions' which characterize the behavior of depressed patients. If the patient is enabled merely to contemplate future positive reinforcements, depressive responses usually diminish or disappear. The time-projection sequence described above makes use of this observation. Any change in emotional tone in which excitatory rather than inhibitory affect predominates (whether due to positive or negative reinforcement) is also likely to impede depressive reactions. When depressed patients are highly refractory to the usual range of positive reinforcers, they are sometimes rendered more amenable to stimulation after undergoing a general regimen of stimulus deprivation. The three methods discussed above are merely a small sample of the many and varied techniques which can be advanced within a general behavioral framework.

Acknowledgments

I wish to thank Dr J.P. Brady, Dr A.T. Beck and Dr T. Schnurer for their comments and advice.

References

ANDREEV, B.V. (1960). *Sleep Therapy in the Neuroses*. New York: Consultant's Bureau.

BAN, T.Z., CHOI, S.M., LEHMANN, H.E. and ADAMO, E. (1966). Conditional reflex studies in depression. *Can. Psychiat. Assoc. J.* **11**, S98–S104.

BLINDER, M.G. (1966). The pragmatic classification of depression. *Am. J. Psychiatr.* **123**, 259–269.

DENGROVE, E. (1966). Treatment of non-phobic disorders by the behavioral therapies. Lecture to the Association for Advancement of the Behavioral Therapies, in New York on 17 December.

FERSTER, C.B. (1965). Classification of behavioral pathology. In Krasner, L. and Ullmann, L.P. (Eds), *Research in Behavior Modification*. New York: Holt, Rinehart & Winston

FREUD, S. (1925). Mourning and melancholia. In *Collected Papers*, Vol. IV. London: Hogarth.

HATHAWAY, S.R. and McKINLEY, J.C. (1951). *Manual of the MMPI*. New York: The Psychological Corporation.

KORA, T. (1965). Morita therapy. *Int. J. Psychiatr.* **1**, 611–640.

LOUCAS, K.P. and STAFFORD-CLARK, D. (1965). Electronarcosis at Guy's. *Guy's Hosp. Reps.* **114**, 223–237.

MADDISON, D. and DUNCAN, G.M. (Eds) (1965). *Aspects of Depressive Illness*. Edinburgh: Livingston.

SKINNER, B.F. (1953). *Science and Human Behavior*. New York: Macmillan.

STENSTEDT, A. (1959). Involutional melancholia. *Acta Psychiatr. Scand. Suppl.* 127, **34**, 1–71.

WOLPE, J. and LAZARUS, A.A. (1966). *Behaviour Therapy Techniques*. Oxford: Pergamon Press.

Chapter 9
Multimodal Behavior Therapy: Treating the 'BASIC ID' (1973)

What follows is the first exposition of Lazarus's 'multimodal' position. If you have read the preceding chapters, the evolution of Lazarus's thinking, which finally crystallised in this 1973 paper, should be evident. When this paper was written, he was Director of Clinical Training at Yale University, but shortly before its publication, he had moved to Rutgers University as Chairperson of their University College Psychology Department. This article underscores several innovative clinical features, such as the specific application of sensory methods, and the use of 'anti-future shock' imagery to offset relapses. In subsequent writings, Lazarus has elaborated on many of the points herein and he has added new ideas, but the major multimodal premises and procedures are clearly articulated in this paper.

Progress in the field of psychotherapy is hindered by a factor that is endemic in our society: an item is considered newsworthy, and accolades are accorded when claims run counter to the dictates of commonsense. Thus, everything from megavitamins to anal lavages and primal screams gains staunch adherents who, in their frenetic search for a panacea, often breed confusion worse confounded. The present paper emphasizes that patients are usually troubled by a multitude of *specific* problems which should be dealt with by a similar multitude of *specific* treatments. The approach advocated herein is very different from those systems which cluster presenting problems into ill-defined constructs and then direct one or two treatment procedures at these constructs. The basic assumption is that durable (long-lasting) therapeutic results depend upon the amount of effort expended by patient and therapist across at least six or seven parameters.

First published in 1973. Reproduced, with permission of Williams & Wilkins, Baltimore, from Lazarus, A.A. (1973). Multimodal behavior therapy: Treating the BASIC ID. *Journal of Nervous and Mental Disease*, **156**, 404–411.

Research into the interaction between technique and relationship variables in therapy has shown that an effective therapist 'must be more than a "nice guy" who can exude prescribed interpersonal conditions – he must have an armamentarium of scientifically derived skills and techniques to supplement his effective interpersonal relations' (Woody, 1971, p. 8). Deliberately excluded from the present formulation is the empathic, non-judgmental warmth, wit and wisdom which characterize those therapists who help rather than harm their clients (Bergin, 1971). If this were an article on surgical techniques and procedures, we would presuppose that individuals who apply the prescribed methods are free from pronounced tremors and possess more than a modicum of manual dexterity. Thus, it is hoped that multimodal behavioral procedures will attract non-mechanistic therapists who are flexible, empathic and genuinely concerned about the welfare of their clients.

The main impetus for all forms of treatment probably stems from the general urgency of human problems and the need for practical assistance. This has lent acceptance to technically faulty work that would not pass muster in other fields, and every informed practitioner is all too well aware of the fragmentary and contradictory theories that hold sway in the absence of experimental evidence. Apart from the plethora of different techniques, systems and theories, we have conflicting models and paradigm clashes as exemplified by the differences between radical behaviorists and devout phenomenologists. Attempts to blend divergent models into integrative or eclectic harmony may often result in no more than syncretistic muddles (Reisman, 1971; Woody, 1971). And yet without general guiding principles that cut across all systems of therapy, we are left with cabalistic vignettes in place of experimental data or even clinical evidence. Multimodal behavior therapy encompasses: (1) specification of goals and problems; (2) specification of treatment techniques to achieve these goals and remedy these problems; and (3) systematic measurement of the relative success of these techniques.

Because all patients are influenced by processes that lie beyond the therapist's control and comprehension, the field of psychological treatment and intervention is likely to foster superstitious fallacies as readily as well established facts. The tendency to ascribe causative properties to the *last* event in any sequence is all too well known (e.g. her stomach pains must be due to the sausage she just ate for lunch). Thus a patient, after grappling with a problem for years, starts massaging his left kneecap while plucking his right ear lobe and experiences immediate and lasting relief from tenacious symptoms. If a therapist happens to be close at hand, a new technique is likely to be born and placed alongside the parade of other 'breakthroughs' with the screamers, confronters, disclosers, relaxers, dreamers and desensitizers. And, if the therapist happens to be sufficiently naïve, enthusiastic and charismatic, we will probably never convince him, his students or his successful patients that the knee-and-ear technique per se is not the significant agent of change. To guard against this penchant, we must insist upon the precise specification of the operations by which systematic assessment of the efficacy of a treatment for a specific problem is made on a regular basis.

The foregoing variables plus the power struggle between psychiatrists and psychologists and the various schools therein tend to hamper progress. The field, over the span of the past 8 years, is described by two leading research clinicians as 'chaotic' (Colby, 1964; Frank, 1971). Part of the confusion may also be ascribed to the fact that there is a human (but unscientific) penchant to search for unitary treatments and cures. How nice if insight alone or a soul-searing scream could pave the way to mental health. How simple and convenient for countless addicts if aversion therapy afforded long-lasting results. And what a boon to phobic sufferers if their morbid fears were enduringly assuaged by systematic desensitization and assertive training methods. But whilst short-lived relief is available to most, we must concur with Lesse that for most syndromes 'there is very little proof at this time that any one given technique is superior to another in the long-range therapy of a particular type of psychogenic problem' (Lesse, 1972, p. 330).

Notwithstanding the biases that lead to theoretical befuddlement, most clinicians would probably agree with the pragmatic assumption that the more a patient learns in therapy, the less likely he or she is to relapse afterwards. Thus, an alcoholic treated only by aversion therapy would be more likely to relapse than his or her counterpart who had also received relaxation therapy (Blake, 1965). The benefits which accrue from aversion therapy plus relaxation training would be further potentiated by the addition of assertive training, family therapy and vocational guidance (Lazarus, 1965). This general statement implies that *lasting change* is at the very least a function of combined *techniques, strategies* and *modalities*. This vitiates the search for a panacea, or a single therapeutic modality. But a point of diminishing returns obviously exists. If two aspirins are good for you, ten are not five times better. When and why should we stop pushing everything from transcendental meditation to hot and cold sitz baths at our clients? Conversely, how, when, where and why do we infer that, in a given instance, meditation plus sensitivity training is preferable to psychodrama and contingency contracting? Above all, how can we wield Occam's razor to dissect the chaos of these diverse psychotherapeutic enterprises into meaningful and congruent components?

Seven Modalities

An arbitrary division created *sui generis* would simply turn back the clock on the composite theories and facts that psychologists have amassed to date. It is no accident that, ever since the publication of Brentano's *Psychologie vom empirischen Standpunkte* in 1874, acts such as ideation, together with feeling states and sensory judgments, have comprised the main subject matter of general psychology. In other words, psychology as the scientific study of behavior has long been concerned with sensation, imagery, cognition, emotion and interpersonal relationships. If we examine psychotherapeutic processes in the light of each of these basic modalities, seemingly disparate systems are brought into clearer focus, and the necessary and sufficient conditions for long-lasting therapeutic change might readily be discerned.

Every patient–therapist interaction involves *behavior* (be it lying down on a couch and free associating, or actively role-playing a significant encounter), *affect* (be it the silent joy of non-judgmental acceptance, or the sobbing release of pent-up anger), *sensation* (which covers a wide range of sensory stimuli from the spontaneous awareness of bodily discomfort to the deliberate cultivation of specific sensual delights), *imagery* (be it the fleeting glimpse of a childhood memory, or the contrived perception of a calm-producing scene) and *cognition* (the insights, philosophies, ideas, and judgments that constitute our fundamental values, attitudes and beliefs). All of these take place within the context of an *interpersonal* relationship, or various interpersonal relationships. An added dimension with many patients is their need for medication or *drugs* (e.g. phenothiazine derivatives and various antidepressants and mood regulators). Taking the first letter of each of the foregoing italicized words, we have the acronym BASIC ID. *Obviously, the proposed seven modalities are interdependent and interactive.*

If we approach a patient *de novo* and inquire in detail about his or her salient behaviors, affective responses, sensations, images, cognitions, interpersonal relationships, and his or her need for drugs or medication, we will probably know more about him or her than we can hope to obtain from routine history taking and psychological tests. Whether or not these general guidelines can provide all that we need to know in order to be of therapeutic service is an empirical question.*

Other Systems

While it is important to determine whether the BASIC ID and the various combinations thereof are sufficiently exhaustive to encompass most vagaries of human conduct, it is perhaps more compelling first to view, very briefly, a few existing systems of therapy in the light of these modalities.

---

*Some may argue that the absence of a 'spiritual' dimension is an obvious hiatus, although in the interests of parsimony, it can be shown that cognitive–affective interchanges readily provide the necessary vinculum.

Most systems deal with the majority of modalities en passant; very few pay specific and direct attention to each particular zone. Psychoanalysis deals almost exclusively with cognitive–affective interchanges. The neo-Reichian school of bioenergetics (Lowen, 1967) focuses upon behavior (in the form of 'body language'), and the sensory–affective dimension. Encounter groups and gestalt therapy display a similar suspicion of the 'head' and are inclined to neglect cognitive material for the sake of 'gut reactions' or affective and sensory responses. Gestalt therapists also employ role playing and imagery techniques. The Masters and Johnson (1970) sex-training regimen deals explicitly with sexual behavior, affective processes, the 'sensate focus', various re-educative features and the correction of misconceptions, all within a dyadic context, preceded by routine medical and laboratory examinations. They do not avail themselves of imagery techniques (e.g. desensitization, self-hypnosis, or fantasy projection), a fact which may limit their overall success rate.

Perhaps it is worth stressing at this point that the major hypothesis, backed by the author's clinical data (Lazarus, 1971a,b), is that *durable results are in direct proportion to the number of specific modalities deliberately invoked by any therapeutic system.* Psychoanalysis, for instance, is grossly limited because penetrating insights can hardly be expected to restore effective functioning in people with deficient response repertoires – they need explicit training, modeling and shaping for the acquisition of adaptive social patterns. Conversely, nothing short of coercive manipulation is likely to develop new response patterns that are at variance with people's fundamental belief systems. Indeed, insight, self-understanding and the correction of irrational beliefs must usually precede behavior change whenever faulty assumptions govern the channels of manifest behavior. In other instances, behavior change must occur before 'insight' can develop (Lazarus, 1971b). Thus, cognitive restructuring and overt behavior training are often reciprocal. This should not be misconstrued as implying that a judicious blend of psychoanalysis and behavior therapy is being advocated. Psychoanalytic theory is unscientific and needlessly complex; behavioristic theory is often mechanistic and needlessly simplistic. The points being emphasized transcend any given system or school of therapy. However, adherence to social learning theory (Bandura, 1969) as the most elegant theoretical system to explain our therapeutic sorties places the writer's identification within the province of behavior therapy – hence 'multimodal behavior therapy'. Perhaps the plainest way of expressing our major thesis is to stress that comprehensive treatment at the very least calls for the correction of irrational beliefs, deviant behaviors, unpleasant feelings, intrusive images, stressful relationships, negative sensations and possible biochemical imbalance. To the extent that problem identification (diagnosis) systematically explores each of these modalities, whereupon therapeutic intervention remedies whatever deficits and maladaptive patterns emerge, treatment outcomes will be positive and long-lasting. To ignore any of these modalities is to practice a brand of therapy that is incomplete. Of course, not every case requires attention to each modality, but this conclusion can only be reached after each area has been carefully investigated during problem identification (i.e. diagnosis). A similar position stressing comprehensive assessment and therapy has been advocated by Kanfer and Saslow (1968).

Problem Identification

Faulty problem identification (inadequate assessment) is probably the greatest impediment to successful therapy. The major advantage of a multi-modal orientation is that it provides a systematic framework for conceptualizing presenting complaints within a meaningful context. A young man with the seemingly monosymptomatic complaint of 'claustrophobia' was seen to be troubled by much more than 'confined or crowded spaces' as soon as the basic modalities had been scanned. The main impact upon his *behavior* was his inability to attend social gatherings, plus the inconvenience of avoiding elevators, public transportation and locked doors. The *affective* concomitants of his avoidance behavior were high levels of general anxiety and frequent panic attacks (e.g. when a barber shop became crowded, and at the check-out counter of a supermarket). The *sensory* modality revealed the fact that he was constantly tense and suffered from muscle spasms. His *imagery* seemed to focus on death, burials and other morbid themes. The *cognitive* area revealed a tendency to catastrophize and to demean himself. At the *interpersonal* level, his wife was inclined to mother him and to reinforce his avoidance behavior. This information, *obtained after a cursory 10- to 15-minute inquiry*, immediately underscored crucial antecedent and maintaining factors that warranted more detailed exploration as a prelude to meaningful therapeutic intervention.

In contrast with the foregoing case, little more than *sensory unawareness* in a 22-year-old woman seemed to be the basis for complaints of pervasive anxiety, existential panic and generalized depression. She was so preoccupied with lofty thoughts and abstract ideation that she remained impervious to most visual, auditory, tactile and other sensory stimuli. Treatment was simply a matter of instructing her to attend to a wide range of specific sensations. 'I want you to relax in a bath of warm water and to examine exact temperature contrasts in various parts of your body and study all the accompanying sensations.' 'When you walk into a room I want you to pay special attention to every object, and afterwards, write down a description from memory.' 'Spend the next 10 minutes listening to all the sounds that you can hear and observe their effects upon you.' 'Pick up that orange. Look at it. Feel its weight, its texture, its temperature. Now start peeling it with that knife. Stop peeling and smell the orange.

Run your tongue over the outside of the peel. Now feel the difference between the outside and the inside of the peel....' These simple exercises in sensory awareness were extraordinarily effective in bringing her in touch with her environment and in diminishing her panic, anxiety and depression. She was then amenable to more basic therapy beyond her presenting complaints.

The multimodal approach to therapy is similar to what is called 'the problem-oriented record approach'. This emphasis upon problem specification is just coming into its own in psychiatry as evidenced in an article by Hayes-Roth, Longabaugh and Ryback (1972). In medicine this approach to record keeping and treatment is slightly older, being best illustrated by Weed's work (1968). Multimodal behavior therapy not only underscores the value of this new approach, but also provides a conceptual framework for its psychiatric implementation. Let us now turn to a case illustration of its use.

Case Illustration

A case presentation should lend substance to the string of assertions outlined on the foregoing pages.

Mary Ann aged 24 was diagnosed as a chronic undifferentiated schizophrenic. Shortly after her third admission to a mental hospital, her parents referred her to the author for treatment. According to the hospital reports, her prognosis was poor. She was overweight, apathetic and withdrawn, but against a background of lethargic indifference, you would detect an ephemeral smile, a sparkle of humor, a sudden glow of warmth, a witty remark, an apposite comment, a poignant revelation. She was heavily medicated (perphenazine (Trilafon, Fentazin) 8 mg three times daily, protriptyline (Vivactil, Concordin) 10 mg three times daily, benztropine mesylate (Cogentin) 2 mg twice daily), and throughout the course of therapy she continued seeing a psychiatrist once a month who adjusted her intake of drugs.

A life history questionnaire, followed by an initial interview, revealed that well-intentioned but misguided parents had created a breeding ground for guilty attitudes, especially in matters pertaining to sex. Moreover, an older sister, 5 years her senior, had aggravated the situation 'by tormenting me from the day I was born'. Her vulnerability to peer pressure during puberty had rendered her prone to 'everything but heroin'. Nevertheless, she had excelled at school, and her first noticeable breakdown occurred at age 18, shortly after graduating from high school. 'I was on a religious kick and kept hearing voices.' Her second hospital admission followed a suicidal gesture at age 21, and her third admission was heralded by her sister's sudden demise soon after the patient turned 24.

Since she was a mine of sexual misinformation, her uncertainties and conflicts with regard to sex became an obvious area for therapeutic intervention. The book *Sex Without Guilt* by Albert Ellis (1965) served as a useful springboard towards the correction of more basic areas of sexual uncertainty and anxiety. Meanwhile, careful questioning revealed the following modality profile:

Modality	Problem	Proposed treatment
Behavior	Inappropriate withdrawal responses	Assertive training
	Frequent crying	Non-reinforcement
	Unkempt appearance	Grooming instructions
	Excessive eating	Low calorie regimen
	Negative self-statements	Positive self-talk assignments
	Poor eye contact	Rehearsal techniques
	Mumbling of words with poor voice projection	Verbal projection exercises
	Avoidance of heterosexual situations	Re-education and desensitization
Affect	Unable to express overt anger	Role-playing
	Frequent anxiety	Relaxation training and reassurance
	Absence of enthusiasm and spontaneous joy	Positive imagery procedures
	Panic attacks (usually precipitated by criticism from authority figures)	Desensitization and assertive training
	Suicidal feelings	Time projection techniques
	Emptiness and aloneness	General relationship building
Sensation	Stomach spasms	Abdominal breathing and relaxing
	Out of touch with most sensual pleasures	Sensate focus method
	Tension in jaw and neck	Differential relaxation
	Frequent lower back pains	Orthopedic exercises
	Inner tremors	Gendlin's focusing methods (Lazarus, 1971a, p. 232)
Imagery	Distressing scenes of sister's funeral	Desensitization
	Mother's angry face shouting 'You fool!'	Empty chair technique
	Performing fellatio on God	Blow up technique (implosion)
	Recurring dreams about airplane bombings	Eidetic imagery invoking feelings of being safe
Cognition	Irrational self-talk: 'I am evil.' 'I must suffer.' 'Sex is dirty.' 'I am inferior.'	Deliberate rational disputation and corrective self-talk
	Syllogistic reasoning, overgeneralization	Parsing of irrational sentences
	Sexual misinformation	Sexual education
Interpersonal relationships	Characterized by child-like dependence	Specific self-sufficiency assignments
	Easily exploited/submissive	Assertive training
	Overly suspicious	Exaggerated role-taking
	Secondary gains from parental concern	Explain reinforcement principles to parents and try to enlist their help
	Manipulative tendencies	Training in direct and confrontative behaviors

The modality profile may strike the reader as a fragmented, or mechanistic barrage of techniques that would call for a disjointed array of therapeutic maneuvers. In actual practice, the procedures follow logically and blend smoothly into meaningful interventions.

During the course of therapy as more data emerged and as a clearer picture of the patient became apparent, the modality profile was constantly revised. Therapy was mainly a process of devising ways and means to remedy Mary Ann's shortcomings and problem areas throughout the basic modalities. The concept of 'technical eclecticism' came into its own (Lazarus, 1967). In other words, a wide array of therapeutic methods drawn from numerous disciplines was applied, but to remain theoretically consistent, the active ingredients of every technique were sought within the province of social learning theory.

In Mary Ann's case, the array of therapeutic methods selected to restructure her life included familiar behavior therapy techniques, such as desensitization, assertive training, role-playing and modeling, but many additional procedures were employed, such as time projection, cognitive restructuring, eidetic imagery and exaggerated role-taking as described in some of the author's publications (Lazarus, 1971a, 1972). The empty chair technique (Perls, 1969) and other methods borrowed from gestalt therapy and encounter group procedures were added to the treatment regimen. Mary Ann was also seen with her parents for eight sessions, and was in a group for 30 weeks.

During the course of therapy she became engaged and was seen with her fiancé for premarital counseling for several sessions.

The treatment period covered the span of 13 months at the end of which time she was coping admirably without medication and has continued to do so now for more than a year.

This case was chosen for illustrative purposes because so often, people diagnosed as 'psychotic' receive little more than chemotherapy and emotional support. Yet, in the author's experience, once the florid symptoms are controlled by medication, many people are amenable to multimodal behavior therapy. It is tragic that large numbers of people who can be reached and helped by multimodal behavior therapy are often left to vegetate.

Conclusions

Those who favor working with one or two specific modalities may inquire what evidence there is to support the contention that *multimodal* treatment is necessary. At present, the author's follow-up studies (e.g. Lazarus, 1971a,b) have shown that relapse all too commonly ensues after the usual behavior therapy programs, despite the fact that behavioral treatments usually cover more modalities than most other forms of therapy. Of course, the run of the mill behavior therapist does not devote as much attention to imagery techniques as we are advocating (even when using covert reinforcement procedures and imaginal desensitization), nor does he or she delve meticulously enough into cognitive material, being especially neglectful of various philosophical values and their bearing on self-worth.

Another fact worth emphasizing is that in order to offset 'future shock', multimodal therapy attempts to anticipate areas of stress that the client is likely to experience in time to come. Thus, imaginal rehearsal may be used to prepare people to cope with the marriage of a child, a possible change in occupation, the purchase of a new home, the process of aging and so forth. In the author's experience, these psychological 'fire drills' can serve an important preventive function.

As each modality is investigated, a clear understanding of the individual and his or her interpersonal context emerges. Even with a 'simple phobia', new light is shed, and unexpected information is often gleaned when examining the behavioral, affective, sensory, imaginal, cognitive and interpersonal consequences of the avoidance responses. Whenever a plateau is reached in therapy and progress falters, the writer has found it enormously productive to examine each modality in turn in order to determine a possibly neglected area of concern. More often than not, new material emerges and therapy proceeds apace.

Acknowledgments

Several colleagues made incisive criticisms of the initial draft. The writer is especially grateful to Bob Karlin, Bill Mulligan, Carole Pearl and Terry Wilson.

References

BANDURA, A. (1969). *Principles of Behavior Modification.* New York: Holt, Rinehart & Winston.

BERGIN, A.E. (1971). The evaluation of therapeutic outcomes. In: Bergin, A.E. and Garfield, S.L. (Eds), *Handbook of Psychotherapy and Behavior Change*, pp. 217–270. New York: Wiley.

BLAKE, B.G. (1965). The application of behavior therapy to treatment of alcoholism. *Behav. Res. Ther.* **3**, 75–85.

COLBY, K.M. (1964). Psychotherapeutic processes. *Ann. Rev. Psychol.* **15**, 347–370.

ELLIS, A. (1965). *Sex Without Guilt.* New York: Grove Press.

FRANK, J.D. (1971). Therapeutic factors in psychotherapy. *Am. J. Psychother.* **25**, 350–361.

HAYES-ROTH, F., LONGABAUGH, R. and RYBACK, R. (1972). The problem-oriented medical record and psychiatry. *Br. J. Psychiatr.* **121**, 27–34.

KANFER, F.H. and SASLOW, G. (1968). Behavioral diagnosis. In: Franks, C.M. (Ed.), *Behavior Therapy: Appraisal and Status*, pp. 417–444. New York: McGraw-Hill.

LAZARUS, A.A. (1965). Towards the understanding and effective treatment of alcoholism. *S. Afr. Med. J.* **39**, 736–741.

LAZARUS, A.A. (1967). In support of technical eclecticism. *Psychol. Rep.* **21**, 415–416.

LAZARUS, A.A. (1971a). *Behavior Therapy and Beyond.* New York: McGraw-Hill.

LAZARUS, A.A. (1971b). Notes on behavior therapy, the problem of relapse and some tentative solutions. *Psychotherapy* **8**, 192–196.

LAZARUS, A.A. (Ed.) (1972). *Clinical Behavior Therapy*. New York: Brunner Mazel.

LESSE, S. (1972). Anxiety – Its relationship to the development and amelioration of obsessive-compulsive disorders. *Am. J. Psychother.* **26**, 330–337.

LOWEN, A. (1967). *The Betrayal of the Body*. New York: Macmillan.

MASTERS, W.H. and JOHNSON, V.E. (1970). *Human Sexual Inadequacy*. Boston: Little Brown.

PERLS, F.S. (1969). *Gestalt Therapy Verbatim*. Lafayette, CA: Real People Press.

REISMAN, J.M. (1971). *Toward the Integration of Psychotherapy*. New York: Wiley.

WEED, L.L. (1968). Medical records that guide and teach. *N. Engl. J. Med.* **278**, 593–600.

WOODY, R.H. (1971). *Psychobehavioral Counseling and Therapy*. New York: Appleton-Century-Crofts.

Chapter 10
Desensitization and Cognitive Restructuring (1974)

Lazarus continued to be concerned about what he regarded as narrow and rigid views espoused by Wolpe and Eysenck respectively, and wrote several critiques, one of which is the following article. (Lazarus's most incisive critique of Professor Eysenck's contributions to behaviour therapy appears in the book *Hans Eysenck: Consensus and Controversy*, edited by S. and C. Modgil and published in 1986 by the Falmer Press, London.) At a time before behaviour therapy had become known (as it is today) as 'cognitive–behaviour therapy', Lazarus was arguing for a cognitive mediational model to replace notions of stimulus–response (S-R) conditioning. It is clear that he is one of the forerunners of cognitive–behaviour therapy.

It is generally agreed that one's therapeutic methods will be determined mainly by one's view of causality. If deviant behavior is considered the terminal manifestation of a basic underlying conflict, the proper focus of therapeutic attention will be aimed at resolving the conflict, whatever ancillary methods may also be employed. If demoniacal possession is postulated, exorcism will be the treatment of choice. Genetic, constitutional and organic hypotheses about maladaptive behavior are inclined to generate medical and chemical interventions. Similarly, the notion that most deviant responses (neuroses) are classically conditioned autonomic responses (Wolpe, 1958) has given rise to a spate of deconditioning techniques.

Obviously, techniques may be effective for reasons other than those which gave rise to them – thus desensitization may 'really' produce change for reasons of perceptual realignment rather than autonomic deconditioning. Nevertheless, the individual practitioner's view of disturbed behavior is apt to determine the methods of treatment he applies or withholds in every case. Consider, for instance, the view that, in

First published in 1974. Reproduced, with the permission of the Editor of *Psychotherapy*, from Lazarus, A.A. (1974). Desensitization and cognitive restructuring. *Psychotherapy: Theory, Research and Practice*, **11**, 98–102.

phobic behavior, 'the original cause of the symptom is a conjunction of a single traumatic event (or several repeated subtraumatic experiences) with the presence of a previously neutral stimulus. Through classical conditioning the previously neutral stimulus (CS) now acquires the properties properly belonging to the traumatic event (UCS) itself, and produces the autonomic disturbances originally produced by the UCS' (Eysenck, 1963). The foregoing appears to be a non-mediational theory of classical conditioning. There is little room in Eysenck's schema for examining the sufferer's assumptions and beliefs, his interpersonal relationships or any operant responses apart from 'the skeletal and muscular activities instrumental in moderating these conditioned autonomic responses' (Eysenck, 1963). Indeed, despite evidence to the contrary (e.g. Miller, 1969), Wolpe (1969) states that 'it is because neurotic behavior is usually primarily a matter of autonomic conditioning that operant techniques have not been prominent in the treatment of neuroses' (p. 219). Even in his more recent writings, Eysenck (1970) refers to people having a 'neurotic attack' and likens this 'attack' to a skier suffering a broken leg. Herein lies the crux of the matter. *A model that appears to account for traumatic neuroses is held to be paradigmatic of neurotic disorders in general.*

Like many writers before him, Rachman (1968) cites studies by Grinker and Spiegel (1945) on combat neuroses, as well as the much over-worked case of Watson and Rayner's (1920) 'little Albert' in accounting for the genesis of phobic responses. Wolpe (1969) also cites Krasnogorski's (1925) induction of experimental neuroses in children by exposing them to ambiguous stimuli, and Campbell, Sanderson and Laverty (1964) have indicated that marked anxiety reactions can be conditioned by a single severe stress due to respiratory paralysis. Two questions arise:

1. How much of the variance seen in general psychiatric syndromes can be accounted for by the abovementioned principles?
2. How many phobic cases seen clinically are due to traumatic or subtraumatic conditioning?

The points elaborated below will highlight the importance of verbal propaganda, irrational assumptions, and the processes of imitation and modeling in the genesis and correction of most aberrant behaviors.

Problems of terminology and definition now enter the picture. Eysenck and Rachman do not define what they mean by a 'single traumatic event' or 'frequent subtraumatic events'. If I approached a child and gently whispered in his or her ear that some laboratory rats carry a deadly plague and that it is best to play it safe by avoiding all rats, would this constitute 'a single traumatic event' if the child thereupon evinced persistent avoidance reactions to laboratory animals? And could the mechanism underlying the child's behavior be construed as conditioning? Although Wolpe (1958, 1969) continually used the term 'conditioning' as a synonym for all kinds of learning, English and English (1958) refer to this practice as 'theory-begging' and argue that 'the term conditioning is best reserved for those forms of learning that bear *close resemblance* to the experimental design of conditioning'.

Perhaps I should get slightly ahead of the argument at this point and emphasize that, in keeping with Marks (1969), less than 3 per cent of my phobic patients recounted a history of traumatic or subtraumatic conditioning (n=100). In the present context, a traumatic event is considered as any major stressful experience, such as a protracted illness, physical injury, overt assault, death of a significant other and loss of financial security. In many instances, the genesis of specific fears and phobias remains uncertain and obscure. Rachman (1968, p. 37) states that 'clinicians frequently encounter phobic patients who cannot recall having undergone any traumatic experiences which may be associated with the object of their fear', and then still adhering to a classical conditioning model he adds that 'the majority of these subjects probably acquired their fears...by second, third or tenth remove'. To infer tenth-order conditioning is not much more scientific than to postulate primary sexual displacements or other unconscious processes. Suffice it to say that, in more than 100 detailed case histories of people suffering from phobia-like hypersensitivities, the author found suggestive evidence that most deviant responses were acquired by processes of verbal communication (not unlike my hypothetical example regarding the child and laboratory rats), and by modeling and imitation (compare Bandura, 1969).

It is noteworthy that experimental studies have shown that modeling techniques appear to achieve more rapid results than desensitization techniques in overcoming children's fears (Bandura, 1969). The points at issue are:

1. The laboratory paradigm of little Albert does not appear to fit the genesis of many children's fears in their natural ecology.
2. Strict desensitization paradigms that are large extrapolations from the behavior of traumatized cats (Wolpe, 1958) produce clinical results that are 'often costly in time and limited in effectiveness' (Marks, 1969).

In the same way that those who consider deviant behavior to be the upshot of unconscious forces will tend to focus upon underlying conflicts in their patients, therapists who maintain that emotional states originate solely in subcortical or hypothalamic brain centers (Wolpe, 1958) view cognitive restructuring as 'merely a background to the specific reconditioning of reactions that usually belong to the autonomic nervous system'. There is evidence to doubt the schism between thoughts and feelings (Arnold, 1960). Rokeach (1960) has claimed that 'every emotion has its cognitive counterpart, and every cognition its emotional counterpart'. Ellis (1962) has cited both clinical and experimental evidence to support the overlapping of reason and emotion. Most of the contributors in Arnold's (1970) book also support this view. It is therefore not surprising that, by adding cognitive retraining to conventional desensitization procedures, clinical results appear to be more rapid and more durable (Lazarus, 1968, 1971). Technically, the combined regimen proceeds as follows: The client, say a 'cardiac neurotic', who is being desensitized to pains-in-the-chest, would be relaxed in the usual way and asked to imagine a graded series of chest spasms ranked from 'very mild' to 'very uncomfortable'. Instead of relying entirely upon the presumed counterconditioning effects of muscular relaxation to inhibit his anxieties, he would also be instructed to think about causes other than a coronary thrombosis that can cause chest pains. 'Perhaps I have indigestion.' 'Maybe I pulled a muscle.' 'It could be fibrositis.'

Before citing further examples of 'cognitive restructuring' and commenting upon the overall clinical results, there are one or two additional theoretical issues that need to be discussed. The classical conditioning notion of aberrant behavior postulates that extinction of the 'neurosis' is prevented by the persistent avoidance behavior that keeps the organism away from the CS. The model is unitary, self-contained and extremely parsimonious but ignores the fact that a host of secondary reinforcers often tend to maintain deviant responses (Bandura, 1969). Apart from the primary gain of avoiding fearful stimuli, the secondary gains of social attention and/or personal manipulation are clinically well known. In short, therapeutic attention usually needs to be directed towards situational *and* interpersonal cues. Finally, although behavior is generally a function of its consequences, it should be strongly emphasized that a person 'can be rewarded or punished by his *own* thinking, even when this thinking is largely divorced from outside reinforcements and penalties' (Ellis, 1962).

A theory of behavior which attaches due credence to a person's cognitions is likely to produce different therapeutic maneuvers from models based largely upon notions of subcortical autonomic conditioning. Consider the treatment of persons hypersensitive to devaluation, disapproval, criticism or rejection. These categories represent almost 30 per cent of the 68 anxiety response habits represented in Wolpe's (1969) table of basic case data (pp. 145–148). Desensitization (plus flooding in one case) was the standard means of treatment. In accord with the author's own findings (Lazarus, 1963), when applying desensitization therapy alone, the mean number of sessions required to overcome each phobia was more than ten (Wolpe, 1969). *The author now has over 30 cases on record to show that when cognitive restructuring was employed, either alone or in conjunction with desensitization, the mean number of sessions per phobia was reduced to 4.2.* It should be noted that in treating classic phobias (e.g. claustrophobia or acrophobia) where social action is precluded, desensitization often remains the treatment of choice. In *social phobias* (e.g. fears of criticism, rejection, disapproval etc.), cognitive restructuring appears to yield faster and more durable results.

The precise operations of 'cognitive restructuring' need to be contrasted with the procedure of systematic desensitization. Let us say that we have a relatively low item on a rejection hierarchy: 'You had lunch with Sally and Jim on Monday and Tuesday. It is now Wednesday at noon and you discover that they have gone off to lunch without you.' The ordinary desensitization sequence has the client relaxing while picturing the foregoing event. If upset or otherwise disturbed by the image, the client so indicates by some prearranged signal, in which case the scene is terminated, relaxation instructions are re-emphasized, and the same scene is presented again and again until the client experiences no subjective units of disturbance (SUDS). The same sequence handled by 'cognitive restructuring' is quite different, as the following dialogue will underscore.

Therapist: Now I want you to imagine that it is Wednesday and you discover that Sally and Jim have taken off for lunch without you. Think about that and tell me how you feel.

Client: Awful! I can feel it right here (points to stomach).

Therapist: Okay, so you must be telling yourself that the reason they went without you is due to some failing or shortcoming in you.

Client: Yes, I think they probably find me boring because I don't know too much about sports and other things that interest them.

Therapist: It sounds to me as if they bore you because you would much rather be with people who share your interests in music and art.

Client: Yes, that's possible. I never thought of it that way.

Therapist: That may be important. Now tell me, apart from alleged shortcomings in you, what other reasons could Sally and Jim have had for going to lunch without you?

Client: Oh, I don't know.

Therapist: Come on, think of some possibilities.

Client: Well, maybe they had something personal to talk about.

Therapist: What else?

Client: Oh, perhaps they saw how much work I had to do and decided not to disturb me. (Pause) Maybe they were going across to the other branch and decided to grab a bite to eat on the way.

Therapist: Very good. So you've come up with several non-rejection alternatives. How's the tension in your gut?

Client: Oh, it's gone.

Therapist: Now in any situation where you feel rejected will you please remember immediately to run through several non-rejecting alternatives? I want you to do this as a matter of course.

Client: I'll try to remember.

Therapist: Good. But now let's assume that they did in fact decide not to have lunch with you because you bore them. Is this so awful? And does it mean you will bore everyone with whom you come into contact?

Client: I see what you're getting at.

Therapist: Instead of shrinking away from confronting Sally and Jim, what course of *action* can you take?

Client: I can ask them why they went to lunch without me.

Therapist: And are you ready for the consequence in case they don't say that you seemed busy or they were off to the other branch, but if they imply that you are a bore?

Client: Yes. I would say that we do seem to have different interests and that it was understandable for them to be turned off by me.

Therapist: Excellent. Now let's take the whole scene over again. Picture yourself at work. On Monday and Tuesday Sally and Jim asked you to join them for lunch and you ate with them. Now it is Wednesday and you are thinking about having lunch. You look for Sally and Jim and discover that they have gone off to lunch without you. Picture it clearly. How do you feel?

Client: Fine. I mean it doesn't bother me.

Therapist: Okay, let's take the next scene. Your boss tells you that he's not satisfied with your work....

The importance of training clients to alter their thoughts, self-verbalizations, and self-instructions is central to rational–emotive psychotherapy (Ellis, 1962) and has gained considerable experimental support from many studies, especially the work of Meichenbaum (1972, 1973). An important note by Davison and Valins (1968) has also underscored the crucial role played by cognitive processes during desensitization therapy. As for traditional behavior therapy, of which it is an extension, cognitive restructuring is essentially an *action therapy* (London, 1964) which teaches the client constructive alternativism (Kelly, 1955) and also provides him or her with assertive and other appropriate responses. In severely anxious cases, relaxation training is added to the sequence. Indeed, formal desensitization may reduce anxiety but it is not geared explicitly to provide the client with a repertoire of adaptive thoughts and actions. Again, in phobic situations where social action is not involved, desensitization is still generally indicated.

To recapitulate: a theory of behavior which postulates a cognitive mediational model of affective responses is bound to utilize different or additional therapeutic strategies than a non-mediational classical conditioning paradigm of aberrant behavior. From a clinical perspective, the most relevant questions are whether or not the resultant methods are more effective than classic desensitization techniques. There is evidence that the use of cognitive restructuring can expedite and enhance desensitization therapy in some cases and circumvent it in others.

References

ARNOLD, M. (1960). *Emotion and Personality*. New York: Columbia University Press.

ARNOLD, M. (Ed.) (1970). *Feelings and Emotions*. New York: Academic Press.

BANDURA, A. (1969). *Principles of Behavior Modification*. New York: Holt, Rinehart & Winston.

CAMPBELL, D., SANDERSON, R.E. and LAVERTY, S.G. (1964). Characteristics of a conditioned response in human subjects during extinction trials following a single traumatic conditioning trial. *J. Abnorm. Soc. Psychol.* **68**, 627-639.

DAVISON, G.C. and VALINS, S. (1968). Self-produced and drug produced relaxation. *Behaviour Research and Therapy* **6**, 401-402.

ELLIS, A. (1962). *Reason and Emotion in Psychotherapy*. New York: Lyle Stuart.

ENGLISH, H.B. and ENGLISH A.C. (1958). *A Comprehensive Dictionary of Psychological and Psychoanalytical Terms*. New York: Longmans Green.

EYSENCK, H.J. (1963). Behaviour therapy, extinction and relapse in neurosis. *Br. J. Psychiatr.* **109**, 12-18.

EYSENCK, H. J. (1970). A mish-mash of theories. *Int. J. Psychiatr.* **9**, 140-146

GRINKER, R.R. and SPIEGEL, J.P. (1945). *Men under Stress*. London: Churchill.

JONES, M.C. (1924). The elimination of children's fears. *J. Exp. Psychol.* **7**, 382-390.

KELLY, G.A. (1955). *The Psychology of Personal Constructs*. New York: Norton.

KRASNOGORSKI, N.I. (1925). The conditioned reflexes and children's neuroses. *Am. J. Dis. Child.* **30**, 753-768.

LAZARUS, A.A. (1963). The results of behaviour therapy in 126 cases of severe neurosis. *Behav. Res. Ther.* **1**, 69-79.

LAZARUS, A.A. (1968). Variations in desensitization therapy. *Psychotherapy: Theory, Research and Practice* **5**(1), 50-52.

LAZARUS, A.A. (1971). *Behavior Therapy and Beyond*. New York: McGraw-Hill.

LONDON, P. (1964). *The Modes and Morals of Psychotherapy*. New York: Holt, Rinehart & Winston.

MARKS, I.M. (1969). *Fear and Phobias*. New York: Academic Press.

MEICHENBAUM, D.H. (1972). Cognitive modification of test anxious college students. *J. Consult. Clin. Psychol.* **39**, 370-380.

MEICHENBAUM, D.H. (1973). Cognitive factors in behavior modification: Modifying what people say to themselves. In: Franks, C.M. and Wilson, G.T. (Eds), *Annual Review of Behavior Therapy*, pp. 416-431. New York: Brunner/Mazel.

MILLER, N.E. (1969). Learning of visceral and glandular responses. *Science* **163**, 434-445.

RACHMAN, S. (1968). *Phobias: Their Nature and Control*. Springfield: Charles C. Thomas.

ROKEACH, M. (1960). *The Open and Closed Mind*. New York: Basic Books.

WATSON, J.B. and RAYNER, R. (1920). Conditioned emotional reactions. *J. Exp. Psychol.* **3**, 1-14.

WOLPE, J. (1958). *Psychotherapy by Reciprocal Inhibition*. Stanford: Stanford University Press.

WOLPE, J. (1968). Learning therapies. In: Howels, J.G. (Ed.), *Modern Perspectives in World Psychiatry*. Edinburgh: Oliver & Boyd.

WOLPE, J. (1969). *The Practice of Behavior Therapy*. New York: Pergamon Press.

Chapter 11
Has Behavior Therapy
Outlived its Usefulness?
(1977)

This article is a more complete and detailed exposition of the cognitive–behavioural position that Lazarus espoused in the preceding chapter. A number of readers misunderstood him to imply that the entire behavioural approach was passé. Instead, his position was that the scientific study of human interaction would proceed more rapidly without the counterproductive loyalties that often accompany school adherence. To say, 'I am a behaviour therapist' has a different flavour and connotes a different trajectory from, 'I am committed to bringing scientific methods to bear upon psychotherapeutic processes'. In essence, what Lazarus was arguing for here was the demise of 'behaviour therapy' and the birth of 'cognitive–behaviour therapy' and 'multimodal therapy'.

There is still a tendency to equate *behavior therapy* with *behaviorism*. This creates confusion and beclouds significant clinical concerns. Many researchers and practitioners have challenged the view that *behavior therapists* are *behaviorists*. Locke (1971) has argued that the methods of behavior therapy contradict 'every major premise of behaviorism'. Indeed, most behavior therapists have extended, if not shed, their behavioristic heritage. They apply methods designed to change images and thoughts, emphasis is placed upon self-management, self-reports are employed for assessment and therapy, and clients' self-attitudes and other covert processes are thoroughly explored (O'Leary and Wilson, 1975; Goldfried and Davison, 1976).

There is a very high degree of diversification among the members of this Association*. Yet there does seem to be one central notion to which we would all subscribe. We place great value on meticulous observation,

First published in 1977. Reproduced with permission from Lazarus, A.A. (1977). Has behavior therapy outlived its usefulness? *American Psychologist*, **32**, 550–554. Copyright © 1977 by the American Psychological Association. It is based on an invited address delivered at the Tenth Annual Convention of the Association for Advancement of Behavior Therapy, New York City, December 5 1976.
*Association for Advancement of Behavior Therapy (AABT).

careful testing of hypotheses, and continual self-correction on the basis of empirically derived data. As Franks (Franks, C.M., 1976, personal communication) has suggested: 'Are we not at this stage in our development basically an *Association for Advancement of the Scientific Study of Human Interaction* – in all its ramifications?'

Characteristic of the thinking in behavior therapy in the early stages of its development were such books as Eysenck's (1960) *Behaviour Therapy and the Neuroses* and Ullmann and Krasner's (1965) *Case Studies in Behavior Modification*. These books cover some basic pioneering efforts, but with the advantage of hindsight, we can now see that, outstanding as these writings were in their time, they are now primarily of historical significance. In terms of current thinking, the points of view expressed in these and several other books would be regarded as naïve. As Kanfer (1976) points out, 'If a practitioner of behavior therapy had decided to take a long leave of absence in 1965, he would be astonished and confused if he returned today'. One need only consult the *Annual Review of Behavior Therapy* (Franks and Wilson, 1973) from 1973 through 1976 to realize how far behavior therapy has evolved. Present-day behavior therapy has

> no universally accepted definition, no consensus as to goals, concepts or underlying philosophy, no agreement as to its purview, no monolithic point of view, no overriding strategy or core technique, no single founding father, no general agreement about matters of training, and there is no single profession to which primary allegiance is declared.
>
> (Lazarus and Wilson, 1976, p. 153)

Generally, to understand the present and to predict the future we must appreciate the past. Yet, as many scholars point out, the first duty of a historian is to be on guard against his or her own sympathies. My sympathies remain firmly committed to 'behavioral' principles – if by that we mean due regard for scientific objectivity, extreme caution in the face of conjecture and speculation, a rigorous process of deduction from testable theories, and a fitting indifference towards persuasion and hearsay. But if we reserve the term 'behavioral' for those who tread the path of empiricism whilst avoiding what Franks (1976) aptly called 'the treacherous slopes of the notional', many of Jay Haley's writings would be considered 'behavioral', even Carl Rogers could be regarded as 'behavioral', and Hans Strupp would be accorded a similar fate.

A major point, therefore, is that several 'non-behavioral' researchers have remained true to the canons of scientific methodology and have furnished data that are open to verification or disproof. Their frameworks, rather than stemming from learning principles or social learning theory, may be derived from group process, systems theory, cybernetics, information processing, communications theory or socioecological sources. With a trenchant distaste for overgeneralization, and a vigilant avoidance of capricious conclusions, these 'non-behavioral' scientists have accumulated clinical notions and therapeutic procedures that we dare not overlook (e.g. Minuchin, 1974; Haley, 1976; Malan, 1976).

The Original Errors

In the 1940s and 1950s, the field of psychotherapy was dominated by psychoanalysis. Even those researchers who clearly recognized that psychodynamic principles and theories were inconsistent and untestable, nevertheless embraced basic psychoanalytic tenets (e.g. Dollard and Miller, 1950). It was erroneously assumed that by translating psychoanalytic concepts into the language of conditioning and learning theory, the latter would gain clinical utility, and psychodynamic principles would achieve scientific respectability. As far back as 1933, French published a paper in the *American Journal of Psychiatry* on the 'interrelations between psychoanalysis and the experimental work of Pavlov'. In 1934, Kubie addressed the relation of the conditioned reflex to psychoanalytic technique, and Shaw (1946) was among the first to provide 'a stimulus–response analysis of repression and insight in psychotherapy'. These writings did little to advance knowledge and merely demonstrated how readily the concepts from one discipline could be transposed into the terms of another.

During the 1920s, a considerable amount of clinical practice was based upon conditioning and deconditioning procedures. Kretschmer's (1922/1934) text on medical psychology described 'systematic habituation therapy' and other 'behavioral' techniques. A book on phobic disorders by Williams (1923) viewed 'reconditioning' as the foundation of psychotherapy, and Jones (1924) devised several 'deconditioning' strategies for overcoming children's fears. Gesell (1938) listed 57 early references to learning and conditioning procedures for overcoming children's clinical problems. But these works failed to rescind the prevailing Freudian zeitgeist and were almost completely eclipsed by it.

It was not until the mid-1950s that a significant number of clinicians developed an enduring interest in the writings of Pavlov, Watson, Hull, Thorndike, Guthrie, Tolman and Skinner. The die was cast. If psychotherapy was essentially a learning process, why not draw upon the major learning theorists of the day? Thus, through massive extrapolation, Hull's reinforcement theory and Guthrie's contiguity theory were drawn into the domain of psychotherapy. An overzealous adoption of stimulus–response theory led these clinical pioneers to embrace *behaviorism* in the same way, and for many of the same reasons, that Watson eschewed all internal constructs in response to the introspectionists of his day. As London (1972) has pointed out, we have yet to live down this unfortunate choice of ideology.

The terms 'behavior therapy' and 'behavior therapist' first appeared in print in the *South African Medical Journal* when the author applied them to Wolpe's 'reciprocal inhibition' framework (Chapter 2). Something had to be done to demonstrate that behavior was often clinically significant in its own right. Most therapists (with the exception of certain hypnotists) remained strongly opposed to 'symptomatic treatment'. Behavior per se was almost completely ignored in favor of 'underlying' dynamics that were viewed as the only respectable domain of intervention. All else was considered mere palliation. Thus, in order to bring behavior back into therapy, we witnessed the birth (or rebirth) of 'behavior therapy' and 'behavior modification'. But less than 20 years later, we seem to be witnessing what Krasner (1976) regards as the premature demise of behavior modification. (The death of behavior modification refers to the *system*, not to the basic principles. Reinforcement and punishment are ubiquitous and exert a continual impact on human conduct. Disputes center around the interpretation, implementation, and application of these fundamental principles.)

Enter Cognitions and Other Covert Processes

The emergence of behavior therapy was presaged by (1) the belief in automatic and autonomic conditioning, (2) the eschewal of most cognitive processes, and (3) constant extrapolation from animal experimentation to human functioning. Over the span of almost three decades, Wolpe (1948, 1958, 1976) has remained dedicated to the proposition that cognitive processes are entirely secondary to subcortical autonomic reconditioning as the *real* basis of emotional and behavioral change. Thus, Wolpe (1976, p. 29) contends that 'in the majority of neuroses, conditioned anxiety habits are the sole problem'. But our current view is that in humans, conditioning does not occur automatically and is in fact cognitively mediated (Bandura, 1974; Brewer, 1974; Mahoney, 1974). The non-mediational model cannot account for vicarious learning, semantic generalization, and other 'exclusively human' functions such as imaginal response patterns and symbolic processes. We need not belabor the fact that the non-mediational model provides an attenuated and truncated view of human functioning. To account for behavior solely in terms of external rewards and punishments overlooks the fact that human beings can be rewarded and punished by their *own thinking*, 'even when this thinking is largely divorced from outside reinforcements and penalties' (Ellis, 1962, p. 16). There are compelling data that demonstrate how self-evaluative and self-produced reactions take precedence over external consequences (Bandura, 1973).

While behaviorists (e.g. Rachlin, 1976) remain staunchly opposed to the notion that behavior, however complex, can be influenced by cognitions, the field of behavior therapy has become increasingly 'cognitive'. (Radical behaviorists still claim that only environmental events and contingencies can directly influence behavior.) Of course, nearly everyone, apart from ESP enthusiasts, will agree that the only way we can know anything about another person is through his or her *behavior* (verbal and non-verbal responses), but those of us who work extensively and intensively with patients or clients find it necessary to make inferences about 'private events' and 'covert processes' in addition to observing, quantifying and modifying overt behaviors. And as one enters the area of 'self-talk' and 'mediating constructs', the existence of *ambiguity* becomes evident. Behaviorism and stimulus–response learning theory have no way of recognizing ambiguity and various levels of abstraction – let alone dealing with them. To cite a simple clinical example, early behavior therapists regarded phobias as conditioned avoidance responses (Rachman, 1968; Wolpe, 1973) and thereby completely overlooked the fact that phobias can be used as manipulative ploys, as face-saving pretexts, and as symbolic retreats (Lazarus, 1971).

Another important outcome of ambiguity is the widespread influence of paradoxical communications in most areas of human interaction. The clinical use of 'paradoxical procedures' (e.g. Watzlawick, Weakland and Fisch, 1974) offers a range of potentially powerful interventions. These methods, whilst easily explained in terms of communications theory, are extremely difficult to interpret according to reinforcement theory. No doubt, a determined learning theorist can 'explain' virtually anything, on a post hoc basis, in a manner congruent with conditioning and radical behavioristic principles. But from a therapeutic standpoint, a theory is only as useful as the effective repertoire of techniques it successfully generates. I recognize, of course, that the therapeutic emphasis is quite separate from the concerns of the research scientist, for whom clinical techniques are quite secondary to the generality of a theory.

As far back as 40 years ago, a number of theorists considered it necessary to draw on cognitive processes when accounting for some kinds of conditioning (Razran, 1935; Woodworth, 1938). Zener (1937) even suggested the necessity of a cognitive theory to account for the Pavlovian conditioning of dogs! Brewer's (1974) scholarly review argues persuasively that behavioristic psychology is unable to explain even simple behavior, and that any convincing evidence for operant or classical conditioning in adult humans is non-existent. The essence of his compelling argument is that in human subjects, conditioning is produced through the operation of higher mental processes – through cognitive mediation. Only a few die-hards would not agree that the stimulus–response 'learning theory' basis of behavior therapy is passé and that a distinctly cognitive orientation now prevails.

Whither Behavior Therapy?

None of the foregoing is meant to gainsay the invaluable services that 'behavioral' orientations have rendered. The inestimable virtues of quantification, replication, specificity and objectivity cannot be overstated. By challenging and questioning the heuristic value of disease analogies and various medical models, behavior therapy has placed psychological change and intervention in its proper context – within education rather than medicine. And by adding foresight to hindsight (as in the formula of behavior as a frequent, but not invariable, function of its consequences), we have learned that etiological or antecedent factors alone are grossly limited in accounting for human interaction. Behavior therapy has pinpointed the need to search for current maintaining factors in addition to antecedent events.

Nevertheless, behavior therapy and behavior modification have acquired a bad press. To receive funding, many hospitals and community agencies have had to drop the label *behavior* from their program proposals. In several quarters, the term 'behavior modification' is an adrenalin-raiser that evokes unfortunate stereotypes. One grows weary of explaining that behavior therapists do not deny consciousness, that they do not treat people like Pavlovian dogs, that they are not Machiavellian and coercive, that aversion therapy (except in the hands of a lunatic fringe) has always been a minor and relatively insignificant part of our armamentarium, and that we are not ignorant of the part played by mutual trust and other relationship factors among our treatment variables.

When making therapeutic recommendations, however, the degree of diversification among behavior therapists appears to be no less extensive than the differences between behavioral and non-behavioural practitioners (Loew, Grayson and Loew, 1975). There are multiple approaches for overcoming human woes, but we require precise knowledge about what is best under specified conditions. All therapists need to be wary of any uncritical acceptance of ideas, while also realizing that their theories and methods must necessarily undergo change. It takes courage to abandon pet notions and favored strategies when the disciplined light of science reveals their shortcomings. I believe that therapists of all persuasions must transcend the constraints of factionalism in which cloistered adherents of rival schools, movements and systems each cling to their separate illusions or unwisely seek solace in volatile blends or overinclusive amalgams.

I am opposed to the advancement of psychoanalysis, to the advancement of gestalt therapy, to the advancement of existential therapy, to the advancement of behavior therapy or to the advancement of any delimited school of thought. I would like to see an advancement in psychological knowledge, an advancement in the understanding of human interaction, in the alleviation of suffering and in the know-how of therapeutic intervention. As a reflection of my evolving commitment to these developments, my own clinical work has grown from a fairly strict behavioral orientation to a broad-spectrum, behavior therapy approach, with a current emphasis on multifaceted interventions that constitute 'multimodal behavior therapy' (Lazarus, 1965, 1971, 1976). Behavioral and interpersonal factors constitute about 28 per cent of the variance in multimodal therapy. The other 72 per cent of assessment–intervention strategies are devoted to affective, sensory, imaginal, cognitive and biochemical/neurophysiological considerations.

If behavior therapy, in keeping with the views of this Association (the AABT), is limited to principles and methods derived from research in experimental and social psychology, it can be seen as a small but significant part of a multimodal therapy approach. Within the confines of this delimitative context, behavior therapy can continue to serve a useful function. But no practitioner who wishes to be effective with a broad range of clients can afford to limit himself or herself in this manner. Strictly speaking, behavior therapy, like psychoanalysis, can only be defended as a research tactic. The real world of human suffering and the vicissitudes of psychological growth demand much more than any of us have offered to date.

Acknowledgments

I am grateful to Allen Fay, Cyril Franks, Peter Nathan, Terry Wilson and Rob Woolfolk for their cogent criticisms of the initial draft.

References

BANDURA, A. (1973). *Aggression: A Social Learning Analysis*. Englewood Cliffs, NJ: Prentice-Hall.

BANDURA, A. (1974). Behavior theory and the models of man. *Am. Psychol.* 29, 859-869.

BREWER, W.F. (1974). There is no convincing evidence for operant or classical conditioning in adult humans. In: Weimer, W.B. and Palermo, D.S. (Eds), *Cognition and the Symbolic Processes*. New York: Halsted Press.

DOLLARD, J. and MILLER, N.E. (1950). *Personality and Psychotherapy*. New York: McGraw-Hill.

ELLIS, A. (1962). *Reason and Emotion in Psychotherapy*. New York: Lyle Stuart.

EYSENCK, H.J. (1960). *Behaviour Therapy and the Neuroses*. Oxford: Pergamon Press.

FRANKS, C.M. (1976). Foreword. In: Lazarus, A.A. (Ed.), *Multimodal Behavior Therapy*. New York: Springer.

FRANKS, C.M. and WILSON, G.T. (Eds) (1973). *Annual Review of Behavior Therapy: Theory and Practice*. New York: Brunner/Mazel.

FRENCH, T. (1933). Interrelations between psychoanalysis and the experimental work of Pavlov. *Am. J. Psychiatr.* 12, 1165-1203.

GESELL, A. (1938). The conditioned reflex and the psychiatry of infancy. *Am. J. Orthopsychiatr.* 8, 19-30.

GOLDFRIED, M.R. and DAVISON, G.C. (1976). *Clinical Behavior Therapy*. New York: Holt, Rinehart & Winston.

HALEY, J. (1976). *Problem Solving Therapy*. San Francisco: Jossey-Bass.

JONES, M.C. (1924). The elimination of children's fears. *J. Exp. Psychol.* **1**, 382–390.

KANFER, F.H. (1976). The many faces of self-control, or behavior modification changes its focus. Paper presented at the 8th International Banff Conference, Banff, Alberta, Canada.

KRASNER, L. (1976). On the death of behavior modification: Some comments from a mourner. *Am. Psychol.* **31**, 387–388.

KRETSCHMER, E. (1934). *Kretschmer's Textbook of Medical Psychology* (E.B. Strauss, Trans.). London: Oxford University Press. (Originally published, 1922.)

KUBIE, L.S. (1934). Relation of the conditioned reflex to psychoanalytic technique. *Arch. Neurol. Psychiatr.* **32**, 1137–1142.

LAZARUS, A.A. (1965). Towards the understanding and effective treatment of alcoholism. *S. Afr. Med. J.* **39**, 736–741.

LAZARUS, A.A. (1971). *Behavior Therapy and Beyond*. New York: McGraw-Hill.

LAZARUS, A.A. (1976). *Multimodal Behavior Therapy*. New York: Springer.

LAZARUS, A.A. and WILSON, G.T. (1976). Behavior modification: Clinical and experimental perspectives. In: Wolman, B.B. (Ed.), *The Therapist's Handbook*. New York: Van Nostrand Reinhold.

LOCKE, E.A. (1971). Is 'behavior therapy' behavioristic? An analysis of Wolpe's psychotherapeutic methods. *Psychol. Bull.* **76**, 318–327.

LOEW, C.A., GRAYSON, H. and LOEW, G.H. (Eds) (1975). *Three Psychotherapies*. New York: Brunner/Mazel.

LONDON, P. (1972). The end of ideology in behavior modification. *Am. Psychol.* **27**, 913–926.

MAHONEY, M.J. (1974). *Cognition and Behavior Modification*. Cambridge, MA: Ballinger.

MALAN, D.H. (1976). *The Frontier of Brief Psychotherapy*. New York: Plenum.

MINUCHIN, S. (1974). *Families and Family Therapy*. Cambridge, MA: Harvard University Press.

O'LEARY, K.D. and WILSON, G.T. (1975). *Behavior Therapy: Application and Outcome*. Englewood Cliffs, NJ: Prentice-Hall.

RACHLIN, H. (1976). *Introduction to Modern Behaviorism*, 2nd edn. San Francisco: Freeman.

RACHMAN, S. (1968). *Phobias: Their Nature and Control*. Springfield IL: Charles C. Thomas.

RAZRAN, G.H.S. (1935). Conditioned responses: An experimental study and a theoretical analysis. *Arch. Psychol.* **28**, No. 191.

SHAW, F. (1946). A stimulus-response analysis of repression and insight in psychotherapy. *Psychol. Rev.* **53**, 36–42.

ULLMANN, L.P. and KRASNER, L. (1965). *Case Studies in Behavior Modification*. New York: Holt, Rinehart & Winston.

WATZLAWICK, P., WEAKLAND, J. and FISCH, R. (1974). *Change: Principles of Problem Formation and Problem Resolution*. New York: Norton.

WILLIAMS, T.A. (1923). *Dreads and Besetting Fears*. Boston: Little, Brown.

WOLPE, J. (1948). *An approach to the problem of neurosis based on the conditioned response*. Unpublished MD thesis, Witwatersrand Medical School.

WOLPE, J. (1958). *Psychotherapy by Reciprocal Inhibition*. Stanford, CA: Stanford University Press.

WOLPE, J. (1973). *The Practice of Behavior Therapy*, 2nd edn. Elmsford, NY: Pergamon Press.

WOLPE, J. (1976). *Theme and Variation: A Behavior Therapy Casebook*. Elmsford, NY: Pergamon Press.

WOODWORTH, R.S. (1938). *Experimental Psychology*. New York: Holt.

ZENER, K. (1937). The significance of behavior accompanying conditioned salivary secretion for theories of the conditioned reflex. *Am. J. Psychol.* **50**, 384-403.

Chapter 12
Toward Delineating Some Causes of Change in Psychotherapy (1980)

> What are the active ingredients of psychotherapeutic change and growth? The
> foregoing question is one that intrigues most counsellors and therapists and is
> one that Lazarus addressed in several of his writings. In this chapter, he talks
> about several superstitions that therapists can develop and he challenges the
> view that common factors, rather than discrete interventions, account for the
> outcome variance with specific types of problems (a view that he amplified in
> many subsequent papers). For example, the reader may want to study this next
> chapter and then read Chaper 14 which brings some of the major issues into
> even clearer focus.

Extreme views have been generated about virtually every position in psychotherapy. Some will argue that relationship factors constitute the
essence of psychotherapy and embody all the necessary conditions for
growth and change. Others adhere to the view that the elements of hope,
faith and belief comprise the only important factors. Yet others think
entirely in terms of tactics, strategies, maneuvers, methods and techniques. And then there are those who argue that only a comprehensive
framework that incorporates all these interactive components into assessment and therapy can possibly delineate the active principles of therapeutic change and eventually lead to a scientific, artistic and humanistic
consensus.

Has any clarity come to the fore since Colby (1964) began his review of
psychotherapeutic processes with the words 'chaos prevails', a sentiment
that was echoed by Frank (1971)? If we were to ask a physician for some
medical facts or turn to a lawyer for legal facts, we would be inundated
with an information blizzard. But when we ask psychotherapists for some
psychotherapeutic facts, we often draw a blank. When certain facts are
proffered, they usually fall outside the sphere of psychology – for example,

First published in 1980. Reproduced with permission from Lazarus, A.A. (1980). Toward delineating some causes of change in psychotherapy. *Professional Psychology*, **11**, 863-870. Copyright
© 1980 by the American Psychological Association.

'It is a fact that lithium is the treatment of choice when dealing with the manic phase of a bipolar affective disorder'. Other people hedge. 'What exactly do you mean by "a fact"?' At what level of confidence does something have to be stated before it can be considered factual?'

In the past decade, researchers and therapists have come to realize that psychotherapy is not a unitary process applied to unitary problems. General questions about the efficacy of something called *psychotherapy* (e.g. Eysenck, 1952) have been replaced by an emphasis on *specificity*: '*what* treatment, by *whom*, is most effective for *this* individual with *that* specific problem, and under *which* set of circumstances' (Paul, 1967, p. 111). Yet many noted researchers still persist in conducting omnibus studies. For instance, Luborsky, Singer and Luborsky (1976) reviewed studies that compared individual psychotherapy with group psychotherapy and examined time-limited vs time-unlimited psychotherapy, behavior therapy vs psychotherapy, psychopharmacotherapy vs psychotherapy, and other equally broad categories. Their dominant conclusion was that 'everybody has won and all must have prizes' (p. 3), because no significant differences were found among the various approaches.

It seems obvious to me that, if you expose common or garden variety 'neurotics' to anything from systematic desensitization to unsystematic chitchat, equally positive outcomes are almost inevitable. The individuals in any mixed or heterogeneous group of troubled people are likely to overcome their problems for a variety of therapeutic and extratherapeutic reasons. Consequently, some experts champion the view that all psychotherapeutic change is predominantly a function of common factors inherent in every therapeutic approach. This strikes me as a particularly dangerous conclusion. It tends to lull therapists into a false sense of security and generates such sentiments as: 'I don't have to do anything specific or bother about apposite interventions. I merely have to remain pleasant and non-judgmental, and allow the patient's increased morale to do the rest.' It also fosters an anti-intellectual and antiscientific outlook. If the common factors are all that matter, why bother to search for significant differences? However, although there may be heuristic virtue in searching for overall principles of change, let us not stop looking for precise and specific treatments of choice. It would be negligent, if not criminal, for a therapist to withhold lithium and offer nothing but a warm, supportive and empathic relationship when consulted by someone with a manic–depressive illness. Similarly, in the treatment of children with nocturnal enuresis, 'the bell-and-pad method appears overwhelmingly more effective than supportive and psychodynamically oriented verbal psychotherapy and routine treatments' (Kazdin and Wilson, 1978, p. 89).

If you are faced with the task of decreasing ritual behaviors in a group of encrusted obsessive–compulsive individuals, a disorder that as Kazdin and Wilson (1978) point out 'has remained refractory to modification by the full panoply of psychiatric treatments, ranging from psychotherapy to chemotherapy and lobotomy' (p. 14), then do not concern yourself with insight, existential encounters, or empathy. And do not waste time with systematic desensitization, thought stopping, progressive relaxation or aversion relief. Do administer a series of performance-based methods such as in vivo flooding, response prevention and participant modeling (Rachman and Hodgson, 1980).

There are additional therapeutic indications and contraindications, as documented in the recent literature on outcomes and designs (e.g. Garfield and Bergin, 1978; Kazdin and Wilson, 1978). For instance, non-orgasmic women are more likely to respond to a 'sexual growth program' (Heiman, LoPiccolo and LoPiccolo, 1976) than to other forms of intervention. And sexually dysfunctional men are more likely to respond to a Masters and Johnson (1970) type of retraining than to conventional or traditional psychotherapy. Phobic disorders are more readily overcome with participant modeling than with other procedures, and conversational therapies generally achieve very little with problems such as stuttering, tics, nail-biting and other 'bad habits' (compare Redd, Porterfield and Andersen, 1979).

In every instance, individual and personal exceptions to these rules may be discerned. Some enuretic children may require a warm and sustained therapeutic interaction with a parent figure rather than the bell and pad. Some obsessive–compulsive cases may actually respond better to traditional therapy than to response prevention techniques. And some premature ejaculators may fare very well with supportive therapy and do poorly with threshhold training such as the 'squeeze technique'. In these instances, only astute and thorough assessment procedures can determine what approach the individual client is likely to require (compare Lazarus, 1976).

Although many confounds and limitations in the vast literature on psychotherapy research models use process and outcome measures, it is important to keep emphasizing specific data on the efficacy of discrete interventions for certain conditions. In addition to those previously listed, Wilson (1980) has discussed many other well-researched treatment effects. Here are a few of the findings he reports:

1. Self-monitoring the caloric content of foods consumed, as opposed to the circumstances under which eating takes place, reliably produces significant reductions in weight, at least in the short term.
2. Cigarette smoking is better reduced by self-monitoring the estimated tar and nicotine content of each cigarette smoked than by merely counting the number of cigarettes smoked.
3. In most instances, therapeutic change appears to follow methods that are performance based, whereas purely cognitive or verbal methods are often less effective.

4. Lasting therapeutic change usually requires the use of explicit maintenance strategies.

In short, it seems that Frank et al. (1978) are quite *incorrect* in concluding that 'while it would be highly desirable to devise specific therapies for specific symptoms, with a few exceptions this goal still eludes us' (p. 172).

Superstition and Deadwood

Many clinicians are inclined to downgrade laboratory research as sterile and irrelevant and prefer to select treatment methods on the basis of subjective appeal. As a direct consequence, professional psychotherapy comprises a large measure of common and uncommon nonsense, and the perpetuation of this nonsense is often harmful. Many leading therapists readily admit that a 'deterioration effect' can ensue, and it is the view of several experts that people may suffer negative effects as the result of undergoing psychotherapy (Strupp, Hadley and Gomes-Schwartz, 1977; Bergin and Lambert, 1978). One thing we seem to know about behavior change and psychotherapy is that the process is not necessarily salubrious. If I am correct in asserting that the field is riddled with superstitition and deadwood, why and how, we might ask, did this situation arise? And how and why is it perpetuated? Let us discuss a few obvious contaminants.

One possibility is that specific changes in a person's life circumstances, unrelated to the therapy, are all too readily overlooked as the real ingredient of constructive change. For example, 3 weeks after I trained an extremely agitated 60-year-old widow in relaxation and meditation, she telephoned and reported a gratifying improvement. 'I feel fine. The tense feelings are gone, my headaches are gone, I am sleeping much better, and I have not taken any Valium.' The therapeutic effects of a combined relaxation–meditation regimen seemed rather impressive. But experience has taught me to ask a simple attribution question. 'Do you think that the relaxation–meditation techniques brought about this improvement?' I inquired. 'Well', she answered, 'to tell you the truth, I think it has more to do with the fact that the couple who lived in the next apartment moved out.' Upon further inquiry I learned that her next door neighbors were 'noisy young hooligans' who harassed her and threatened physical violence if she complained to anyone. She was so terrified of them that she made no mention of it to me and, even though they had moved away, she was still reluctant to discuss it. A 'nice young married couple' had moved into the vacant apartment. 'It's a lot easier to sleep without that stereo going all night', she added.*

---

*The glib acceptance of a client's facile explanations may be equally hazardous, because clients as well as therapists may readily confuse correlation with causation and falsely ascribe improvement to variables that were incidental rather than active.

Had I failed to look into the reasons for her therapeutic improvement, it would have been credited to the synergistic properties of relaxation and meditation. Although this is a simple and clear-cut example, I am implying that too many clinicians are apt to give credit where it really is not due and thereby obfuscate the issues.

In recent years, there has been a spate of professional and popular literature outlining our developmental phases from birth through childhood, puberty, adolescence, adulthood, middle age, old age and advanced old age. It is hypothesized that there are many different variations within phases and that at each level we face unique crises, and are capable of shedding old habits and of acquiring new ones. Paradoxically, we become more malleable and more rigid, more vulnerable and more secure in essential respects, as each phase is reached.

Again, it is all too easy for therapists to overlook a 'phase change' that coincides with treatment improvement and attribute all credit to the ongoing techniques. For example, Wolpe and Lazarus (1966) reported that

> when one of us (J.W.) left Johannesburg, he handed over to A.A.L. a patient suffering from severe agoraphobia and fears of group situations that had been improving very slowly on systematic desensitization. For a time A.A.L. continued in the same way, and then began to try out variations with no good effect, until he introduced the 'shock-avoidance' modification of 'anxiety-relief' conditioning, which led to complete and lasting recovery in a matter of 3 weeks.   (pp. 20–21)

In retrospect, I now wonder what role the 'shock-avoidance' technique played in the final recovery. At the time I introduced this 'new technique', the client's daughter was about to marry and her son had graduated from high school. This was a 'phase change'. She was no longer needed in the home, her children were adults and her 'mothering phase' was over. Now she was free to travel, to become mobile, to give up her agoraphobia. But at the time that I wrote *Behavior Therapy Techniques* with Wolpe, I was so fixated on techniques that I failed to think beyond them. Today, there are still many practitioners who make the same mistake.

There are many similar confounds. If a therapist happens to apply a favorite tactic or technique when a positive shift in a client's biological functioning is occurring, it will be difficult to persuade either the client or the therapist that the beneficial outcome was largely unrelated to the psychological interventions. Or, to cite yet another example, one of my colleagues attributed all the gains in an 8-year-old child, whom she had treated since he was 4, to her specific psychological ministrations. Since, with children, the passage of time permits the complex processes of maturation to take place, it seems to me that anyone who achieves results after treating a child for a year or two should give some of the credit to nature.

How does this jibe with the aforementioned emphasis on applying discrete interventions to particular problems? How can we tell, for instance, whether response prevention, rather than some unidentified process, intrinsic or extrinsic to the therapy, was the real basis for change with a particular obsessive–compulsive individual? Science offers no ultimate or absolute answers, but experiments can control for the impact of relationship and placebo effects, suggestion, biological shifts and other forces, and parcel out the active independent variables. But it would be a boon to the profession if psychotherapists embraced the null hypothesis and contended that their results were probably due to factors other than their favorite interventions – unless they had data to the contrary.

The point being emphasized is that many people resolve their conflicts, solve their problems and overcome their disturbances as the result of processes that lie outside their therapists' attributions. I have alluded to extratherapeutic factors such as environmental changes, phase changes, biological shifts and maturation. A proclivity to refer to them as 'non-specific treatment factors' masks the existence of eminently specifiable ingredients that require specific elaboration (Wilson, 1980). I am guilty of this myself. In 1961, I wrote a paper in which I termed the deliberate use of counterconditioning techniques 'specific reciprocal inhibition' and relegated everything else (interview situations, verbal interchange and relationship factors) to the heap of '*non-specific* properties for inhibiting neurotic responses' (Chapter 3). Scientific advances within psychology and psychotherapy have shown that we need to distil the active ingredients of these non-specific factors and deliberately incorporate them into our clinical repertoires (compare Wilson and Evans, 1977). The same holds true for the catch all term 'spontaneous remission'.

Some Additional Causes of Change

The major thesis being presented in this paper is that, apart from numerous well-researched treatment effects, many specious psychotherapeutic methods have received credit for improvements that would either have occurred in any case or that were due to identifiable factors outside the therapy. An allied point is that some of psychotherapy's most cherished truths have not stood up under proper scientific scrutiny. For example, the therapist's warmth, empathy and genuineness are widely regarded as demonstrably related to the effective practice of psychotherapy. Yet some studies indicate that, although these attributes may facilitate client-centered therapy, they do not distinguish good and poor therapists of other schools (Frank et al., 1978). And even client-centered therapists report that these so-called facilitative conditions are less potent and are neither as general nor as great as once thought (Mitchell, Bozarth and Krauft, 1977). Another widely held notion is that therapist expectancies significantly determine the course and outcome of psychotherapy, but Wilkins (1978) showed that 'very little evidence exists to support the popular assumption that therapist expectancies play a contributory role in causing therapeutic change' (p. 350). Caution should be exercised in uncritically accepting any assumption.

An issue that has withstood critical scrutiny is that any interaction that engenders a high level of faith and hope is particularly potent. Frank's (1961) classic book, *Persuasion and Healing*, clearly documented the inestimable power of suggestion, hope, faith and persuasion. This subsequently led to the development of specific methods of relationship enhancement and to the development of several well-researched procedures for successfully increasing therapist attraction and influence (e.g. Goldstein, 1971, 1975). Following Schofield (1964), some therapists regard psychotherapy as a formalized 'friendship industry where trained and highly qualified experts in friendship offer ongoing care, awareness and responsible guardianship' (Abramovitz, A., 1979, personal communication). I can support this notion if 'responsible guardianship' implies the systematic application of critical research findings and data-based clinical essentials (Goldfried and Davison, 1976; Wilson, 1980).

It is becoming widely recognized that sustained and positive treatment outcomes are predicated on the feeling of mastery and control the client acquires. Bandura (1977) refers to this important process as 'self-efficacy'. Alfred Adler, in his discussions of a striving for superiority and the achievement of mastery in overcoming a sense of inferiority and helplessness, stressed that clients must be brought:

> through various devices to the point where they necessarily acquire faith in their own mental and physical powers.... One must put tasks in their way which they can accomplish and from the accomplishment of which they gain faith in themselves.
>
> (Ansbacher and Ansbacher, 1956, p. 400)

All practicing therapists are faced with a constant and immediate dilemma – how to consolidate the evanescent goals of therapy in the face of numerous presenting complaints, implicit and explicit expectations, hidden agendas and other conflicting information. Since each individual is a complex system in which his or her idiosyncratic features may take precedence over commonalities in specific contexts, the final orchestration of psychotherapy remains an art. Certain stylistic aspects can be taught – when and how to pay attention or to appear inattentive, what level of activity or inactivity to display at a given moment, what degree of directiveness or non-directiveness to adopt, how to implement homework assignments and how to present a convincing therapeutic rationale. But many aspects of 'psychotherapeutic grammar' are exceedingly difficult to teach (Grinder and Bandler, 1976).

Colby (1962) captured the essence of the art and science of psychotherapy extremely well.

> It is a practical art, a craft like agriculture, or medicine, or in wine-making in which an artisan relies on an incomplete, fragmentary body of knowledge and empirically established rules traditionally passed on from master to apprentice ... He looks to science for help, not to make him an applied scientist which cannot be done anyway – but to elucidate acute difficulties in the art. (p. 95)

Unfortunately, some influential psychotherapists do not see themselves as practical artists, as wine-makers or agriculturalists. Religious zeal tends to characterize their outlook, and after assuming a messianic role, replete with disciples who uphold their dogma, they form a cult and promote their doctrine with vigor and vehemence. Fortunately, strong indications now show that these creeds are being superseded by responsible professionals who are intent on discovering and disseminating facts, even when they run counter to their own self-interest. On the whole, there are persuasive reasons for a sense of optimism and hope.

Acknowledgments

The writer is grateful to Arnold Abramovitz, Allen Fay, Irene Rhodes, Terry Wilson and Rob Woolfolk for their constructive criticisms.

References

ANSBACHER, H. and ANSBACHER, R.R. (Eds) (1956). *The Individual Psychology of Alfred Adler*. New York: Basic Books.

BANDURA, A. (1977), Self-efficacy: Toward a unifying theory of behavior change. *Psychol. Rev.* **84**, 191–215.

BERGIN, A.E. and LAMBERT, M.J. (1978). The evaluation of therapeutic outcomes. In: Garfield, S.L. and Bergin, A.E. (Eds), *Handbook of Psychotherapy and Behavior Change: An Empirical Analysis*. New York: Wiley.

COLBY, K.M. (1962). Discussion of papers on therapist's contribution. In Strupp, H.H. and Luborsky, L. (Eds), *Research in Psychotherapy II*. Washington, DC: American Psychological Association.

COLBY, K.M. (1964). Psychotherapeutic processes. *Annu. Rev. Psychol.* **15**, 347–370.

EYSENCK, H.J. (1952). The effects of psychotherapy: An evaluation. *J. Consult. Psychol.* **16**, 319–324.

FRANK, J.D. (1961). *Persuasion and Healing*. Baltimore, MD: Johns Hopkins Press.

FRANK, J.D. (1971). Therapeutic factors in psychotherapy. *Am. J. Psychother.* **25**, 350–361.

FRANK, J.D., HOEHN-SARIC, R., IMBER, S.D., LIBERMAN, B.L. and STONE, A.R. (1978). *Effective Ingredients of Successful Psychotherapy*. New York: Brunner/Mazel.

GARFIELD, S.L. and BERGIN, A.E. (Eds) (1978). *Handbook of Psychotherapy and Behavior Change: An Empirical Analysis*. New York: Wiley.

GOLDFRIED, M.R. and DAVISON, G.C. (1976). *Clinical Behavior Therapy*. New York: Holt, Rinehart & Winston.

GOLDSTEIN, A.P. (1971). *Psychotherapeutic Attraction*. New York: Pergamon Press.

GOLDSTEIN, A.P. (1975). Relationship-enhancement methods. In: Kanfer, F.H. and Goldstein, A.P. (Eds), *Helping People Change*. New York: Pergamon Press.

GRINDER, J.E. and BANDLER, R. (1976). *The Structure of Magic*. Cupertino, CA: Science and Behavior Books.

HEIMAN, J., LOPICCOLO, L. and LOPICCOLO, J. (1976). *Becoming Orgasmic: A Sexual Growth Program for Women*. Englewood Cliffs, NJ: Prentice-Hall.

KAZDIN, A.E. and WILSON, G.T. (1978). *Evaluation of Behavior Therapy: Issues, Evidence and Research Strategies*. Cambridge, MA: Ballinger.

LAZARUS, A.A. (1976). *Multimodal Behavior Therapy*. New York: Springer.

LUBORSKY, L., SINGER, B. and LUBORSKY, L. (1976). Comparative studies of psychotherapies. In: Spitzer, R.L. and Klein, D.F. (Eds), *Evaluation of Psychological Therapies*. Baltimore, MD: Johns Hopkins University Press.

MASTERS, W.H. and JOHNSON, V.E. (1970). *Human Sexual Inadequacy*. Boston: Little, Brown.

MITCHELL, K.M., BOZARTH, J.D. and KRAUFT, C.C. (1977). A reappraisal of the therapeutic effectiveness of accurate empathy, nonpossessive warmth, and genuineness. In: Gurman, A.S. and Razin, A.M. (Eds), *Effective Psychotherapy: A Handbook of Research*. New York: Pergamon Press.

PAUL, G.L. (1967). Strategy of outcome research in psychotherapy. *J. Consult. Psychol.* **31**, 109–118.

RACHMAN, S. and HODGSON, R. (1980). *Obsessions and Compulsions*. Englewood Cliffs, NJ: Prentice-Hall.

REDD, W.H., PORTERFIELD, A.L. and ANDERSEN, B.L. (1979). *Behavior Modification: Behavioral Approaches to Human Problems*. New York: Random House.

SCHOFIELD, W. (1964). *Psychotherapy: The Purchase of Friendship*. Englewood Cliffs, NJ: Prentice-Hall.

STRUPP, H.H., HADLEY, S.W. and GOMES-SCHWARTZ, B. (1977). *Psychotherapy for Better or Worse: The Problem of Negative Effects*. New York: Aronson.

WILKINS, W. (1978). Expectancies in applied settings. In: Gurman, A.S. and Razin, A.M. (Eds), *Effective Psychotherapy: A Handbook of Research*. New York: Pergamon Press.

WILSON, G.T. (1980). Toward specifying the 'nonspecific' factors in behavior therapy: A social learning analysis. In: Mahoney, M.J. (Ed.), *Psychotherapy Process*. New York: Plenum.

WILSON, G.T. and EVANS, I.M. (1977). The therapist–client relationship in behavior therapy. In: Gurman, A.S. and Razin, A.M. (Eds), *Effective Psychotherapy: A Handbook of Research*. New York: Pergamon Press.

WOLPE, J. and LAZARUS, A.A. (1966). *Behavior Therapy Techniques*. Oxford: Pergamon Press.

Chapter 13
Resistance or
Rationalization? (1982)

In 1972 Lazarus began collaborating with Dr Allen Fay, a New York psychiatrist. They co-authored books, chapters and scientific papers. The Lazarus/Fay chapter on 'resistance' is one of their most provocative, insightful, astute and clinically relevant co-authored contributions. They have managed to pinpoint factors across a broad range of conditions which can lead to resistance and counter-control. Critics and reviewers were extremely positive about this chapter. Many were impressed by their discussion of the way in which a patient's individual characteristics and his or her family processes interact with the therapist, and influence the therapeutic relationship. Today, problems of non-compliance, and the difficulties that all clinicians experience in achieving treatment adherence, occupy a more and more central position in much of the literature.

The concept of 'resistance' is probably the most elaborate rationalization that therapists employ to explain their treatment failures. When their efforts are frustrated, they frequently postulate the existence of internal forces or make causal assignment to a 'frustrator', thus reducing dissonance at the patient's expense. Spoken or unspoken, the sentiment is: 'It is not my own inadequate assessment or faulty diagnosis, nor the limitations of my theories or methods, but instead the patient's stubbornness, unwillingness, or inability to cooperate that accounts for his or her lack of progress.' At the outset, we would like to underline our view that 'resistance' is generally a function of the limitations of our knowledge and methods and the constraints of our personalities. These are the major factors that create difficulty in dealing successfully with the special therapeutic problems individuals bring to our attention.

All therapists in the course of their professional activities encounter remarkably recalcitrant problems in patients who *appear* to have vested

This was written with Allen Fay and first published in 1982. Reproduced, with the permission of Plenum Publishing Corp., from Lazarus, A.A. and Fay, A. (1982). Resistance or rationalization? A cognitive–behavioral perspective. In: Wachtel, P.L. (Ed.) *Resistance: Psychodynamic and Behavioral Approaches*, pp. 115–132. New York: Plenum.

interests in some form of 'stasis'. Indeed, the course of therapy seldom follows a smooth, monotonic progression; setbacks and reversals often impede progress. Nevertheless, the notion that some internal process (resistance) is responsible for most or many treatment failures or setbacks is simply an unfortunate though convenient evasion of clinical responsibilities.

A patient disagrees with the therapist's interpretations, refuses to comply with his or her suggestions, comes late or misses appointments, fails to carry out homework assignments, 'forgets' to take prescribed medication, withholds important information, becomes evasive when asked pertinent questions, tells deliberate lies, or displays oppositional tendencies in other ways. What prevailing forces can account for these 'resistant' behaviors? Is resistance inevitable? Is it intrapsychically determined, interpersonally specific, a manifestation of the therapist's incompetence, an indication of incompatibility or poor matching between patient and therapist, or evidence of secondary gain? Sometimes patients may ardently *resist* all the therapist's suggestions, interpretations and ministrations, and yet achieve rapid and lasting improvement. Would such patients' cognitive non-acceptance and behavioral non-compliance still be viewed as 'resistance'? If a therapist gives poor advice, the patient does not comply, and a favorable outcome ensues – must we then assume that the patient improved in order to show up or demean the therapist? Surely we would have to elaborate some kind of procrustean explanation to get us off the hook!

It is necessary to separate resistance as a postulated mechanism explaining a clinical phenomenon (negative outcomes) from resistance as a clinical phenomenon itself. Clearly, it begs the question to speak of resistance whenever positive outcomes are not achieved. Furthermore, labeling all non-compliant behavior 'resistance' obscures the essential importance of teasing out specific antecedent and maintaining factors that generate uncooperative behaviors in specific contexts.

Another relevant issue concerns the distinction between the *patient* being resistant and the *problem* being resistant. We frequently talk about certain patterns and symptoms being notoriously refractory (e.g. severe obsessive–compulsive states), regardless of who the patient is or who the therapist is.

Is resistance ubiquitous? Does every therapist's attempt to produce change lead to resistance in some form and to some degree? Or does resistance exist in specific relationships and only in particular contexts? Many clinicians contend that a certain degree of resistance is inevitable because all clients or patients are ambivalent. On the one hand, patients wish to acquire more productive and adaptive attitudes and behaviors, but, on the other hand, they cling to the protection and security of their current styles, despite the negative consequences.

As a psychodynamic mechanism, resistance is inevitable. The analytic model of personality relies heavily on the unconscious and its repressive barriers, and one of its intrinsic ideas about human functioning is that there *must* be opposition to anyone or anything that attempts to expose unconscious processes. Its avowed purpose is to prevent the discharge of energy associated with unconscious material. From this point of view, resistance represents an active force within the patient that prevents him or her from understanding the true but threatening significance of specific symptoms. 'Everything that prevents the patient from producing material derived from the unconscious is resistance' (Fenichel, 1945, p. 27).

Empirically, it is obvious that people may tend to shy away from painful revelations about themselves and that they can disown or deny unacceptable impulses, feelings or cognitions. To avoid facing these disagreeable things, they may come late for their appointments or miss them entirely, they may overintellectualize, rationalize, refuse to carry out prescriptions, and display other negative attitudes towards therapy and the therapist. The danger lies in concluding that these behaviors are, ipso facto, evidence of 'resistance' instead of searching for the *actual* reasons behind them. Thus, some chronic latecomers may have a very poor ability for scheduling time – a problem in its own right, not based on the avoidance of painful material or on antagonism towards the therapy.

By insisting on an unconscious locus for resistance, some therapists compound the difficulty of understanding and resolving intricate clinical problems. A patient may intentionally withhold information and otherwise refuse to participate in treatment because of fear, shame or distrust of the therapist. Unfortunately, those who maintain that unconscious resistance invariably lies behind these deliberate factors deflect responsibility back onto the patient's intrapsychic forces instead of examining situational events (e.g. the therapist's failure to create a climate of trustworthiness for a particular confidence to be shared).

One of the dangers inherent in the notion of the inevitability of resistance is that it leads clinicians to be suspicious of rapid improvement in patients who have not manifested 'resistance'. As a consequence, ad hoc concepts such as 'flight into health' and 'transference cure' emerge that may lead a therapist to withhold positive reinforcement for rapid clinical change. We are not suggesting that all rapid remission is durable, but we would not automatically be suspicious of such a felicitous event.

Is the *locus* of resistance always within the patient? Not if one looks at the problem in terms of *systems*, in which case the process will be seen as a function of the patient–therapist–family network as a whole. (We will discuss some of the 'game' aspects of therapist–patient transactions where 'resistance' seems to be a problem.)

Failure to Carry Out Homework Assignments

From our perspective, one of the most significant signs of 'resistance' is the patient's failure to complete homework assignments: 'I forgot'; 'I didn't have the time'; 'I wasn't sure exactly what you wanted me to do'; 'I didn't feel up to it'; 'The opportunity didn't present itself'. Many other excuses may be offered, but whenever in vivo assignments are entirely bypassed or attempted half-heartedly, progress is generally slow or non-existent. There is persuasive evidence that, in most instances, therapeutic progress follows methods that are performance based, whereas purely cognitive or verbal methods are usually less effective. We therefore dwell most heavily on *action*, on *doing*. We typically ask our patients: 'What have you *done* differently this week?' If the answer is 'Nothing' we assume an absence of progress. In some instances, the answer 'I've been doing a lot of thinking' may signify some positive shift, but we prefer to hear such answers as, 'I applied to seven colleges', or 'I stood up to my husband', or 'I took the risk and went out on three dates', or 'I stopped eating candy and ice cream'. Similarly, therapists' preoccupation with how the patient felt or what the patient thought can impede progress.

Homework assignments are geared to enhance positive shifts in patients' main areas of concern. The timid, reticent, inhibited individual will not acquire a repertoire of assertive skills merely by talking about it, any more than someone will learn to speak a foreign language or play a musical instrument without practice. Homework assignments are dispensed along a graduated hierarchy. 'Over the next week how about making sure that you simply say "thank you" to any compliment you receive, instead of diminishing yourself as you usually do? And will you make a note of how many compliments you receive and exactly how many times you say "thank you" instead of lapsing into your self-downing behaviors?' These instructions were given to an intelligent, attractive, well-groomed, stylishly attired, 20-year-old woman who invariably responded to the frequent compliments she received with overly modest, self-deprecatory statements. At a subsequent session, she reported no opportunity to carry out her homework assignment because she had received no compliments during that week. Likewise, a 32-year-old man stated that he had had no opportunity to ask his employer for a raise. A 15-year-old boy 'forgot' to ask his father if he would attend a few family therapy sessions.

Before leaping to the conclusion that some unspecified 'resistance' lies behind most instances of non-compliance, we find it profitable to examine a variety of more concrete possibilities.

● Was the homework assignment incorrect or irrelevant?
● Was it too threatening?
● Was it too time-consuming in terms of its 'cost effectiveness'?

● Does the patient not appreciate the value of and rationale behind homework exercises? (Is the patient opposed to or unaware of the educational, self-help thrust of our ministrations?)
● Is the therapeutic relationship at fault? (If so, the patient may display passive–aggressive behaviors towards the therapist.)
● Is someone in the patient's social network undermining or sabotaging the therapy?
● Is the patient receiving far too many secondary gains to relinquish his or her maladaptive behavior?

It must be understood that homework assignments are not delivered in an authoritarian manner. The therapist suggests what appears to be a reasonable course of action. Patient and therapist discuss the advisability and feasibility of the assignment, so that the final prescribed tasks appear mutually meaningful. Nevertheless, after leaving the consulting room, the patient may have second thoughts about the advisability of therapists' recommendations. And some of these objections may rest on solid facts that emerged only after the patient seriously contemplated engaging in a specific behavior. By exploring the possibilities raised by each of these alternatives, it is often possible to reframe the assignments, re-educate the patient and, if necessary, re-examine the therapeutic relationship, and re-evaluate the patient's family system or social network.

Control and Countercontrol

When treatment does not proceed apace, falters or fails to get off the ground, several specific and clearly delineated reasons may be discerned. When a treatment impasse is reached, we assume that one or more of the following factors is operative:

1. Inappropriate matching or absence of rapport. (In this instance, instead of insisting that this problem can and must be worked through, it is often advisable to effect referral to a more compatible resource.)
2. Therapist's failure to identify relevant antecedents and/or maintaining factors. (A thorough and accurate assessment is often an indispensable condition for effective therapy.)
3. Therapist's failure to deal with the social network. (All too often therapy is undermined within the patient's system or social network. To dwell only on intraindividual factors leaves ample room for interpersonal saboteurs.)
4. Therapist's use of incorrect techniques. (Includes all errors and blunders that the therapist may commit.)
5. Therapist's faulty or incorrect use of appropriate techniques. (Insufficient training or experience is reflected by this factor.)

6. Extreme excesses or deficits in the patient's biological or psychological functioning. (There are some people who, for numerous reasons, manifest what appears to be irreversible dysfunction.)
7. The desired outcome is not valued highly enough by the patient. (Thus there is an unwillingness to expend the necessary effort to effect change.)

We believe that these seven factors cover the range of explanations for most treatment impasses. It will be noted that, in our view, much of the variance rests with the therapist. In regard to the seventh factor, we have deliberately avoided the term 'motivation'; but there is clearly a wide range of individual differences that patients bring to their therapy in terms of their willingness or ability to invest the necessary time and effort to effect change. It is *largely* the therapist's responsibility to inspire the patient to take the necessary steps, but it is unrealistic to place the *entire* onus on the clinician.

Undoubtedly, we have all encountered patients who simply withdrew from therapy when basic issues were about to be confronted or when substantial changes were in the offing. There are people who seek therapy solely to find an ally who will support their dysfunctional styles. If one attempts to 'normalize' them, they leave. Similarly, others may enter therapy not in order to change, but to form an alliance against a significant other (e.g. a husband tries to team up with a therapist against his wife). There are, in short, people who do not want help, or for whom there may be too many competing factors. Whether or not we should or could devise methods to change their minds remains debatable. Salter (1949) was quite clear about these cases:

> But what shall be done with the persons who do not let you turn the wheels? Often they should be chased from the office with a broomstick, although they are not to be blamed for their personalities.
>
> I explain to them that my appointment book is like a life raft. There is room for only a limited number of people, and I do not intend to waste my time trying to convince any of the bobbing heads around me to get on board. There are others drowning who are only too happy to cooperate in their rescue.

One might be inclined to add: and beware especially of those who not only refuse one's helping hand but try to drag one off the raft in order to drown along with them. It needs to be underlined that some people who come to therapists for help are not seeking any change in their own behavior, but instead are looking for comfort and reassurance. Indeed, such support is the essence of their concept of therapy.

The most puzzling cases are not the outright resisters or deliberate saboteurs. What about those people who never miss appointments, are always punctual and who avidly attend to our ministrations, follow our logic, carry out our assignments, but fail to change and keep coming back?

Some of these cases may be highly accomplished 'passive-resisters' who derive an enormous sense of power and gratification from the therapist's frustration. In these instances, paradoxical procedures such as 'symptom prescription' and 'reframing' often prove effective (Watzlawick, Weakland and Fisch, 1974; Haley, 1976).

Generally, our successful clients come regularly to their sessions, are willing to be as 'transparent' as possible during these sessions (i.e. they do not deliberately lie, distort or withhold information), and are amenable to trying a variety of procedures on for size (e.g. they will role-play when appropriate, practice relaxation, meditation, confrontation, study pre-scribed books and other reading materials, take medication when recom-mended, keep activity charts, and share their reactions, thoughts and feelings with the therapist). Our model is essentially *educational* and we liken ourselves to a music teacher or an athletic coach – we supply guid-ance, offer specific training exercises, correct misconceptions, try to mod-ify faulty styles, provide up-to-date information, display caring, support and encouragement; still, most of the responsibility rests with the 'trainee' to practice between training sessions. We spend an average of an hour per week with each patient and emphasize that actions performed during the other 167 hours will determine the success or failure of the therapy

It is quite obvious that many patients display oppositional behaviors. Indeed, most people are inclined to resist efforts by others, be they overt or covert, to modify their behavior. The tendency to counteract attempts to influence or control us makes it incumbent on therapists to establish a *cooperative* climate wherein change is predicated on mutual goals and shared objectives. The field of social psychology has shown that coopera-tive behaviors are more likely to occur when someone is requested, rather than directed, to perform (or refrain from) specific acts. *Telling* a client to relax, imagine scenes, act more assertively, self-monitor specific behaviors or agree on contingency management is likely to foster some degree of opposition or countercontrol (Davison, 1973; Wilson and Evans, 1977). *Asking* for the same performance-based responses is less likely to evoke opposition. Thus resistance or countercontrol may be a direct function of the therapist's manner and style. In our experience, at least 80 per cent of patients follow our *requests* or suggestions without travail.

Still, it is important to emphasize that, no matter how tactful, supportive or cooperative the climate of therapy may become, in the final analysis, dur-ing the helping process, the therapist will attempt to *influence* the client. As Johnson and Matross (1977) point out, 'persons who are interacting are con-stantly influencing and being influenced by each other'. Yet many feel there is a fine line between constructive and destructive influence. For example, coercion readily truncates one's freedom, and so does exploitation (i.e. the use of unfair, dishonest or insidious means for one's own purposes or advant-ages). Thus there is a widespread tendency to beware of 'influence' – no matter how benignly or constructively intended. Therapists are therefore required to build and maintain trust throughout the course of therapy.

Who is the patient?

All too frequently, individuals present themselves for therapy who are not positively disposed towards change. In our experience, it is often useful to view the patient as the person who wants change and is willing to work for it. The patient is *not* necessarily (as in the medical model) the individual with the identifiable symptom, although even in medicine there is room for a systems perspective. In clinical practice, one commonly sees a family containing a 'non-functioning' grown offspring living with parents.

> A young man lived a life of idleness at his parents' expense. In response to their pressuring, he made abortive attempts to find work but usually slept late, ate enormous quantities of food, and intimidated his parents into buying him a car, subsidizing expensive vacations ('From what?' we inquired), and in general tolerating sloth, slovenliness and abusiveness. The parents were somewhat puzzled when therapy was made conditional on the whole family being seen together. They were told, 'Billy is not the patient – you are the patient. You are the ones who desire the change. Why should he work? He could not begin to support himself in the style you have made possible. When *you* change, he will change.' Although this point may seem hackneyed to therapists schooled in learning principles, systems theory and behavior modification techniques, the young man over a 12-year period had seen four therapists and had even been given a course of ECT. Twelve visits later (mainly by the parents, because Billy did not attend half the sessions), striking changes were evident in the parents' demeanor and approach, accompanied by corresponding increases in the young man's adaptive behaviors.

Value differences and the definition of normalcy

> A 24-year-old man received enough support from a small trust to live in a shabby residential hotel without having to work. Therapy was also paid for. Whereas initially the patient had phobic complaints, he was now improved and felt therapy was no longer needed. He was encouraged to get a job, but he clearly had no interest in working. 'I've tried a couple of jobs and find them boring and not terribly rewarding financially. I'm really enjoying life. I can eat for about a dollar fifty a day [stale bread, canned soup etc.] and spend my time taking long walks, going to museums and libraries, and socializing with friends. I date women who enjoy what I enjoy. When I need a few bucks I baby-sit.' We asked if it would not be better to get some kind of training for work that might be more satisfying, and we suggested the long-range adaptive value of a different living pattern. He replied that he would take his chances on the future and insisted that he was perfectly content, despite the family's view that his lifestyle was grossly pathological. We were inclined to view this individual as a *non-patient* rather than a 'resistant patient'.

The Varieties of Resistance

As we have indicated, four different factors can lead to 'resistance' in therapy: (1) resistance as a function of the patient's individual characteristics;

(2) resistance as a product of the patient's interpersonal relationships (systems or family processes); (3) resistance as a function of the therapist (or the relationship); and (4) resistance as a function of the state of the art (and science).

We will now briefly discuss each of these factors.

Individual characteristics

A clear distinction must be drawn between unresponsive cases and resistant individuals. Let us take a person with low intelligence who fails to comply with a therapist's interventions simply because of an inability to comprehend specific recommendations. This non-compliance is not a function of 'resistance', since the term implies some deliberate or unconscious *opposition*. (The dictionary meaning involves some exertion aimed at counteracting or defeating a force.) In addition to individuals with poor cognitive ability, there are patients whose genetic endowment and cultural heritage have rendered them so arid, with such a paucity of coping responses, that therapy at best amounts to a caretaking and supportive function.

As Goldstein, Heller and Sechrest (1966) have said, it is incumbent on therapists to investigate their lack of success with certain classes of patients, 'working toward the goal of developing new techniques and improving old ones to expand [their] usefulness beyond its present narrow range' (p. 152).

Clinically, some simple tactics often succeed with seemingly 'unmotivated' or 'resistant' clients: 'As far as I'm concerned, psychology and psychiatry is worth nothing. You guys are the real nuts who should be locked away. I'm here to get my goddamn parents off my back. So cure me!' How does one 'motivate' or overcome the 'resistance' of a 16-year-old boy who snarls these words the moment his mother and father step into the waiting room so that the therapist and he can have a private, heart-to-heart meeting? It is easier to say how one can *fail* to overcome such resistance. Failure is almost guaranteed if one remains passive, reflective or becomes interpretive: 'You seem to be an angry and frightened young man who has problems with authority'. Of course, there is no way to be sure that a particular repsonse from the therapist will prove facilitative, neutral or negative. The therapist may sit quietly, sagaciously nodding his or her head, and thereby trigger a positive capitulation simply because an angry outburst from the patient met with not an iota of condemnation. Conversely, stepping out of an expected role and saying something like, 'Shut up you little jerk! I'm interested only in getting paid. I couldn't care less about you or your goddamn parents!' might prove enormously helpful in other instances. Such situations highlight the importance of the therapist's ability to assume different roles – in short, to be a convincing actor in his or her own consulting room. A broad array of techniques and a capacity for style change are essential if a therapist is to be successful with a variety of problems and personalities (Lazarus, 1976, 1981).

Our own clinical rule of thumb is generally to start with a logical, supportive, empathic approach. 'Most people get angry when forced into things they don't want to do.' This statement has a reasonable chance of eliciting a positive reaction from the patient. 'Well, Doctor, how would you feel if you were always put down by your parents?' But what if the hostility merely escalates? 'Quit that phony "I understand you" act!' That was the exact response from an actual case in point. The following rejoinder broke the impasse: 'Look fellow. I have very little time for this bullshit myself. But I do have a few tricks up my sleeve that might help get your parents off your back – if that is what you really want.'

Openly defiant patients are generally easier to manage than those seemingly cooperative individuals who employ subtle or facile tactics that undermine one's efforts. An 18-year-old girl referred by a Pretrial Intervention Community System for shoplifting said: 'I don't need a shrink. I need somebody to teach me how not to get caught.' She was startled when the therapist said: 'Nobody has ever caught me and I've been ripping things off much longer than you. Perhaps I can be your teacher.' This approach is a variant of a well-known method commonly called 'siding with the resistance' (Sherman, 1968). The girl soon dropped her façade and said: 'I know you're kidding. Maybe I could use some help with my hangups.'

Along similar lines, the following dialogue ensued when a 37-year-old woman arrived for her second visit:

Patient: I've decided to drop out of therapy.
Therapist: Good-bye. I hope all goes well with you.
Patient: Just like that?
Therapist: Pardon?
Patient: Aren't you supposed to try and talk me into being in treatment?
Therapist: I'm not a secondhand car salesman. I only work with people who want to receive help from me.
Patient: Well what makes you think I don't want to be helped?

Fay (1978) describes the successful application of paradoxical procedures to an extremely resistant 37-year-old man who had frustrated all rationally based attempts to overcome his general inertia and withdrawal.

Patient: I should really be getting up every morning like everyone else and going to work.
Therapist: Why should you?
Patient: Any normal person would do that and I want to be normal.
Therapist: Is it so normal to drag yourself out of bed every morning and do some boring work all day with all the pressures and hassles and the miserable commuting?

Patient: But other people do it.
Therapist: Is it necessary for you to do something simply because other people do it?
Patient: Well, I want to be good at something.
Therapist: You *are* good at something. You are superb at eating and sleeping.
Patient: I don't think that's right. I should get a job and function like other people.
Therapist: I think you should do what you enjoy and what you do best and that is eating, sleeping and watching television.
Patient: But what I'm doing is sick.
Therapist: What's sick about doing the things you want to do? I think you're doing just fine. I don't see any sickness, and if you *were* sick, I would certainly be the one to know it.

Within 2 weeks the patient had a job and, in spite of early misunderstandings with his employers, he was still working 6 months later.

Patients can undermine therapy at various points. For example, when using systematic desensitization, therapists open themselves to patients' non-compliance at several stages (Rhoades and Feather, 1972). When faced with a patient who is resisting and not responding to desensitization methods, the therapist has several alternatives. The reasons behind the resistance can be explored; a collaborative set may be invoked by asking the patient to design a modified desensitization procedure that would be tailored to his or her specific needs and expectancies (for example, one seemingly resistant patient, when asked to modify the procedure, suggested bringing along a cassette recording of some of his favorite music in the hope that 'music plus relaxation' would offset the anxieties generated by the specific hierarchical scenes – a tactic that proved most effective); and the therapist with a broad array of techniques at his or her disposal can always introduce a different procedure when one is not working, just as a skilled hypnotist slips effortlessly and gracefully from one trance-induction method to another.

Interpersonal, systems or family processes

From a cognitive–behavioral standpoint, an important question is: 'Who or what is maintaining the behavior?' Many patients receive intermittent reinforcement for their aberrant behaviors from significant others who deliberately or inadvertently foster the problematic styles and symptoms. It is common to find several 'emotional saboteurs' within the patient's social network, but it is not necessary to become embroiled in some of the convoluted explanations and theories that certain systems and family analysts have offered. Nevertheless, it is well documented that family members often undermine a therapist's endeavors when they fear that a change in an individual will threaten their own security. Hence couples therapy and family therapy have become an important medium to offset such sources of resistance. By seeing all the principals together, 'resistance' can more easily be detected and overcome.

Resistance often lies in the dyadic transactions.

We were treating an anxious, unassertive and somewhat depressed woman, age 35, who was married and had two children. Although she came for sessions regularly and punctually, we were unable to make therapeutic headway. She was seemingly compliant, yet managed to frustrate all our attempts to effect change. After 2 months of weekly sessions she was a little less anxious and a trifle more assertive, but no significant gains had accrued. A thorough interpersonal analysis revealed that she was extremely reluctant to achieve a non-anxious, assertive and optimistic lifestyle for fear of destroying her marriage and thereby damaging her children. It appeared that her reticence, self-downing utterances and fears tended to bolster her husband, who seemed to enjoy the role of her comforter and protector. She felt (and on meeting her husband, we concurred) that she could easily outstrip him. Developing her potential and abandoning her anxious and dependent games would probably destabilize her marital relationship to the point of rupture. 'I would rather sacrifice myself than risk my marriage and the happiness of my children.' It also became apparent that her marital interactions were an exact copy of her parents' style. They had always voiced strong opposition to divorce on religious grounds.

The foregoing is a typical example of what we consider resistance. The patient's reluctance to change had little to do with resistance as traditionally conceived, but was integrally tied to her own values and those of her social milieu. This case poses several treatment dilemmas. Can a way be found wherein this woman would become self-fulfilled without damaging her marital relationship? If not, is it best to teach her to accept her lot in life? Can some of her problems be mitigated by upgrading the marital relationship so that at least partial fulfillment and some degree of independence are achieved? Should therapy aim to actualize and emancipate this woman regardless of family repercussions? Regardless of the answers to these questions, one basic objective would be to eliminate needless guilt so that decisions are based on rational choice rather than neurotic constraints.

For us the essence of the systems approach to therapy is that individuals influence and are influenced by the people with whom they come in contact (especially relatives and friends), and hence a change in one person is likely to have repercussions on significant others. If a positive change in an individual is inclined to have a negative impact on someone else in his or her network, some form of reluctance or resistance to change may be foreseen. If the individual him- or herself does not actively resist the change process, some member of the family or social network will probably find a way of preserving the status quo. Being alert to these interactive processes is often an indispensable condition for therapeutic success.

The therapist (or the relationship)

It is always important to realize that a seemingly resistant patient may in fact simply be avoiding a particular suggestion of a particular therapist at a particular time. The patient may be very selective about accepting ideas, suggestions or recommendations. In that case, we would prefer to call the patient *selective* rather than *resistant*.

If we say to a client 'John, since you are attracted to Mary, why not ask her for a date?', is he manifesting resistance if he does not do it? Perhaps he lacks the requisite social skills to accept our advice or perhaps he has not been desensitized to the rejection he anticipates.

The point is that different therapists obviously vary in their interpersonal skills, their knowledge, perceptiveness and other facilitative attributes. When a patient is 'resistant', it often means that he or she is being treated incorrectly or is seeing the wrong therapist.

> A psychiatric resident was making no headway with a female patient whom he was treating along traditional psychodynamic lines. She was constantly asking him personal questions - whether or not he was married, his taste in music and art, his favorite books, and other likes and dislikes. He invariably sidestepped the questions and reflected the presumed motives behind them. His analytic supervisor encouraged him to continue in the same manner, but at a general meeting where we were present, the resident expressed the fear that his patient was about to stop seeing him. 'Answer her questions like a human being', we advised him. 'Play it straight, and while you are at it, offer her an apology for having behaved toward her like a computer.' Subsequently, we were told that he followed our advice, the treatment impasse was overcome, close rapport was established, and therapeutic progress ensued.

> A number of years ago, a female patient who was terrified of sexual penetration had failed to respond to a panoply of cognitive–behavioral techniques. We decided to provide a 'modeling experience' in the form of one of the early sex therapy films. The objective was to enable her to become more comfortable with her body and with masturbation. Unfortunately, the particular film, which showed a very experienced, creative and free-spirited woman masturbating, did not produce the desired result but had the effect of intimidating the patient. It was only after she had left therapy, having achieved only modest gains, that we fully appreciated the importance of using coping models rather than mastery models (a film of a somewhat inept couple achieving a desired result, albeit through some fumbling and imperfect maneuvers, is likely to encourage and motivate certain patients far more than the depiction of bedroom athletes who enact a sexual encounter of interminable ecstasy).

Thus, the more a therapist knows, the fewer 'resistant' patients he or she will have. Perhaps ignorant therapists or therapists who restrict themselves to the methods and techniques learned during their formal training, regardless of the requirements of the clinical situation, are the ones who are resistant.

The theme of this chapter is that what appears to be 'resistance' may often have its locus within the therapist. Did the therapist fail to introduce an essential ingredient into the therapy? Again we would ask: 'Was the client's social network excluded and hence some powerful maintaining factors overlooked?' 'Was exhortation relied on without first administering the necessary modeling experiences?' 'Was instruction offered without first applying behavior rehearsal or other preparatory methods, such as coping imagery or stress inoculation?'

We have alluded to the fact that there is a difference in the content and quality of 'resistance' when a client deliberately countermands a therapist's endeavors because of disrespect, anger, fear or mistrust as opposed to an inadvertent failure to comply with a therapist's ministrations. To lump a myriad of different behaviors under the heading 'resistance' or 'countercontrol' misses the fact that specific messages have specific meanings and call for specific (different) interventions.

If a client's non-compliance stems from his or her perception of the therapist as a parent figure and reflects the network of parent–child expectations and implications, successful therapy will hinge on a resolution of these symbolic impediments. On the other hand, different therapeutic tactics are required where the client's struggles with the therapist rest on the interpersonal ramifications inherent in the specific therapy situation with the particular therapist. 'I dislike Dr A. because he reminds me of my father' is quite different from 'I dislike Dr A. because he betrayed my confidence'. Concerning the former point, Franks and Wilson (1973) state:

> If a person as a child has been able to maintain his identity only by resisting or fighting parental authority, there is no reason why we should not suspect that he will attempt to treat his behavior therapist with similar defensive tokens. These may never interpose themselves in outright defiance; rather they may take the more subtle form of an inability to respond to remedial promptings.

Therapists may unwittingly reinforce particular maladaptive behaviors and then claim that the patient is resistant. For example, a patient who consistently threatens suicide and receives a great deal of attention from the therapist for these dysfunctional utterances may continue to be 'resistant' until the therapist stops responding to the suicidal threats and instead dispenses positive reinforcement for more rational pronouncements.

When therapeutic impasses arise because of the incompatibilities between patient and therapist, we strongly recommend a judicious referral to a colleague whose personality and methodology seem better suited to the needs of the patient.

The state of the art (and science)

Obviously, there are people who cannot be helped by the methods currently at our disposal. Only with reluctance have we learned to concede that some people are beyond help, at least for the present. Yet we hang on. Even when consulted by people with malignant self-hate, intent on self-destruction, incapacitated by encrusted obsessive–compulsive rituals, with a pervasive sense of helplessness and hopelessness, we ply our balms and are intermittently rewarded for our ardent efforts. But when we fail to help these individuals, or when less floridly disturbed people (whose psychological ground is nevertheless a marsh of anhedonia and self-denunciation) fail to change, we need to parcel out the patient's *inability* vs his or her *refusal* to derive benefit.

We treated an extremely unhappy woman in her mid-thirties who had been a battered child. We had no methods in our repertoire that were capable of removing her numerous 'psychic scars'. Similarly, the best individual and combined efforts we could muster were unable to shatter the web of misery that pervaded a woman in her late forties. After failing to respond to several traditional therapies and one inpatient treatment regimen, she consulted us. We exhausted the range of our combined armamentaria, which included everything from drug treatment to biofeedback, and the patient eventually committed suicide.

On the positive side, we (like all therapists) have succeeded with seemingly intractable cases who had been declared untreatable and unreachable by several experts and authorities. To be able to articulate the exact ingredients that lead to failure or success is a worthy but lofty goal that our present knowledge does not even approach.

Although we have acknowledged that the concept of resistance has a measure of legitimacy, we nevertheless feel that its general usage is more likely to obfuscate than illuminate the course of therapeutic endeavors. In conclusion, we can only urge our colleagues to avoid confusing resistance with rationalized failure.

References

DAVISON, G.C. (1973). Counter control in behavior modification. In: Hamerlynck, L.A., Handy, L.C. and Mash, E.J. (Eds), *Behavior Change: Methodology, Concepts and Practice*. Champaign, IL: Research Press.

FAY, A. (1978). *Making Things Better by Making Them Worse*. New York: Hawthorn Books.

FENICHEL, O. (1945). *The Psychoanalytic Theory of Neurosis*. New York: W.W. Norton.

FRANKS, C.M. and WILSON, G.T. (1973). *Annual Review of Behavior Therapy: Theory and Practice*, Vol. 1. New York: Brunner/Mazel.

GOLDSTEIN, A.P., HELLER, K. and SECHREST, L.B. (1966). *Psychotherapy and the Psychology of Behavior Change*. New York: Wiley.

HALEY, J. (1976). *Problem-solving Therapy*. San Francisco: Jossey-Bass.

JOHNSON, D.W. and MATROSS, R.P. (1977). Interpersonal influence in psychotherapy: A social psychological view. In: Gurman, A.S. and Razin, A.M. (Eds), *Effective Psychotherapy: A Handbook of Research*. New York: Pergamon Press.

LAZARUS, A.A. (1976). *Multimodal Behavior Therapy*. New York: Springer.

LAZARUS, A.A. (1981). *The Practice of Multimodal Therapy*. New York: McGraw-Hill.

RHOADES, J.M. and FEATHER, B.W. (1972). Transference and resistance observed in behaviour therapy. *Br. J. Med. Psychol.* **45**, 99–103.

SALTER, A. (1949). *Conditioned Reflex Therapy*. New York: Farrar, Straus.

SHERMAN, M.H. (1968). Siding with the resistance versus interpretation: Role implications. In: Nelson, M.C., Nelson, B., Sherman, M.H. and Strean, H.S. (Eds), *Roles and Paradigms in Psychotherapy*. New York: Grune & Stratton.

WATZLAWICK, P., WEAKLAND, J. and FISCH, R. (1974). *Change: Principles of Problem Formation and Problem Resolution*;. New York: W.W. Norton.

WILSON, G.T. and EVANS, I.M. (1977). The therapist–client relationship in behavior therapy. In: Gurman, A.S. and Razin, A.M. (Eds), *Effective Psychotherapy: A Handbook of Research*. New York: Pergamon Press.

Chapter 14
The Specificity Factor in Psychotherapy (1984)

The need to find appropriate treatments for particular patients (specific treatments for specific people, administered by specific therapists, for specific problems, under specific sets of circumstances) became one of Arnold Lazarus's main clinical concerns early in his career. This penchant will already have been evident in previous chapters, but in this particular presentation, he discusses explicit tactics and well-matched strategies to replace global or generalised treatment methods. He challenges omnibus theories, overgeneralisations and certain fads in psychotherapy.

It is well known that systems, methods and techniques of psychotherapy continue to proliferate at an astonishing rate. Herink's (1980) potpourri of more than 250 therapies purports to represent only a fraction of extant treatment approaches. Perusal of this bewildering array of psychic nostrums reveals what may be termed a 'generalization fallacy'. Instead of providing remedies or strategies for overcoming specific problems, the majority claim to have the answer for all victims of 'neurotic suffering', or 'emotional disturbance', or other global dysfunctions. Thus, Holden (1980), a primal therapist, states that only the full re-experience of childhood pain 'is the way to reverse neurosis'. Mowrer (1980) offers 'integrity groups', a type of secular confessional, as another all-encompassing solution. Rogerian counselors provide all comers with identical sets of 'facilitative conditions'. Which particular treatment the consumer receives appears to depend mainly on whose consulting room he or she happens to enter, whether or not this is what he or she requires.

If the same mode of dispensing services pertained to the practice of medicine (psychiatry excluded), we might picture the following scenario:

A woman with a sore throat consults a physician whose name she picks out of the telephone book. The MD into whose consulting room she is ushered turns out to

First published in 1984. Reproduced, with the permission of The Haworth Press, from Lazarus, A.A. (1984). The specificity factor in psychotherapy. *Psychotherapy in Private Practice*, **2**, 43–48.

be a gynecologist. Consequently, the patient undergoes a routine pelvic examination during which a mild infection is discovered. An antibiotic is prescribed resulting in the serendipitous remission of her throat ailment. This felicitous result might lead the patient to seek gynecologic assistance for all future throat ailments. To analogize further from the field of psychotherapy, we would then have a doctor who would insist that the pelvis was the royal road to the pharynx.

In an attempt to avoid the manifold traps of overgeneralization, I have developed a carefully structured set of multimodal assessment procedures (Lazarus, 1981). A brief case presentation will illustrate how multimodal tactics focus on personalistic variables.

Ms WR, a 32-year-old woman, complained of 'panic attacks' that she attributed to her divorce 4 years earlier. At least twice a month, she would experience mounting anxiety for no apparent reason. Occasionally, if sufficiently distracted at the time, she would calm down; if not, her anxiety would escalate into what she termed 'a panic attack' replete with intense tachycardia, dizziness, shortness of breath, and nausea. She first consulted her family doctor, who diagnosed her condition as 'episodic, acute hyperventilation' and advised her to breathe into a paper bag before her symptoms reached panic proportions. When this proved ineffective, he referred her to a psychiatrist who prescribed a tricyclic antidepressant and, later, a monoamine oxidase inhibitor. This lessened the intensity of her panic attacks but not their frequency. Her next consultant, a psychodynamic psychotherapist, intimated that it was necessary to understand the underlying causes of her anxiety and panic, but indicated that this might take several years, with no guarantees. Instead, she joined a biofeedback clinic and received training in electromyography (EMG), galvanic skin response (GSR) and thermal control, with little benefit.

I was her fourth mental health consultant. She was referred to me by a former client who said that I 'dabbled in hypnosis'. Instead of 'dabbling' with her, or 'hypnotizing' her, I conducted a fairly typical initial interview and asked her to complete and mail back my Multimodal Life History Questionnaire (Lazarus, 1981). By the end of our second meeting, two significant findings were apparent:

1. Her divorce was but one of several antecedent factors. Three events that predated her divorce were the death of a close friend, job insecurity due to non-promotion, and a bout with pneumonia and pleurisy that left her physically debilitated for several months after being hospitalized for more than 2 weeks.

2. Close questioning of Ms WR revealed that her anxiety and panic followed a fairly distinctive pattern: something would bring her dead friend to mind and/or her thoughts would drift back to her own spell of physical debilitation. If these thoughts lingered, her mind would immediately flash back to scenes of her friend's funeral and her own hospitalization. If not interrupted at this juncture, she tended to focus

on real or imagined negative sensations, which would finally culminate in panic, especially if she got in touch with physical reactions that predominated during her illness and convalescence.

In multimodal terms (Lazarus, 1981) her modality 'firing order' usually occurred in the following sequence: negative cognitions were followed by distressing mental images, which in turn elicited unpleasant physical sensations, culminating in an affective anxiety response. We would term this a 'C-I-S-A pattern' (cognition–imagery–sensation–affect). Our experience is that such a patient would respond better to an initial cognitive intervention. Had she followed, say, an S-C-I-A pattern – in which the *sensory mode* initiated the sequence – biofeedback would probably have been an effective initial treatment. But in this case, where the sensory modality follows cognition and imagery, a predominantly sensory intervention such as biofeedback would not be expected to prove especially helpful until her dysfunctional cognitions and aversive images were brought under control. Please note the treatment specificity that is being addressed here.

First, the client's insight into her own 'firing order' enabled her to realize that her 'panic attacks' were precipitated by predictable events. Secondly, she learned that to ward off future episodes it was essential to disrupt her negative thoughts and replace them with positive self-statements. Next, her gloomy images were to be deliberately counterposed by scenes that evoked joie de vivre. Finally, she was to cultivate subjectively pleasant sensory responses that yielded calm and tranquil emotions (e.g. relaxation, diaphragmatic breathing, and autogenic warmth, heaviness, and peace). These specific objectives were achieved in four sessions. Ms WR has not suffered a panic attack for almost 4 years. (She has since enrolled in an EdD program in counseling psychology.)

Gordon Paul (1967) was the first to underscore the specificity factor. He asked, '*What* treatment, by *whom*, is most effective for *this* individual with *that* specific problem, and under *which* set of circumstances?' (p. 111). Studies have indicated that patients with identical psychiatric diagnoses fare better when treatment is tailored to individual response patterns. For example, phobic patients may be divided into two broad categories, behavioral reactors and physiological reactors. Clients with social phobias who are 'behavioral reactors' responded better to social skills training than to applied relaxation, whereas the latter proved more effective with 'physiological reactors'. Claustrophobic patients were more responsive to relaxation than to exposure if they were 'physiological reactors' whereas 'behavioral reactors' found exposure significantly more effective (Öst, Jerrelmalm and Johansson, 1981; Öst, Johansson and Jerrelmalm, 1982).

The specificity factor is clearly exemplified by some of the latest findings in the treatment of obsessive–compulsive disorders. In vivo exposure is almost an indispensable condition for effective outcomes (Marks, Hodgson and Rachman, 1975; Rachman and Hodgson, 1980; Steketee, Foa and Grayson, 1982). Severely incapacitated patients often require supervision in a psychiatric setting where trained personnel apply *response prevention* (i.e. they ensure that the patients refrain from carrying out their rituals). Three specific findings have emerged:

1. The actual exposure component tends to reduce anxiety.
2. Response prevention reduces the ritualistic behaviors.
3. *Imagined* exposure facilitates the maintenance of therapeutic gains.

(See Foa, Steketee and Milby, 1980; Foa, Steketee and Turner, 1980.)

Basically, the specificity factor is concerned with the age-old dictum of finding appropriate treatments for particular patients, instead of performing procrustean maneuvers that force one and all into the same preconceived system. In theory, nearly all therapists appear to be in agreement with the need for flexibility and respectful attention to individual differences. In practice, they often tend to violate the specificity factor. For example, Haley (1976) eloquently stresses that 'any standardized method of therapy, no matter how effective with certain problems, cannot deal successfully with the wide range that is typically offered to a therapist....A skillful therapist will approach each new person with the idea that a unique procedure might be necessary for this particular person and social situation' (pp. 9–10). In direct contradiction to the foregoing, Haley then states: 'Today it is assumed that to begin therapy by interviewing one person is to begin with a handicap' (p. 10).

I recently interviewed a 24-year-old man who, in his quest for psychotherapy, had telephoned a well-known treatment center for an appointment. He was referred to an 'intake receptionist' who ascertained that he was living at home with his parents and younger sister, and insisted that the entire family be present. Unbeknownst to the client, he had called a family therapy center that presumably wished to avoid 'beginning therapy with a handicap'. For reasons that I will not go into here, in my opinion it would have been a grave mistake for this young man to be seen in family therapy.

The specificity factor goes far beyond attempts to match clients to the best (individually compatible) therapy and therapist. Let us assume that a therapist, fully cognizant of specificity, has asked and affirmatively answered each of the following questions: Am I well suited to this person? Do we appear to have established rapport? Would it not be in the client's best interests to be referred elsewhere? Do I feel confident that my ministrations will prove effective? Have I deduced what type of treatment style, form, speed and cadence to adopt? Have we agreed upon the initial frequency and duration of the treatment sessions? Given positive responses to each of the foregoing, the therapist now deduces that the client will derive benefit from relaxation training. A new set of questions arise. Some of the more obvious ones are: Which of the many types of relaxation training programs is this particular client likely to respond to most favorably? How frequently, and for what length of time, should the client practice the selected relaxation sequence? Will compliance be augmented or attenuated by the supplementary use of cassettes for home use?

These types of questions are generally not pondered by Freudians, Jungians, Adlerians, Sullivanians, Rogerians and most other psychotherapeutic disciplines. In my view, this omission has given rise to the omnibus theories, overgeneralizations and the many fads that characterize the field. In this age of accountability, with new demands for cost-effective and cost–benefit analyses being foisted on the profession by outside agencies, our survival may depend on our ability to arrive at specific answers to highly specific questions.

Most of my own professional endeavors have focused on attempts to develop an assessment structure that would permit clinicians to ask the right questions in order to reach the most plausible solutions. While artistry and clinical intuition remain indispensable, a worthwhile goal is to have sufficient 'checkpoints' and 'markers' to minimize reliance on subjective factors. As long as the field of psychotherapy continues to spawn systems, schools and other non-specific and all-embracing orientations, there is little hope of achieving far-reaching scientific respectability. The need for greater specificity cannot be overstated.

References

FOA, E.B., STEKETEE, G. and MILBY, J.B. (1980). Differential effects of exposure and response prevention in obsessive–compulsive washers. *J. Consult. Clin. Psychol.* **48**, 71-79.

FOA, E.B., STEKETEE, G. and TURNER, R.M. (1980). Effects of imaginal exposure to feared disasters in obsessive compulsive checkers. *Behav. Res. Ther.* **18**, 449-455.

HALEY, J. (1976). *Problem-solving Therapy*. San Francisco: Jossey-Bass.

HERINK, R. (1980). *The Psychotherapy Handbook*. New York: New American Library.

HOLDEN, E.M. (1980). Primal therapy. In: Herink, R. (Ed.), *The Psychotherapy Handbook*, pp. 494-496. New York: New American Library.

LAZARUS, A.A. (1981). *The Practice of Multimodal Therapy*. New York: McGraw-Hill.

MARKS, I.M., HODGSON, R. and RACHMAN, S. (1975). Treatment of chronic obsessive compulsive neurosis by in vivo exposure. A two-year follow-up and issues in treatment. *Br. J. Psychiatr.* **127**, 349-364.

MOWRER, O.H. (1980). Integrity groups. In: Herink, R. (Ed.), *The Psychotherapy Handbook*, pp. 313-315. New York: New American Library.

ÖST, L-G., JERRELMALM, A. and JOHANSSON, J. (1981). Individual response patterns and the effects of different behavioral methods in the treatment of social phobia. *Behav. Res. Ther.* **19**, 1-16.

ÖST, L-G., JOHANSSON, J. and JERRELMALM, A. (1982). Individual response patterns and the effects of different behavioral methods in the treatment of claustrophobia. *Behav. Res. Ther.* **20**, 445-460.

PAUL, G.L. (1967). Strategy of outcome research in psychotherapy. *J. Consult. Psychol.* **31**, 109–118.

RACHMAN, S. and HODGSON, R. (1980). *Obsessions and Compulsions.* Englewood Cliffs, NJ: Prentice-Hall.

STEKETEE, G., FOA, E.B. and GRAYSON, J.B. (1982). Recent advances in the behavioral treatment of obsessive compulsives. *Arch. Gen. Psychiatr.* **39**, 1365–1371.

Chapter 15
The Multimodal Approach with Adult Outpatients (1987)

Of the many chapters that Lazarus has written on multimodal therapy, this one was selected as an exemplar due to the nature of much of the clinical material throughout. In this chapter, Lazarus not only presents most of his fundamental tenets, but he cites case vignettes that are especially illuminating. Many clinical interchanges have been transcribed directly from cassette recordings and enable one to sit in with Lazarus, as it were, and observe him in action.

Theoretical Model of Behavior Disorders

In a broad sense, we are products of the interplay among our genetic endowment, our physical environment and our social learning history. Adolf Meyer (1915) was among the first to emphasize the need to assess and treat biological, psychological and sociological factors, instead of resorting to mind–body dichotomies. We all recognize that conflicts, traumas and other adverse environmental factors play a role in psychological disturbance (behavior disorders), but this is far too global. What specific constructs, theories, principles, terms and concepts are needed to account for the vagaries of human conduct? The multimodal orientation is predicated on the following assumptions:

1. Human disquietude is multileveled and multilayered – few, if any problems have a single cause or a unitary 'cure'.
2. We are beings who move, feel, sense, imagine, think and relate to one another. At base we are biochemical/neurophysiological entities. Our personalities are the products of our ongoing *b*ehaviors, *a*ffective processes, *s*ensations, *i*mages, *c*ognitions, *i*nterpersonal relationships, and biological functions (wherein psychotropic *d*rugs are most commonly used to remedy dysfunctions). The first letters of each of these modalities form the acronym BASIC ID (or the preferred acronym BASIC I.D.). It is

First published in 1987. Reproduced, with the permission of Guilford Press, from Lazarus, A.A. (1987). The multimodal approach with adult outpatients. In: Jacobson, N.S. (Ed.) *Psychotherapists in Clinical Practice*, pp. 286–326. New York: Guilford Press.

crucial to realize that 'D' stands not only for drugs, medication, or pharmacological intervention, but also includes nutrition, hygiene, exercise, and all basic physiological and pathological inputs.

3. Psychological disturbances are a product of one or more of the following: (a) conflicting or ambivalent feelings or reactions; (b) misinformation; (c) missing information (includes skill deficits, ignorance and naiveté); (d) maladaptive habits (includes conditioned emotional reactions); (e) interpersonal inquietude (e.g. undue dependency, misplaced affection, excessive antipathy); (f) issues pertaining to low self-esteem; (g) biological dysfunctions.

4. At the physiological level, the concept of *thresholds* is most compelling. People have different frustration-tolerance thresholds, different stress-tolerance thresholds, different pain-tolerance thresholds – all of which are largely innate. While hypnosis and other psychological methods can modify certain thresholds, the genetic diathesis will usually prevail in the final analysis.

5. The main learning factors responsible for behavior disorders are conditioned associations (respondent and operant responses); modeling, identification, and other vicarious processes; and idiosyncratic perceptions (addressing the fact that people do not respond to some *real* environment, but rather to their *perceived* environment, thus factoring in the personalistic use of language, semantics, expectancies, encoding and selective attention).

6. Because much of our learning is neither conscious nor deliberate (Shevrin and Dickman, 1980), it is necessary to include *non-conscious processes* (not to be confused with 'the unconscious' that has become a reified entity). We are merely noting that (a) people have different levels and degrees of self-awareness, and (b) that unrecognized (subliminal) stimuli can nevertheless influence one's conscious thoughts, feelings and behaviors.

7. People defend against or avoid pain, discomfort, or negative emotions such as anxiety, depression, guilt, and shame. The term 'defensive reactions' avoids the surplus meanings that psychodynamic theory attaches to 'defense mechanisms'. It is not necessary to fall into the quagmire of Freudian constructs when acknowledging that a truly comprehensive understanding of human personality needs to address the fact that people are capable of denying, disowning, displacing and projecting various thoughts, feelings, wishes and impulses.

8. As we examine dyadic and more complex interactions, another explanatory construct is required. People do not only communicate, they also *metacommunicate* (i.e. communicate about their communications). Communication tends to break down when one is incapable of stepping back, as it were, and examining the content and process of ongoing relationships.

The foregoing are the main theoretical tenets that underlie multimodal assessment and therapy. For more detailed accounts see Lazarus (1981, 1984a, 1985).

Theory of Therapeutic Change

Rationale for treatment approach

Given the preceding theoretical model of behavior disorders, it follows that multimodal practitioners have a pluralistic conception of etiology and treatment. A fundamental premise is that clients are usually troubled by a multitude of specific problems which should be dealt with by a similar multitude of specific treatments. It is assumed that durable results are in direct proportion to the number of different modalities deliberately addressed, that lasting change is at the very least a function of combined *techniques*, *strategies* and *modalities*. Basically, the more a client learns in therapy, the less likely he or she is to relapse afterward. This vitiates the search for a panacea, or a single overriding therapeutic modality. In essence, the multimodal position is that comprehensive treatment at the very least calls for the correction of deviant behaviors, unpleasant feelings, negative sensations, intrusive images, irrational beliefs, stressful relationships and possible biochemical imbalance. Of course, not every case requires attention to each modality, but this conclusion can be reached only after a thorough assessment of each area has been conducted (i.e. comprehensive problem identification). To the extent that interactive problems in behavior, affect, sensation, imagery, cognition, interpersonal relationships and biological functioning are systematically explored, the diagnostic process is likely to be thorough. And to the extent that therapeutic intervention remedies whatever deficits and maladaptive patterns emerge, treatment outcomes are likely to be positive and long-lasting.

The 'idiosyncratic perceptions' alluded to in the preceding section call for the adoption of various treatment styles, and place heavy emphasis on flexibility and specificity. Multimodal therapy calls for a precise tailoring of the therapeutic climate to fit each client's personal needs and expectancies. The term 'bespoke therapy' has been used to describe the multimodal orientation (Zilbergeld, 1982) and aptly conveys the custom-made emphasis. The form, cadence and style of therapy are fitted, whenever possible, to each client's perceived requirements. The basic question is 'Who or what is best for this particular individual, couple, family or group?'. With some clients, it is counterproductive to offer more than a sympathetic ear; with others, unless therapy is highly structured, active and directive, significant progress will not ensue (Davison, 1980). By endeavoring to determine what works, for whom, and under which conditions, multimodal assessments try to spell out when to treat family systems rather than individuals, and vice versa. Even effective therapists will make mistakes relative to gauging the foregoing complexities, but capable therapists, on observing these errors, will usually make adjustments to change the course of therapy.

Overall strategy for bringing about behavior change

Assessment procedures

In multimodal therapy, the initial interview and the use of the Multimodal Life History Questionnaire (Lazarus, 1981)* are the mainstay of assessment and problem identification. The initial interview is used to arrive at 12 determinations:

1. Were there signs of 'psychosis' (e.g. delusions, thought disorders, bizarre or inappropriate behaviors, incongruity of affect)?
2. Were there signs of organicity, organic pathology or any disturbed motor activity (e.g. rigid posture, tics, mannerisms)?
3. Was there evidence of depression, or suicidal or homicidal tendencies?
4. What were the presenting complaints and their main precipitating events?
5. What appeared to be some important antecedent factors?
6. Who or what seemed to be maintaining the client's overt and covert problems?
7. What did the client wish to derive from therapy?
8. Were there clear indications or contraindications for the adoption of a particular therapeutic style? (Did a basic directive or non-directive initial stance seem preferable?)
9. Were there any indications as to whether it would be in the client's best interests to be seen individually, as part of a dyad, triad, family unit and/or in a group?
10. Could a mutually satisfying relationship ensue, or should the client be referred elsewhere?
11. Why was the client seeking therapy at this time – and why not last week, last month or last year?
12. What were some of the client's positive attributes and strengths?

In multimodal assessment, there is no slavish attention to order. When intervening in a crisis situation, the clinician may offer no more than immediate support, reassurance and perhaps guidance. A primary purpose of the initial interview is to determine how to fit the treatment to the client (and not vice versa). Whenever there is any suspicion of organicity, a typical mental status examination is performed. When neuropsychological impairment is suggested, a thorough testing of the client's attention, comprehension, grasp, reasoning, judgment and other neuropsychological factors is called for. The client's interests are best

*The Multimodal Life History Questionnaire is published by Research Press, Box 3177, Dept. G, Champaign, Illinois, 61821, USA.

protected when the therapist has a network of competent physicians (e.g. psychiatrists, neurologists, internists, endocrinologists) for consultation.

Information derived from the initial interview and the 12-page Multimodal Life History Questionnaire usually provides the therapist with information sufficient to design a comprehensive treatment program. The questionnaire, in addition to obtaining routine background information, contains a 'Modality Analysis of Current Problems' via behavior, affect, sensation, imagery, cognition, interpersonal relationships and biological factors. In tandem with observations obtained during the initial interview, after the client completes the Multimodal Life History Questionnaire, the therapist constructs a BASIC I.D. chart or modality profile – a distinctive feature of multimodal therapy. The modality profile establishes a clear nexus between assessment and therapy. It seldom takes longer than 15–20 minutes for the construction of a comprehensive modality profile. Each item on the profile is viewed as a specific problem that calls for direct therapeutic attention. These problem checklists serve as 'working hypotheses' which may be modified or revised as additional factors come to light.

Clients are frequently asked to draw up their own modality profiles; it is sometimes particularly valuable for therapist and client to perform this exercise independently and then compare notes. Clients are provided with a brief explanation of each term in the BASIC I.D. A typewritten instruction sheet with the following information usually suffices:

Behavior This refers mainly to overt behaviors: acts, habits, gestures, responses and reactions that are observable and measurable. Make a list of those acts, habits and so on that you want to increase, and those that you would like to decrease. What would you like to start doing? What would you like to stop doing?

Affect This refers to emotions, moods and strong feelings. What emotions do you experience most often? Write down your unwanted emotions (e.g. anxiety, guilt, anger, depression etc.). Note under 'behavior' what you tend to *do* when you feel a certain way.

Sensation Touching, tasting, smelling, seeing, and hearing are our five basic senses. Make a list of any negative sensations (e.g. tension, dizziness, pain, blushing, sweating, butterflies in stomach etc.) that apply to you. If any of these sensations cause you to act or feel in certain ways, make sure you note them under 'behavior' or 'affect'.

Imagery Write down any bothersome recurring dreams and vivid memories. Include any negative features of the way you see youself, of your 'self-image'. Make a list of any 'mental pictures', past, present or future, that may be troubling you. If any 'auditory images' – tunes or sounds that you keep hearing – constitute a problem, jot them down. If your images arouse any significant actions, feelings or sensations, make sure these items are added to 'behavior', 'affect' and 'sensation'.

Cognition What types of attitudes, values, opinions, and ideas get in the way of your happiness? Make a list of negative things you often say to yourself (e.g. 'I am a failure', 'I am stupid', 'Others dislike me' or 'I'm no good'). Write down some of your most irrational ideas. Be sure to note down how these ideas and thoughts influence your behaviors, feelings, sensations and images.

Interpersonal relationships Write down any bothersome interactions with other people (relatives, friends, lovers, employers, acquaintances etc.). Any concerns you have about the way other people treat you should appear here. Check through the items under 'behavior', 'affect', 'sensation', 'imagery' and 'cognition', and try to determine how they influence and are influenced by your interpersonal relationships. [Note that there is some overlap between the modalities; don't hesitate to list the same problem more than once (e.g. under 'behavior' and 'interpersonal relationships')].

Drugs/biology Make a list of all drugs you are taking, whether prescribed by a doctor or not. Include any health problems, medical concerns, and illnesses that you have or have not had.

Table 15.1 presents a modality profile that a client drew up on her own after reading the foregoing instructions.

In addition to modality profiles (i.e. specific problems and proposed treatments across a client's BASIC I.D.) the use of structural profiles (Table 15.2) often yields important information, especially in couples therapy. The following instructions are sufficient for drawing up these structural profiles:

Here are seven rating scales that pertain to various tendencies that people have. Using a scale of 0 to 6 (0 means that it does not describe you, or you rarely rely on it; 6 means that the description characterizes you, or you rely on it greatly) please rate yourself in the following areas.

Table 15.1. Modality profile

Behavior	Procrastination
	Disorganized/sloppy
Affect	Self-blame, guilt, jealousy, fear
	I'm especially afraid of criticism and rejection
Sensation	Tension, especially in my jaws
	Low back pain
	Fatigued a lot of the time
Imagery	Lonely images
	I picture myself failing at many things
	I often picture myself appearing foolish
Cognition	Trouble making decisions
	I'm often thinking about negative things
	I don't feel entitled to happiness
	I think of myself as less competent than most others
Interpersonal relationships	Basically suspicious and non-trusting
	I don't speak up when I am hurt or angry
	I feel that I am too dependent on my parents
	I don't have any good, close friends
Drugs/biology	Insufficient exercise
	Smoke ±2 packs of cigarettes a day
	Use Valium from time to time

Table 15.2.   Structural profile

1. *Behavior*: How active are you? How much of a 'doer' are you? Do you like to keep busy?

                  Rating: 6 5 4 3 2 1 0

2. *Affect*: How emotional are you? How deeply do you feel things? Are you inclined to impassioned, or soul-stirring inner reactions?

                  Rating: 6 5 4 3 2 1 0

3. *Sensation*: How much do you focus on the pleasures and pains derived from your senses? How 'tuned in' are you to your bodily sensations – to sex, food, music, art?

                  Rating: 6 5 4 3 2 1 0

4. *Imagery*: Do you have a vivid imagination? Do you engage in fantasy and day-dreaming? Do you 'think in pictures'?

                  Rating: 6 5 4 3 2 1 0

5. *Cognition*: How much of a 'thinker' are you? Do you like to analyse things, make plans, reason things through?

                  Rating: 6 5 4 3 2 1 0

6. *Interpersonal relationships*: How much of a 'social being' are you? How important are other people to you? Do you gravitate to people? Do you desire intimacy with others?

                  Rating: 6 5 4 3 2 1 0

7. *Drugs/biology*: Are you healthy and health conscious? Do you take good care of your body and physical health? Do you avoid overeating, ingestion of unnecessary drugs, excessive amounts of alcohol, and exposure to other substances that may be harmful?

                  Rating: 6 5 4 3 2 1 0

These subjective ratings are easily depicted on a graph. Despite their arbitrary nature, these ratings often enable one to derive useful clinical information. Important insights are gained when the therapist explores the meaning and relevance of each rating. In couples therapy, when husband and wife each fill out a structural profile, various differences and areas of potential incompatibility are readily discerned. With couples, it is also useful to have them rate how they think their spouse would depict them. This metacommunication usually provides additional inputs that can be put to good effect. Furthermore, it is also useful to determine the way a person rates him- or herself and to compare this with the way he or she rates his or her spouse. (At present, a standardized instrument is being designed to obtain structural profiles.)

When necessary, the multimodal therapist may call for standardized tests and additional diagnostic and assessment procedures (in the same technically eclectic spirit as a therapeutic method may be employed) but the mainstay of multimodal assessment centers on modality profiles and structural profiles.

Typical stages of treatment

The emphasis on flexibility and idiosyncratic necessity produces a high degree of heterogeneity on the part of the multimodal therapist. There are some clients who first require weeks or months of 'trust building' before any techniques or assessment procedures can be broached. Others are too depressed or too anxious to cope with the rigors of filling in a 12-page Multimodal Life History Questionnaire. Some clients require immediate advice, guidance and behavior rehearsal to deal with a current and pressing problem. Bearing in mind that there are exceptions to every rule and procedure (aside from two absolutes – sexual contact with clients is taboo, and clients should never be deprived of their dignity) most people nevertheless follow a similar therapeutic path.

Typically, initial interviews focus on the establishment of rapport, on assessing and evaluating presenting complaints, and on arriving at the best course of treatment. By dwelling on who or what is best for the client, the first question centers on whether or not alliance building and the development of a mutually satisfying relationship are likely, or whether referral to a different therapist or resource would be of greater benefit to the client. Sometimes, a definite mismatch is evident between client and therapist (e.g. in terms of the client's expectations, or clashpoints vis-à-vis their respective 'personalities'), and rather than 'work through' these differences, my associates and I prefer to effect referral to a more compatible resource. Earnest attempts to match the client to the type of therapist and therapy that he or she seems most likely to profit from makes *referral* an important procedure.

On what basis are referrals determined? It has been argued that there are three kinds of clients: good clients, who get better no matter who the therapist is; bad clients, who are untreatable regardless of how good the therapist is; and those clients who respond only to certain therapies and specific therapists. Clearly, the need for referral would apply to the second and third categories. There are often clear-cut indications for effecting a judicious referral. Sometimes, it seems obvious that a client will relate better to a therapists who is younger, older, of the opposite sex, whose background and race are more in keeping with the client's, who speaks Spanish (or another language that would facilitate rapport), or someone with specific expertise in a given area or with a particular population (e.g. children, adolescents or geriatric clients).

Recently, while seeing a 19-year-old man who was experiencing difficulties at home and at college, I felt myself 'rowing upstream' for three sessions. In essence, we did not seem to be getting anywhere. Consequently, I referred him to an associate who was much closer to him in age, on the hunch that he might be able to achieve a better alliance. I was correct. In the initial session, the client addressed issues he had withheld from me – the fact that he smoked marijuana daily, and a basic fear that he might be homosexual. When my colleague inquired why he had not shared this information with me, the client said, 'Dr Lazarus reminds me too much of my father, and I was unable to open up to him, just as I am unable to discuss things with either my mother or father'.

Given the absence of untoward features that would undermine the development of a therapeutic alliance, relationship building becomes an integral part of the problem-identification sequence. In other words, while eliciting information from the client, while searching for antecedent factors, ongoing problems and maintaining variables, and while ferreting out those subtle and elusive clues that point to appropriate technique selection (to be discussed in greater detail elsewhere in this chapter), one reflects empathy when appropriate, provides evidence of genuine caring, understanding, acceptance and similar basic facilitative conditions. For a small minority of clients, 'relationship therapy' is both necessary and sufficient; for the majority, the context of client–therapist rapport is the soil that enables the techniques to take root (Lazarus and Fay, 1984).

Armed with data from modality profiles, structural profiles, and other sources, the sessions become task oriented as emphasis is placed on mitigating the specific problems across the client's BASIC I.D. The therapist endeavors to pinpoint the types of interventions that are most likely to be of specific help in each instance. Whether or not the practitioner who carried out the multimodal assessment will perform the necessary treatments depends on his or her technical armamentarium. For example, a client may be referred to a biofeedback expert for help with sensory problems, while the primary therapist continues to work with the client in other areas.

Whereas many psychotherapeutic systems refer to a beginning phase, a middle phase and a sequence devoted to terminating therapy, in most instances multimodal therapy does not follow this typical format. After establishing the working alliance and developing the problem checklists, therapy continues until most of the major items on the modality profile no longer constitute a problem, at which point the treatment comes to a logical and operational end. Much more frequently, clients elect to terminate therapy long before each and every entry on their problem profile has been addressed and successfully resolved. In most cases, when the more disturbing or debilitating features have been overcome, the client will decide to 'go it alone'. He or she usually feels capable of living with the remaining problems, or has acquired sufficient coping skills from the therapy to apply them in a self-help capacity and thereby further attenuate residual difficulties. It is not my practice to discourage clients from discontinuing therapy unless I have good reason to suspect that serious consequences may result. It might also be mentioned that some clients elect to undergo several different courses of therapy, preferring to deal with

different problems at different times (and perhaps with different therapists). In several instances, booster or check-up sessions are necessary at
3-month or less frequent intervals, and this may be required for several
years. I have clients with whom ongoing therapy has long since terminated, who consult me from time to time for situational crises, or who
request 'annual check-ups'. There have been some clients, who, despite
the goal-directed and task-oriented nature of the approach, have nonetheless developed undue dependency and with whom treatment termination
became a problem unto itself. These cases are very much the exception
rather than the rule.

The fact that many clients are inclined to leave before all problems
throughout the BASIC I.D. have been dealt with may suggest that our treatment plans are too elaborate, and that the goals we set for our clients are
loftier than their goals for themselves. It should be understood that the
modality profile (BASIC I.D. chart) endeavors to list a wide range of problems, and that the goal of therapy is very rarely to eliminate each and
every item. To aim for a completely problem-free way of life is at best
unrealistic. (Perhaps this is what is meant by 'self-actualization'.) Rather,
the aim of multimodal therapy is to deal with as many specific problem
areas as seem feasible, cost-effective and worthy of attention. Thus, a
client who has overcome debilitating anxiety, whose interpersonal dealings are no longer sources of emotional anguish, and who has triumphed
over previously incapacitating guilt reactions might say, 'I know that I am
still a little too concerned about public opinion, and I do still tend to fuss
over my kids more than I should, and I have one or two other hang-ups,
but nobody's perfect, and I can live with myself just the way I am'.

Thus, it should be clearly understood that the modality profile provides
the total 'blueprint' of the major and minor problem areas, and that the
specific treatment goals are then selected from the total list. In some
instances, the goal might be to focus on one or two of the main problematic modalities; in other cases, we would shoot for all seven (without
necessarily aiming to *eliminate all*) problem items. It is most important
for the therapist to avoid suggesting treatment goals that clients are
unlikely to attain.

Structure of treatment sessions

Typically, treatment sessions begin by asking the client for an update.
'What has happened this week?' If specific homework assignments had
been suggested, the session would probably open by addressing these
issues. 'Did you have that conversation with your brother-in-law, and did
you count calories and note them down?' I take notes during sessions,
usually jotting down reminders to review certain issues, check-up on
assignments and raise particular matters that may clarify hitherto obscure

points. Sometimes clients have pressing problems or other immediate agenda items that supersede the ongoing treatment plan. Reticent clients may have to be prodded to bring additional matters to light. 'Before we continue with the relaxation and imagery exercises, is there something you'd like to talk about?'

A caveat at this juncture seems timely. Many years ago, one of my supervisors erroneously stated that whatever a client elects to discuss is important. Nonsense! Some clients may dwell on trivial events as a smokescreen, blotting out and avoiding the real issues. They may ramble or babble on tediously about irrelevant matters. There are gentle and effective ways of cutting into the flow. 'You have told me a good deal about Paul and Amy's marriage, but I'd much rather hear about your own relationship, particularly how you feel about Ron's new job.' With some clients considerable vigilance is required to ensure that the therapy remains on target. In this regard, a technique called 'bridging' has proved most effective.

Bridging refers to a procedure in which the therapist deliberately tunes into the client's preferred modality before branching off into other dimensions that seem likely to be more productive. Thus, if the theapist is eager to hear about the client's feelings, emotional reactions to a given incident, but is receiving no more than intellectual barriers from the client, the bridging maneuvers might proceed as follows:

Therapist: How did you feel when Sol just walked out and drove away?

Client: Well Sol probably inherited his irascible nature from his mother. I could speak for hours about his family background.

Therapist [trying to remain problem focused]: Did his behavior upset you, the way he just got up and left?

Client: His brother behaves the same way. They learned it from their mother. The old man, their father, was a sweet guy ...

Comment At this juncture, many therapists might be inclined to interrupt the client by pointing out that she is not answering the question, by challenging her intellectualizations, or perhaps by interpreting her 'resistance'. In many instances, these onslaughts are counterproductive. Clients often feel hurt, misunderstood, criticized or attacked when therapists countermand their flow of ideas. In this example, we have a therapist who wishes to enter the client's affective domain, while the client is insistent upon remaining in the cognitive modality. Gaining access to the affective modality via the bridging tactic would require the therapist to go along with the client's cognitive content (usually for no more than 2–5 minutes) and then switch to a less threatening modality (e.g. the sensory area) before finally addressing the affective reactions. Thus, the interchange might continue as follows:

Therapist [continuing to join the client's cognitive output]: So Sol in some ways is a carbon copy of his mother.

Client: He has a few more redeeming features or I would never have married him, but it is interesting how Sol and his brother took after the mother, whereas their sister is just like her father – the Freudians would have a field day analyzing the family identifications. Mildred, that's the sister, chose to marry a man who is a lot like Sol in some ways.... [The discussion remains focused on Sol's family dynamics for the next several minutes.]

Therapist   [bridging]: By the way, while we've been talking about Sol and his family, have you noticed any particular *sensations* anywhere in your body?

Client: Sensations? [pause] I don't know what you mean exactly, but I would say that my chest, well really it's more my throat and jaws feel tensed up.

Therapist: Let's just pay attention to those tense sensations in your throat and jaws. Would you mind closing your eyes and studying those sensations for a few moments?

Client   [complies; sits with eyes closed for about 45 seconds]: I notice that my breathing is very shallow.

Therapist: Is the tension and the shallow breathing in any way connected to feelings and emotions?

Client   [opens her eyes]: I don't know what you mean. [pause] Damn! I think I'm going to cry! He can be such a bastard! [tearfully] Let me tell you something. I don't deserve to be mistreated by him. [cries]

Therapist: So I guess you feel both sad and angry.

Client   [sobbing]: And I feel abandoned. [continues crying] Oh well, I guess there's no point in sniveling about it.

Therapist: Well, have you expressed these feelings to Sol, or have you continued to pretend that it doesn't bother you?

Client: [drying her tears]: I think you and I ought to rehearse a little speech, like we did that time with Margery [her employer].

Comment It should be re-emphasized that a therapist's failure to tune into the client's presenting modality can lead to feelings of alienation – the client may feel misunderstood, or may conclude that the therapist does not speak his or her language. Thus, multimodal therapists *start where the client is* and then bridge into more productive areas of discourse. Usually, I would have stayed with the affective reactions until I felt fairly convinced that the client had fully accepted her feelings, but since she obviously wanted to move towards an action-oriented solution that seemed quite relevant and appropriate, we launched into assertiveness training.

Second-order BASIC I.D. assessments

The initial BASIC I.D. chart (modality profile) translates vague, general or diffuse problems (e.g. depression, anxiety, unhappiness) into specific, discrete and interactive difficulties. Thereafter, while avoiding pushbutton panaceas, the initial selection of techniques is usually straightforward. Relaxation training is applied when undue physical tension is evident; dysfunctional beliefs will call for the correction of misconceptions; timid and unassertive behaviors suggest the application of assertiveness training. Nevertheless, treatment impasses arise – for example, when a client's unassertive reactions are not being changed despite the diligent application of role-playing, behavior rehearsal, modeling and other assertiveness training. When this occurs, a more detailed inquiry into associated behaviors, affective responses, sensory reactions, images, cognitions, interpersonal factors, and possible biological considerations, may shed light on the situation. This recursive application of the BASIC I.D. to itself adds depth and detail to the macroscopic overview afforded by the initial modality profile. Thus, a client who was not responding to assertiveness training, when asked to examine, in detail, the repercussions of assertive responses across the BASIC I.D., revealed a significant 'cognition' that seemed to account for his 'resistance'. In essence, it seemed that he did not feel *entitled* to certain rights and privileges. Consequently, 'cognitive restructuring' was required before role-playing and other behavioral measures proved effective.

Hypothesized active ingredients of treatment approach

In most forms of effective therapy, clients receive a desideratum not usually available in many situations, i.e. an active listener who is essentially non-judgmental, accepting, tolerant, patient, considerate, honest and non-pejorative. For some, the mere exposure to a respected professional who displays genuine caring and sustained good-will is sufficient to induce what Franz Alexander (1932) called 'a corrective emotional experience'. Indeed, for a number of clients, therapy seems to be a constructive reparenting experience.

The main hypothesized ingredients of change, from a multimodal perspective, may be listed as follows:

- *Behavior*: Positive reinforcement. Negative reinforcement. Punishment. Counterconditioning. Extinction.
- *Affect*: Admitting and accepting feelings. Abreaction.
- *Sensation*: Tension release. Sensory pleasuring.
- *Imagery*: Coping images. Changes in self-image.
- *Cognition*: Greater awareness. Cognitive restructuring.
- *Interpersonal relationships*: Non-judgmental acceptance. Modeling. Dispersing unhealthy collusions.
- *Drugs/biology*: Better nutrition and exercise. Substance abuse cessation. Psychotropic medication when indicated.

Specific Techniques

Behavioral strategies

Multimodal therapists are technically eclectic (as opposed to theoretically eclectic) and endeavor to select methods from diverse disciplines without necessarily subscribing to the theoretical doctrines that gave rise to them. The evidence (e.g. Rachman and Wilson, 1980) points to the efficacy of behavioral and cognitive–behavioral procedures over most (but not all) other interventions. Consequently, the majority of techniques employed by multimodal therapists are the standard fare of routine behavior therapy, and certainly fall comfortably within the realm of cognitive–behavior therapy. (The role of non-behavioral and non-cognitive strategies will be discussed in a later section of this chapter.)

The differences between technical eclecticism and theoretical eclecticism need to be underscored. Basically, the theoretical eclectic (also known as 'synthetic eclecticism') attempts to integrate diverse theories, whereas the technical eclectic uses a variety of techniques within a carefully selected and delimited blend of compatible theories. The main problem with theoretical eclecticism is that it ends up with a haphazard mixture of incompatible notions. Technical eclecticism (or 'systematic eclecticism') uses a variety of techniques within a theoretical structure that is open to verification or disproof. Many theoretical systems rest on entirely different and incompatible epistemological foundations. Attempts to integrate these systems are as futile as trying to mix oil and water. Technical eclecticism sidesteps the syncretistic muddles that arise when attempting to blend divergent models into a super-organizing theory. As the introduction to the present chapter implies, the multimodal framework rests on *social learning theory*, *general systems theory* and *group and communications theory*. These theoretical systems blend harmoniously into a congruent framework.

As Wilson (1980) underscored, 'the most potent methods of therapeutic change appear to be those that are performance based' (p. 291). The essence of effective therapy seems to be the capacity to persuade our clients to do different things, and to do things differently. There are two major components that enter into the successful application of behavioral techniques:

1. The therapist should be well versed in the specifics of the various procedures so that he or she displays an aura of genuine knowledge, confidence and competence.
2. An effective practitioner should know how to instigate clients to adhere to treatment prescriptions. The first condition is relatively simple. Many paraprofessionals have been adequately trained to conduct in vivo desensitization, to administer token economies, to employ stimulus control, modeling, non-reinforcement and to assist clients who are recording and self-monitoring various behaviors. Technique proficiency per se is not at all difficult to achieve. There is, however, another level that involves knowing when and when not to use a particular procedure, how to introduce it and, if necessary, 'sell it' to

the client, and whether to make modifications that will jibe with a client's idiosyncratic perceptions. These skills demand special knowledge and training. And as for achieving cooperation and compliance from one's clients, this is no less a problem in the practice of medicine than it is in psychotherapy, and entire books have addressed this crucial topic (e.g. Shelton and Levy, 1981; DiMatteo and DiNocola, 1982).

To illustrate some of the foregoing points, the case of Mrs Graham, a 32-year-old dental assistant who complained of depression and general anxiety since her divorce 7 months earlier, should underscore some important elements. She had consulted a psychiatrist, but discontinued therapy with him when he had recommended an antidepressant. 'I don't believe in drugs!' she declared. The second therapist she consulted was fired when he attempted to introduce imagery techniques. 'I don't believe in mind games', Mrs Graham stated. Next, she saw a therapist whose psychoanalytic penchant was a turn-off. 'I don't believe in rehashing my childhood!' she said. What did Mrs Graham believe in? It was simple to ascertain that she was a firm believer in astrology, the occult and especially in the impact of 'magnetic field forces' vis-à-vis sickness and health.

My assessment revealed that Mrs Graham was extremely tense and suffered from various muscular aches and pains that seemed to be a direct consequence of her inability to relax. Even more importantly, she satisfied most of the diagnostic criteria of a major depressive episode as listed in DSM-III: her appetite was poor and she had lost weight; her sleep was light and fitful; she had lost interest in many formerly enjoyable activities; she complained of chronic fatigue; she blamed herself for the breakup of her marriage and was filled with self-reproach; she complained of a diminished ability to concentrate. Moreover, there was a family history of depression, her mother and two paternal aunts having received courses of electroconvulsive therapy.

There were other problem areas, but in order to achieve significant inroads, it seemed necessary to overcome her debilitating depression and chronic tension as rapidly as possible. Significantly, before consulting me, she had purchased a popular book on the cognitive treatment of depression. 'I soon realized that that stuff would not work for me', she said. I concurred with the psychiatrist who had recommended antidepressant medication. It was also my opinion that Mrs Graham would derive benefit from training in deep muscle relaxation. Given her negativism, the clinical challenge was how to gain her cooperation and compliance. The obvious answer was to provide a context that made sense in terms of her expectancies and addressed her phenomenological perspective.

Therapist: Are you familiar with the concept of homeostasis?
Client: It's sort of like equilibrium isn't it?

Therapist: Right. Our bodies, our physiological processes endeavor to keep things balanced, stable, somewhat constant. But various factors can disrupt this process and throw us off balance.

Client: Like what

Therapist: Well, let's talk about electromagnetism. Physicists have been studying the magnetic properties of electrical currents for many years. As you know, our central nervous system generates and works through electrical impulses. Our brains are partly made up of neurotransmitters and receptor sites. Now if something goes wrong with the way these electromagnetic impulses travel to and from certain parts of the brain, psychophysiological disorders result. We end up feeling depressed, anxious, tense and fatigued. Are you following me?

Client: More or less. It seems to make a great deal of sense to me.

Therapist: Have you ever heard of Mesmer?

Client: Can't say that I have.

Therapist: Well he was one of our psychiatric forefathers who practiced what he called 'animal magnetism' in the late eighteenth century. Anyhow, if he were alive today, he might say that the break up of your marriage plus various other stressors have thrown your magnetic field forces off-center, and that we have to remedy this situation before you can start feeling better.

Client: Well, I must say that you're the first therapist who has talked sense to me.

Therapist: Thank you. But you haven't asked me how we go about changing your magnetic field forces.

Client: Well you're the doctor.

Therapist: Ah, but I don't think you will like or agree to one of my remedies.

Client: What's that?

Therapist: Let's first talk about biofeedback. Do you know what that is?

Client: Like EEG machines?

Therapist: Yes, and there are EMG machines – that's short for electromyogram – and many other devices that can measure your magnetic field forces. But even without these machines, if you are willing to practice certain relaxation exercises, and if you work to acquire the skill of relaxing, letting go of tense muscles several times a day, it will modify your electromagnetic impulses and begin to get back to a state of neuromuscular and central and autonomic nervous system equilibrium, and this could make a big difference.

Client: So why would I disagree with that?

Therapist: There's another component. The two go hand in hand. In the same way that you require positive and negative terminals for electricity to be conducted, I don't think that one strategy alone will work. While you are altering the electromagnetic impulses in your neuromuscular areas through specialized relaxation training, it is also necessary to deal directly with the neurotransmitters and receptor sites in your brain. As I said, either method alone will not do the trick – we need the synergistic properties of both.

Client: Are you suggesting that I need brain surgery?

Therapist [laughing]: Brain surgery? No, no. There are certain medications that directly alter the receptor sites in the brain. But you told me that you refuse to take medication.

Client: That's what they give to schizophrenics. Are you saying that you think I'm schizophrenic?

Therapist: Many schizophrenics are treated with medicines called 'phenothiazines'. I am talking about something entirely different. I believe that a first rate psychopharmacologist, that is a psychiatrist who specializes in the use of psychotropic or neuroleptic medication, will prescribe either a monoamine oxidase inhibitor, or a tricyclic, but since you refuse to go this route, frankly I feel like an electrical engineer with one wire instead of two, and with half a magnet.

Client: When I said that I was anti-drugs, I was referring to tranquilizers and those sorts of things that make you into a zombie.

Comment Is there anything unprofessional or unethical about bending the truth to achieve compliance and obtain a salubrious result? I think not. The package in which the technique is wrapped will often determine if it remains unopened, is opened and discarded, or put to good use. For example, it has been established that the effective treatment of obsessive–compulsive disorders requires such techniques as response prevention and flooding (e.g. Steketee, Foa and Grayson, 1982). However, as already stated, technique selection is one facet; how techniques are introduced, the manner in which they are delivered and the way they are implemented will make the difference between compliance and non-compliance.

In behavior therapy, one of the most central aspects, regardless of the problem being treated, is the use of homework assignments. Certainly, the way I practice therapy renders most of the behavioral strategies applied in my office preludes to excursions, confrontations and other activities that will take place in the client's day-to-day milieu. Thus, the first article on 'behavior rehearsal' (Chapter 6) suggested that when clients role-play and rehearse appropriate, albeit difficult, interpersonal encounters, they are far more likely to put these skills to good effect in vivo than when they are merely given advice, or when they receive a non-directive reflection of their fundamental feelings. As already stated, it is the extent to which clients engage in new or different activities between therapy sessions that usually constitutes the difference between success and failure. Certainly, the evidence from many outcome studies (see Wilson et al., 1984) suggests that without specific homework assignments (in vivo activities), it is unlikely that phobic disorders, social skills problems, obsessive–compulsive behaviors or sexual dysfunctions could be significantly changed.

Giving homework assignments with which clients are likely to comply calls for attention to specific details (Shelton and Ackerman, 1974; Shelton and Levy, 1981) among which the more obvious are:

1. Be explicit and extremely clear about the precise actions you wish the client to carry out.
2. Specify the exact frequency, time, duration of each assignment.

3. Ascertain that the client regards the assignment as pertinent and relevant.
4. Determine that the client does not view the assignment as too time-consuming in terms of its 'cost effectivness'.
5. Ensure that what is being asked of the client is not too threatening. (First provide direct skill training when necessary.)
6. Commence with assignments that are easy to carry out.
7. When giving homework assignments, present them as requests, or as suggestions, rather than as orders or instructions.

The following clinical excerpt illustrates some of these points:

Therapist: Do you think it makes sense for you to talk to your husband about that incident with his secretary?

Client: I know there was nothing serious going on between them, but even though I know this, and even though she no longer works there, I feel I want to let him know exactly how I was feeling at the time.

Therapist: I agree with you. I think that if you just let it slide and said nothing more about it, history will repeat itself simply because your husband won't be aware of a basic groundrule in your marriage.

Client: I should have brought it up two weeks ago, but I've kept putting it off. I guess I'm waiting for the right time or something.

Therapist: Actually, after you and I rehearsed what you would say I thought you would go straight home and discuss it then and there.

Client: That would have made sense. I don't know why I keep putting it off.

Therapist: Well, something is making it difficult for you. What's the worst thing that could happen?

Client: I don't know. [pause] I guess I don't want to seem picky.

Therapist: Do you think your opinion on the matter is picayune? It seems to me that you have a valid point, that you are entitled to your feelings and that you have every right to express them.

Client: No, I agree.

Therapist: Well, does it make sense if, right after dinner tonight, you tell him that you want to discuss an important issue with him?

Client: Yes. Basically, my point is that there are other ways of building up employee morale than by going out for private lunches, and leaving the office to drive someone's else's kids home from school is above and beyond the call of duty.

Therapist: Tell me truthfully, is your main objection that this could have turned into a romantic interlude? What I am asking is whether the fact that he was doing this for a woman is the main objection.

Client: Not really. My point is that Bill tries so hard to be Mr Nice Guy that he may end up a dead-end street. Like the time he left the conference to drive Martin, that kid who had just joined the firm, to the train station....

Therapist: Fine. So let's make sure that you don't merely talk about the secretary but that you also bring up other matters that concern you about his going too far to please other people. Let's role-play it again. Okay? Let me play the part of your husband. We have finished our dinner and you tell me that you have something important to discuss with me. [Role-playing and behavior rehearsal continue for about 10 minutes.]

Client: Well, Professor Higgins, I think I've got it.

Therapist: Good! So when will you *do* it? No more procrastination.

Client: Tomorrow evening, for sure. I don't want to get into it tonight because we're having dinner with some friends, and I'd rather not bring it up before going to bed in case it turns into a lengthy discussion.

Therapist: Are you afraid that it will lead to an argument?

Client: No, but I want to be sure that Bill really sees my point and doesn't humor me, or pretend to agree just to get me off his case.

Therapist: Fair enough. Let's see. Today is Tuesday. [opens appointment book] Can you give me a call on Thursday between one and two just to let me know how it went?

Client: Sure.

Therapist: I have the feeling that you will discuss those issues with Bill because I am pushing you, prodding you, and that you will do it mainly to get me off your back. I want you to do it for *you* not for me.

Client: No, no. It's for me all right. As you know, I procrastinate and I need a little shove from time to time.

Comment Most therapists seem to agree that the role of new experiences provided to the client is crucial for facilitating change. Davison (1980) stated: 'In my own clinical work, I view the therapy situation as one in which the client can try out new ways of thinking, feeling, and behaving, both within the therapy relationship (that is, to myself) and outside the consulting room...As for *how* such experiences are created, I sometimes become more heavy-handed under certain circumstances' (p. 273). Behavior change requires *work* – both from client and therapist.

The role of cognitive therapy

In late 1969 and early 1970, a detailed and systematic follow-up inquiry of 112 cases, randomly selected, led me to question the durability of 'pure' behavior therapy. The findings revealed that 36 per cent had relapsed anywhere from 1 week to 6 years after therapy. However, certain clients had maintained their therapeutic improvements despite the intrusion of inimical circumstances. Referral to the case notes of these individuals revealed that their improvements were often contingent upon the apparent adoption of a different outlook and philosophy of life and increased self-esteem – in addition to an increased range of behavioral skills. *Thus, the synergy of behavioral and cognitive methods became evident.* These findings were published in my book *Behavior Therapy and Beyond* (Lazarus, 1971), which advocated a 'broad-spectrum' approach and was one of the first texts on 'cognitive–behavior therapy'.

Clinicians who limit themselves to conditioning procedures, and who eschew cognitive processes, will soon find that people are capable of overriding the best-laid plans of contiguity, reinforcements and modeling by their own thinking. The cognitive domain addresses the subjective use of language, semantics, expectancies, problem-solving competencies, goals and the selectivity of perception, as well as the specific impact of beliefs, values and attitudes on overt behavior. Some of the main cognitive errors include overgeneralization, dichotomous reasoning, perfectionism, categorical imperatives, non sequiturs, misplaced attributions, 'catastrophizing', jumping to conclusions and excessive approval seeking. To the extent that our clients engage in one or more of these dysfunctional cognitions, they will be prone to a variety of behavioral problems and affective disturbances.

Many years ago, Ellis (1962) stressed that a human being, unlike an animal, 'can be rewarded or punished by his *own* thinking, even when this thinking is largely divorced from outside reinforcements and penalties' (p. 16). Beck (1976) in his classic text on cognitive therapy underscored that 'the specific content of the interpretation of an event leads to a specific emotional response' (p. 51). He then emphasized that 'we can generalize that, depending on the kind of interpretation a person makes, he will feel glad, sad, scared, or angry – or he may have no particular reaction at all' (pp. 51–52).

The following dialogue illustrates typical cognitive interventions:

Client: When people first meet me they think I'm sweet, charming, lovable and kind, but when they get to know me better, they discover that I'm a nasty bit of work.

Therapist: What does your nastiness consist of?

Client: I can be spiteful. I get envious and jealous when other people do better than I do. I have a sharp tongue and can use it like a knife to cut other people down. I can act considerate and concerned, and good-hearted, but the real me is the opposite – nasty, selfish – that's what I really am.

Therapist: Instead of believing that there is one *real you*, and that this true and basic you is a negative, nasty, spiteful or even hateful person, I'd like you to consider that you have different facets to your personality, that each aspect is just as real as any other. Thus, the kind, warm, loving, giving, accepting part is no more or less real than the nasty part. So I am saying that in certain situations, and at various times, the positive components are brought out, and at other times, in different settings, under other circumstances, the negative aspects come to the fore. But each is equally 'real'. What do you think about that?

Client: Well, I'm pretty sure I know where and how I learned to dislike myself. I had two, not just one, overly critical parents. 'You're bad!' 'You're nasty!' 'You're a wicked child!' That's what I grew up with.

Therapist: Okay, so now it's time for you to unlearn that faulty labeling and reframe your own thinking. If your parents understood logical and rational thinking, they would never have called you bad. They would have pointed to a specific thing that you did and they would have called that behavior 'bad'. Do you understand that fundamental distinction?

Client: Yes, but instinctively I look at things more...what's the word?...globally. Here's a perfect example. I caught my girlfriend out on a lie, and as far as I'm concerned, that makes her a liar, and I want nothing to do with liars. Don't you agree that if she has told a lie once, it follows that she can and will lie again and again?

Therapist: Here are two quick reactions. First, it would depend on the magnitude of the lie and the motive behind it. And secondly, if your girlfriend tells lies 10 per cent of the time, that makes her 90 per cent honest.

Client: Isn't that like being a little bit pregnant?

Therapist: All or none? Not at all. Tell me, if someone is selfish 20 per cent of the time, and distinctly unselfish the other 80 per cent, is this person selfish or unselfish?

Client [pause]: I see what you're getting at.

Therapist: You do? Tell me.

Client: Well I sort of get this idea of a balance scale, and you weigh everything to see which is greater or more frequent.

Therapist: My analogy of your style of thinking is that you reach into a basket of apples, pull out a rotten one, and conclude that the entire basket is made up of rotten apples instead of looking further. So your definition of a liar is anyone who ever told a single lie. If someone acts stupidly on a given occasion you would conclude that the person is totally stupid.

Client: But that's the way I was raised....

Therapist: I'm not blaming you for being the way you are. Whether or not the reason you think as you do is 100 per cent due to your critical parents is beside the point. Let's get you to change your way of thinking here and now and forever more. Try this sentence on for size. Will you close your eyes and repeat this five or six times? 'The nice part of me is just as real as the nasty part.' Will you say that aloud and then think it silently?

Client [complies and, after a pause, says]: I'm going to have to work to let that sink in.

Therapist: True. It will take some effort from you. I'm going to give you a book that I wrote with a good friend and colleague [Lazarus and Fay, 1977], which lists some of the common mistakes that many people make in the way they think and act. I'd like you to read it carefully and tell me which of the mistakes you identify with. Will you do that?

Client: Sure.

Therapist: If a picture is worth a thousand words, certain books can be worth, not a thousand sessions, but give or take a dozen.

Comment In multimodal therapy, cognitive restructuring is seldom a necessary and sufficient intervention, but modifying dysfunctional beliefs is often essential if constructive change is to ensue. To be pedantic, I use 'bibliotherapy' fairly extensively with clients who enjoy reading, and it certainly has expedited the treatment process with innumerable individuals. Readers who are familiar with Albert Ellis's treatment procedures will note from the foregoing excerpt that while I concur completely with his reasoning, my therapeutic style is rather different. As an aside, I have seen many of Ellis's trainees trying to emulate his style – right down to his Bronx/New York accent – instead of learning from this giant and remaining themselves. My style also differs from Beck's Socratic method of asking questions, although clients who are averse to didactic instruction would be treated in the Beckian manner. In general, I find a directive stance more rapid and effective; it exemplifies the psychoeducational thrust of multimodal therapy. I find no difficulty in integrating cognitive and behavioral strategies. If, for instance, while teaching a client to dispute his or her own dysfunctional beliefs a significant degree of anxiety seems to occur, it is simple and natural to shift to a relaxation or desensitization sequence. If, while examining irrational ideas, we come upon response deficits, the use of behavior rehearsal is readily introduced. In short, it is my experience that cognitive and behavioral methods are positively synergistic.

The role of non-behavioral and non-cognitive strategies

The most obvious caveat concerns the use of any psychological technique by itself in the face of major biological disturbances that are amenable to somatic interventions. People who are grossly psychotic – delusional, extremely confused, markedly withdrawn and behaviorally inappropriate, homicidal or suicidal – usually require drug therapy to become amenable to psychological interventions. From a multimodal standpoint, as Fay (1976) underscored, 'It is clear that the taking of drugs is affected by the six other modalities and in turn produces results which affect the other modalities' (p. 66). A client with a clear-cut bipolar depressive disorder in the manic phase of the illness is referred to a psychiatrist who most probably prescribes lithium. When the medication has taken effect, one or more of the following interventions are administered: behavioral, sensory, imagery, cognitive, interpersonal.[*] The 'D' modality also involves the encouragement of health habits – good nutrition, exercise and recreation.

Outside of the biological modality, is any intervention non-behavioral or non-cognitive? Surely, nearly all forms of psychotherapy try to teach people to think, feel and act differently. Nevertheless, I employ techniques that are regarded as outside the purview of cognitive–behavior therapy by certain authorities (e.g. Kazdin and Wilson, 1978; Wilson, 1982; Wolpe, 1984) and have been criticized for polluting the system by so doing. Thus, I shall describe some of these 'non-cognitive–behavioral' techniques and attempt to justify their value.

---

[*]Unlike other modalities – behavior, sensation, imagery, cognition, interpersonal relationships, biological considerations – affect cannot be treated directly. Affect is a product of the reciprocal interaction of the other six modalities, and can be worked with only indirectly. 'I arouse emotion directly by getting people to scream while pounding foam rubber cushions', one therapist informed me. 'No', I replied, 'you are arousing emotions via behaviors (screaming and pounding are not emotions) and by generating sensations and images.' Affect is derived from and can only be reached through behavior, sensation, imagery, cognition, interpersonal relationships and biological processes. This conception is the core of the multimodal position. Regardless of the affective disorder under scrutiny, it holds that thoroughness in assessment requires an inquiry into the other six modalities: B-S-I-C-I-D.

Time projection (forwards and backwards)

Clients with fairly vivid imaginations can readily picture themselves going forwards or backwards in time. By going several months into the future and picturing themselves adding more and more rewarding events to their daily lives, some depressed individuals experience a diminution in negative affect (Lazarus, 1968). 'Time tripping' into the past can help clients relive, modify and work through various events. Here is an example:

Client: I was a kid when all this garbage was shoved into my head. What the hell does a 5 year old know? How could I stand up to my parents and tell them that they're talking crap? So these tapes are still there, and often play on 'automatic'. Today, as a 24 year old I realize the truth, but back then I had no measuring stick to show me that it was all clap-trap that they were handing me, and somehow there must be a part of me that still believes it.

Therapist: Would you mind trying out a little fantasy excursion? Sit back and relax, let yourself ease comfortably into the chair. [pause] Now please close your eyes, and imagine that we have a Time Machine that can transport you into the past, and then bring you right back into the present. I'd like you to pay a visit to yourself in the past. You can visit little Michael aged 10, 9, 8 or whatever. At what age would you like to visit yourself in the past?

Client: Say around 5 or 6.

Therapist: Okay. You step into the Time Machine, and instantly you go back and visit yourself at age 5. The 5-year-old Michael looks up and sees a man walking towards him. Of course, he doesn't realize that this is himself, grown up, 24 years of age, coming back out of the future. But he senses something special about that man, he feels a deep affinity for him, and so he will listen to him. Can you get into that picture?

Client   [pause]: Yes. The 5-year-old me is playing in the yard and the 24-year-old me comes up to him, puts a hand on his shoulder, and says, 'Michael, I want to talk to you'.

Therapist: Excellent! Now talk to him. What do you want to tell him?

Client: Michael, your mom and dad have told you a lot of things about sin, and the devil, and hell, and all that sort of thing. That's all nonsense, Michael, just nonsense! Don't believe it. Just pretend to go along with it because if you tell them it is nonsense, they will punish you. But listen to me, Mike. You're a good kid. [pause]

Therapist: Can you explain to 5-year-old Mike that it's all right if he doesn't do brilliantly at school? [The session continues in this vein for about another 5 minutes.]

Client   [very emotional at this juncture]: Mike, remember what I'm telling you. It's the truth.

Therapist: I guess it's time to come back to the present now. Do you have any final words of wisdom for little Michael?

Client: Just remember that Mom and Dad are wrong. They mean well, but they talk a lot of crap about religion.

Comment Imagery procedures that metaphorically tap 'right brain' material are often effective in achieving what pure 'left brain' cognitive disputation and rational reasoning are unable to do. Elsewhere (Lazarus, 1985), I described the case of a man who went back in time and enacted several imaginary dialogues with his father and grandfather (to whom he attributed his current lack of self-confidence). In these dialogues, he persuaded his father and grandfather (and thus convinced himself) that their standards of manliness were irrational and obsolete. In my view, these and several other imagery techniques (Lazarus, 1984b) can readily be seen as being within the compass of cognitive–behavior therapy, but since they did not emanate from laboratory studies, and since their value is purely clinical and anecdotal (as opposed to experimental and confirmed via controlled studies) many behavioral practitioners tend to 'boycott' them.

The deserted island fantasy technique

Here is another 'non-cognitive–behavioural' technique that I have found extremely useful and that I have been taken severely to task for employing (because it too lacks an empirical database vis-à-vis its controlled clinical effectiveness). Many years ago, a particularly frustrating client led me to remark that I'd need to observe her 24 hours a day to get beyond her enigmatic façade. She retorted, 'Well, let's go and spend a few months on a desert island'. Ignoring the possible seductive undertones, I asked her what I would learn about her on the island. She painted a verbal picture that proved highly informative. Her fantasies about our island sojourn enabled me to infer a great deal about her. Despite the subjective nature of this interaction, I had indeed emerged with considerable knowledge about her significant thoughts, feelings and actions. Subsequently, I found that this fantasy journey yielded important clinical information with many clients. Initially (Lazarus, 1971), I used to refer to it as a *desert* island, but the term 'deserted' seemed more accurate (i.e. it was not a barren wilderness, being lush and green but uninhabited). Secondly, there are advantages to conjuring up a person other than the therapist on the island. An entire chapter replete with an actual therapy transcript has spelled out this technique in considerable detail (Lazarus, 1981).

Basically, the client is enjoined to enter into a fantasy experiment wherein a magician tells him or her, 'When I wave my magic wand you will instantly appear on a deserted island and you will remain there for 6 months'. The client is informed that while he or she is on the island, the rest of the world will remain in suspended animation: time will stand still. Being a magic island, there are no dangers and there is an adequate supply of food and provisions. 'Now, before waving his magic wand, the magician gives you a choice: he allows you to choose company or solitude. Would you prefer spending 6 months alone, or would you rather find a pleasant person of the opposite sex [or, when dealing with homo-sexuals, a person of the same sex] waiting for you on the island?' Thereafter, the client is encouraged to 'run with the fantasy', with less imaginative clients being given prompts to help them along: 'How will you occupy your time?' 'What will happen?' 'Do you think you'll be bored?' One gets a clear picture from this procedure of the client's capacity for developing and maintaining close, genuine relationships. With this technique, one can readily detect how much manipulation, deception, asocial, antisocial and other maladaptive patterns are likely to be present.

There are several other techniques drawn from various non-behavioral disciplines that I use fairly extensively – but within a cognitive–behavioral framework. For example, the well-known 'empty chair technique' drawn from psychodrama and gestalt therapy is particularly useful in many cases for instigating assertive behavior. Another non-behavioral technique is Rogerian reflection. Frequently, it is judicious merely to make clear by mir-roring for the client the affective impact of his or her meandering. This seems to be especially helpful when clients express conflicts and other ambivalent feelings. In these instances, by holding up a 'psychic mirror', the therapist is often more facilitative than when offering direct advice. Unlike Rogerians, we seldom find empathic reflection, genuineness, unconditional positive regard and so on, both necessary and sufficient for effecting behavioral change. Rather, when the client has been helped to clarify certain areas of confusion and uncertainty via non-intrusive accep-tance and reflection, it is time to take action. At this juncture, we revert to behavioral rehearsals, assignments and other objective coping strategies. But the point is that while adopting a Rogerian stance, we are into a 'non-behavioral' realm.

Let me stress again, that while drawing on Rogers, or Perls, or Freud, or any other personage or system for particular techniques, we do not necessarily subscribe to the theories that are embraced by any of the specific school adherents. We may have a client reclining on a couch, free associating, for reasons that are entirely different from those that Freud and his followers espouse. I consider it a serious error for a therapist to bypass or ignore techniques that do not emanate from or readily fit into his or her theoretical predilections. As McFall (1985) has underscored: 'Most psychologists probably would agree that no single existing theory, perspective, or approach in psychology is capable of explaining everything observed in human behavior' (p. 28). As London (1964) emphasized: 'However interest-ing, plausible, and appealing a theory may be, it is techniques, not theories, that are actually used on people. The study of the effects of psychotherapy, therefore, is always the study of the effectiveness of techniques' (p. 33).

Role of the Therapist

Clinical skills and other crucial therapist attributes

Obviously, from what I have said in the preceding section, in my book, a good therapist will have at his or her disposal an arsenal of many different techniques. But there is more. Knowing how to administer various techniques must go hand in hand with knowing *when* to select a given procedure. One must also know how to introduce it into the therapy so that the client understands the rationale and is most likely to cooperate. Also, a good therapist is, at the very least, an intelligent consumer of research in the field. For example, therapists who treat phobias with Rogerian reflection, or with psychodynamic insights, or with cognitive disputation, are unlikely to make significant clinical headway, because, as the research evidence has shown, some form of *exposure* – imaginal and/or in vivo – is called for. In the successful treatment of obsessive-compulsive disorders response prevention and flooding techniques are a sine qua non (Steketee, Foa and Grayson, 1982). Several specific behavioral techniques are the treatments of choice for the management of sexual problems such as impotence, orgasmic dysfunction, premature ejaculation and dyspareunia (Leiblum and Pervin, 1980). Marital dysfunction usually requires techniques aimed at teaching more positive and productive interpersonal behaviors (Jacobson and Margolin, 1979). A therapist who is not *au courant* with the pertinent literature on treatment effectiveness will often end up wasting his or her clients' time and money, will fail to help many who could have benefited from someone more knowledgeable, and may even exacerbate matters in certain instances (Mays and Franks, 1985).

Technical proficiency should neither be minimized nor underestimated, yet it has often been said that the client–therapist relationship is paramount, and that techniques per se are of little consequence. There are some clients for whom, as Schofield (1964) emphasized, psychotherapy is essentially the purchase of friendship. In my experience, if measurable gains are to be achieved, client and therapist have to *work*, not merely *relate*. Those for whom a warm, empathic, genuine and caring relationship is both necessary and sufficient to achieve significant gains, constitute a very small minority. Nevertheless, as already mentioned earlier in this chapter, without a client–therapist rapport, the best engineered techniques are unlikely to take effect. Thus the mechanisms of change cannot be divorced from the person administering the particular procedures. As surgeons are apt to point out, it is the person wielding the scalpel who can use it as an instrument of destruction or of healing. In psychotherapy, it is virtually impossible to separate specific mechanisms and techniques from the person administering them.

Certain common characteristics have been very apparent to me among all highly successful therapists I have been privileged to know. The term 'hostile' could not be applied to any one of them. On the contrary, their degree of patience, tolerance and non-judgmental acceptance was sometimes astonishing. This is not to say that they lacked assertiveness. However, when they took a firm stand with a client, it was done in a supportive, non-attacking manner. In thinking about these clinical virtuosos, their genuine respect for people stands out, as does their flexibility and fundamental responsibility. And each one of them is fun-loving, articulate and unpretentious, with a delightful sense of humor. There is more. They practice what they preach; they are authentic and congruent, and they are unafraid of revealing their shortcomings. Interestingly, the majority of these spectacular therapists are unknown beyond the confines of the small towns or large cities in which they practice. They are not internationally revered giants who bask in the limelight of their colleagues' admiration. Indeed, they have been too busy practicing good therapy to find time for self-serving promotions of their wares. I have met many of them by chance – at clinical meetings, at workshops and through the happenstance of being co-therapists or consultants for certain enmeshed couples and families.

Many people resolve their conflicts, solve their problems and overcome their disturbances as a result of processes that lie outside their therapists' attributions. Extratherapeutic factors such as environmental changes, biological shifts and various fortuitous effects (Chapter 12) will produce salubrious outcomes, perhaps even in those instances where the therapist is a somewhat noxious human being. Thus, even the poorest practitioner is likely to develop a coterie of supporters. The truly gifted clinician is exemplified by a demonstrable capacity to be of help to a wide variety of clients, while remaining fully cognizant of his or her limitations, and constantly seeking for the active ingredients of psychological change – instead of taking credit for unintentional influences. Let us take a close look at the 'bad guys'.

Common treatment errors leading to 'bad therapy'

It is my impression that 'bad therapy' is often carried out by well-intentioned but poorly trained practitioners who apply incorrect techniques or, perhaps, select the correct techniques but administer them incorrectly. While ignorance and incompetence on the therapist's behalf do not constitute desirable attributes, they are infinitely less pernicious than narcissism, hostility, seductiveness and a need to exploit the client due to greed, insecurity or downright sadism. Unfortunately, I have encountered more than a small number of therapists whose personalities are well suited to tossing hand grenades into enemy bunkers, and who treat their patients as dangerous adversaries or antagonists. They use diagnostic labels like bayonets. 'My doctor said that I have a borderline personality.' 'She said that I was an obsessive and passive–aggressive something or other.' 'Dr K. said that I have schizophrenic tendencies.' The foregoing are literal quotes from three clients who were members in the same therapy group led by 'Dr K'.

Among my trainees, perhaps the most common error is that of trying too hard to effect change. The students are often eager to prove to their supervisors (and to themselves) what effective change agents they are, so that they tend to rush their clients to take action – very prematurely at times.

Another common error is that of pursuing a favorite line of inquiry, or employing a particular procedure despite no evidence of change. I find this especially true of those who are strongly devoted to cognitive therapy. They tend to continue to argue, cajole, dispute, challenge, explain, interpret and reframe. Instead of switching to a different modality (e.g. imagery) they seem of the opinion that a change in cognition is the be-all and end-all.

In listening to one of my student's therapy tapes, I noted that he had launched into a lengthy self-disclosure regarding some of his own shortcomings and limitations. When asked to justify this procedure, he claimed that he was modeling anti-perfectionism and the virtues of fallibility. While selective self-disclosure is often an effective strategy, it was evident to me that the student's motive was more one of receiving, than of giving, therapy. I pointed this out and after a few moments of reflection he admitted that I was correct. It is most important for therapists to be aware of their own motives – otherwise the possibilities of making endless errors are rampant.

Wolf, Wolf and Spielberg (1980) have addressed the most salient helpful and harmful responses that typify good and bad therapy. At the top of their list of destructive responses are examples of grossly judgmental and intolerant attitudes. Therapists who display disgust, disdain, impatience, blaming, disrespect, intolerance and guilt-induction are included in this category. Here are some typical responses:

- *Disdain*: 'Yes, I know what you are all about alright. Unfortunately, your type is all too common.'
- *Guilt*: 'Why didn't you wake up and do something *before* your son got hooked on drugs?'
- *Blame*: 'You made a mess of that situation and now you expect me to pick up the pieces.'

Next, Wolf, Wolf and Spielberg refer to 'blatant insensitivity and inaccuracies', wherein the therapist fails to appreciate the client's feelings, or is highly inappropriate in the timing of his or her remarks. They also mention the destructive impact of the clinician's anger and defensiveness, as well as the fostering of dependence. A classic example of the latter is the following statement: 'You've come a long way during these past 18 months, but if you terminate therapy now, you'll be right back to square one before you know it.' Less damaging, but nonetheless disruptive, are instances of poorly timed or irrelevant questions, confusing remarks and false reassurance.

To end this section on a positive note, Wolf, Wolf and Spielberg (1980) point out that 'very helpful responses' and 'extremely helpful responses' share a number of common features. They include: concise and accurate phrasing, perceptiveness, sensitivity to relevant and highly charged emotional issues, the display of profound respect and significant understanding, and the appropriate use of humor. Their major facilitative conditions include empathy, respect, genuineness, warmth, concreteness, self-disclosure and immediacy. Whether or not these facilitative core qualities can be taught or 'techniqued' is an open question. Personally, it is my belief that these are attributes that students bring with them into their training programs. Those who do not possess them to start with will inevitably end up without them – regardless of their academic credentials or the excellence of the clinical training programs to which they are exposed.

Common Clinical Issues

Preventing resistance and non-compliance

Throughout this chapter, several allusions have been made regarding the attainment of the client's active cooperation. There is an additional strategy that has not been mentioned: *tracking the 'firing orders' of the specific modalities*. This refers to the fact that different people tend to generate negative affect through individualistic perceptions of the BASIC I.D. Thus, some clients dwell first on aversive images (I) (pictures of dire events and a variety of horrors), followed by unpleasant sensations (S) (tremors, sweating, palpitations and shortness of breath), to which they attach negative cognitions (C) (ideas about their impending death), leading to maladaptive behavior (B) (withdrawal, avoidance and isolation). This ISCB firing order (imagery–sensory–cognitive–behavioral) will tend to require a different treatment strategy from that employed with say a CISB reactor (cognitive-imagery-sensory-behavior), or with someone with yet a different sequence. For example, our clinical findings suggest that it is usually better to select techniques that adhere to the client's chain reaction. When someone reports that he or she starts with the *sensory modality*, it is usually advisable initially to introduce biofeedback, relaxation, and so on. 'My anxieties usually begin to develop when I tune into the fact that my body is feeling a little "off", such as a queasy feeling in my stomach, or a little tension in my neck. This sets off the chain. These feelings grow stronger as I attend to them, and then new ones develop, and pretty soon I start *thinking* that something dreadful is going to happen to me. These thoughts start up a whole series of *memories and pictures* of the time I came down with pneumonia – which went undiagnosed for 6 weeks.' Here we have a sensory–cognitive–imagery pattern. Thus, after teaching the client several sensory techniques (relaxation, specific biofeedback, breathing exercises etc.), the cognitive modality is attended to (e.g. instructing the client in positive self-talk) followed next by imagery methods (e.g. the use of specific pictures wherein the client sees him- or herself being healthy, warding off disease etc.).

However, if a client's anxiety is triggered first by cognitions ('I'm doing fine when suddenly I start thinking of all the things that could possibly go wrong'), followed by images ('Then I see myself, quite vividly, passing out and making a complete fool of myself'), leading to negative sensations ('My hands get clammy, my chest tightens up, and I get butterflies in my stomach'), the use of biofeedback/relaxation as a first line of attack would usually not be especially effective, because the sensory mode is the *third* sequence in the chain. My clinical observations suggest that when one selects techniques that follow the client's individual sequence, the therapeutic impact is augmented. And in my experience, most clients have little difficulty tracking their respective 'firing orders' when asked to do so. Some clients demand a rationale for technique selection and, by explaining that their own patterns of response will be matched to the specific ordering of techniques, many thereby prove less resistant.

Some additional tactics for overcoming resistance

At times, a client's resistance or non-compliance may be a function of his or her view that the therapist's investment and involvement with and interest in resolving his or her problems is insufficient (i.e. below his or her expectations). Under these circumstances, some remedies proposed by Fay and Lazarus (1982) include:

● An unsolicited telephone call by the therapist to follow up on something that was discussed in the session.
● Shifting the locus of therapy to outside the office, such as outdoor walking sessions, a session in the park or, under certain circumstances, a home visit by the therapist.
● Sharing a mutual avid interest such as playing tennis or chamber music together.

We must not continue making the same mistakes with clients who are not responding, repeat the mistakes other therapists have made, or in general fit the client in a procrustean fashion into a unimodal framework.

Many therapists believe that contact with the client outside the normal confines of a therapist's office creates 'boundary' problems. The personalistic emphasis of the multimodal tradition would oppose any such blanket taboo. There are indeed clients with whom all dealings should always be strictly 'professional' and who would take unkindly to extramural contact. In my experience, these people are in the minority, and have usually comprised the more seriously disturbed individuals who have consulted me.

The most uncooperative clients are generally those individuals who are not seeking therapy voluntarily, but who have been coerced into coming. People referred by the courts, and children reluctantly dragged in by their desperate parents, fall into this category. In these instances, practicing paradoxical techniques, or simply doing something that is out of character, thereby violating the client's expectations, can initiate a major change. Thus, the following dialogue ensued with a hostile 16-year-old boy who had been cutting class, fighting with his two siblings and allegedly using marijuana to excess:

Therapist: I decided to ask your parents to remain in the waiting room so that you and I could talk privately. I gather that you've been having a pretty rough time of it at home and at school. If you'd like to fill me in, share with me what's been going on with you, I might be able to help.

Client: I don't need any help.

Therapist: Well, it seems to me that a lot of people are on your back. Is that true?

Client: No.

Therapist: How's school?

Client: School's school.

Therapist: They said you were cutting classes.

Client: That's their problem, not mine.

Therapist: Nothing and nobody is bugging you?

Client: Right.

Therapist: So your parents brought you to me under false pretenses. I see people who are unhappy in some way, shape or form, and together we figure out ways and means of overcoming their problems. With you, I'm going to earn my fee the easy way – without working. If I simply discharge you and tell your parents that you have no troubles or problems, they will take you to another shrink. So here's what I'm going to do. I have a lot of work and reading to catch up on. You just sit here until the hour is up while I do my reading. Then I charge your parents for my time anyway. This way, we both come out ahead. I get to do my reading, and you are not pestered by a therapist trying to help you. [selects a book and starts to read]

Client [after 2-3 minutes]: How much do they pay you?

Therapist: Who?

Client: Like my parents.

Therapist: At least $80 an hour. Isn't that nice? I'm getting paid by your parents to catch up on my reading. I wish all my clients were like you.

Client: Do you ever *really* help anyone?

Therapist: Unfortunately I don't get paid by other people simply to sit here and read my books – I have to work hard and really help them.

Client: Yeah, but all this garbage of going back into my childhood and examining my dreams, I don't see how that can help.

Therapist: I don't work that way. I prefer to stick to the here-and-now and to get into real problem solving. I believe simply that two heads are better than one, and that when my clients and I look at problems from different angles, we usually come up with solutions.

Client: Yeah, but you don't know my parents.

Therapist: True, but if you fill me in, maybe I can come up with something useful.

Client: What if I said my mother's a real ball-buster.

Therapist: I'd believe you and I'd try to help you figure out a way of coping with her.

Client: Well she's always on my case.

Therapist: Does she treat you differently from the way she treats your sister and brother?

Client: You're damn right she does. She's always played favorites. My sister can do nothing wrong....

Comment We were soon off and running, and within 15 minutes had established a working liaison. After a few additional individual sessions with the young man, it became evident to me that family therapy was indicated. I had no trouble shifting from an individual therapy format to a family systems arrangement, although working with the five of them made me feel that I was indeed earning my fee the hard way!

Typically, when a treatment impasse is reached, one or more of the following factors seems to be operative:

1. An absence of rapport or inappropriate matching. (In these instances, referral to a more appropriate resource is usually the best solution.)
2. Inaccurate assessment (especially the therapist's failure to identify relevant antecedents and/or maintaining factors).
3. An exclusive focus on intraindividual factors, thereby leaving ample room for saboteurs in the client's social network to undermine the therapy.
4. Therapist errors and blunders (especially the use of inappropriate techniques).
5. The faulty or incorrect use of appropriate techniques – usually a function of inadequate training.
6. Extreme degrees of 'psychopathology' in the client.
7. The client's unwillingness to expend the necessary effort to effect meaningful change.

Note that most of the variance, in my view, rests with the therapist, and pertains to his or her skills, or the lack thereof. Only the last two items reflect possible excesses and deficits within the client. (For comprehensive coverage of these and other aspects of 'resistance', see Chapter 13.)

Fostering generalization and maintenance of therapeutic gains

As already stated in several places throughout this chapter, to facilitate in vivo transfer from the client–therapist relationship to significant others and to ensure generalization from the treatment setting to work, home and social environments, one of the major tactics has been the systematic use of *homework assignments*. Furthermore, generalization may be enhanced by involving important members of the client's social network. Involvement of the social network permits the therapist to mitigate negative attitudes within the family towards change in the client. Moreover, by bringing family members into the office, one is better able to control noncontingent reinforcement in the client's natural environment. Collaboration by therapist, identified patient and social network facilitates many aspects of behavioral retraining, emotional growth and value transformation.

While it is not routinely feasible for therapists to go into the client's natural environment, extramural excursions are sometimes necessary for generalization to occur. At times, a paraprofessional or auxilliary therapist works with the client at home or in work or recreational settings under the therapist's direction. Participant modeling and reinforced practice in vivo may be particularly helpful in this situation.

It is often valuable for the therapist to maintain telephone contact with the client in the interval between sessions. For example, a client may practice social skills in an individual or group therapy setting, but frequently will not take emotional risks in life unless prompted, exhorted, monitored, reinforced and encouraged by daily telephone calls.

One of the most useful tactics for generalizing control of punitive responses in couples is the use of a tape recorder at home, on vacations, in the car or even when talking on the telephone. Couples and families quickly learn to refrain from aggressive exchanges in the therapist's office but revert to destructive habits in other settings. The use of a tape recorder heightens self-awareness and tends to inhibit destructive communication in natural settings. Clients may bring in the tapes for review during the sessions to facilitate further the learning of prosocial and effective communication styles, and the unlearning of dysfunctional ones.

Two of the most effective techniques that provide an important prelude to the transfer of therapeutic gains are *behavior rehearsal* and *coping imagery*. Behavior rehearsal, using audiocassettes or even videotapes as ancillary aids, employs role-playing to ensure that the client develops appropriate interpersonal skills. Coping imagery consists of evoking systematic mental pictures in which the client sees him- or herself dealing with inimical situations, and yet managing to get through them. The rationale for recommending several brief coping imagery practice sessions per day is that most of us need to see ourselves performing adequately in our mind's eye *before* we can venture forth into the real-life situation with any sense of confidence.

In terms of *maintenance*, it is generally accepted that, with addictions, frequent booster sessions and careful after-care tactics are required if relapse is to be avoided. In general, however, my follow-up inquiries have shown that a number of clients retain their recoveries until significant, but often predictable, circumstances take them by surprise. Relapse would often not have occurred had clients been prepared to cope with events that resided in their future. This can be achieved through rehearsal via projected imagery. By taking stock of challenges that are most likely to occur and by encouraging the client to visualize him- or herself coping with these events, one can enhance the client's capacity to deal with them effectively. These 'emotional fire drills' tend to ward off the hazards of 'future shock'.

In essence, comprehensive therapy probably offers the best prevention against relapse, thus maximizing the likelihood of long-term maintenance. When treatment outcomes and therapeutic gains were shortlived, follow-ups (Lazarus, 1981) revealed not that therapy was too shallow, but that an insufficient number of areas had been covered (i.e. therapy was too narrow).

Other populations

While I have confined my comments throughout this chapter to the multimodal treatment of adult outpatients (since that is the population I deal with in most instances) it should not be thought that the approach has no value with different populations in various settings. Brunell and Young (1982) have edited a compelling volume detailing the application of multimodal assessment and therapy to psychiatric inpatients. Keat (1979) described multimodal therapy with children. Pearl and Guarnaccia (1976) discussed multimodal therapy and mental handicap. Slowinski (1985) described the use of multimodal methods with two recalcitrant 'ghetto clients'. Ridley (1984) commented on the specific virtues of the multimodal approach for the non-disclosing black client. Edwards and Kleine (1986) have addressed multimodal consultation with gifted adolescents. There is scarcely a clinical entity for which multimodal assessment and therapy cannot be proposed and implemented. The BASIC I.D. paradigm has even been applied to community disasters (Sank, 1979).

Multimodal therapists are drawn from the full range of 'health service providers'. Psychiatrists, psychologists, social workers, pastoral counselors and other mental health workers have members who are well versed in and employ multimodal methods. This is consonant with the trend in current psychotherapy toward multifaceted, multidimensional and multidisciplinary interventions. Multiform and multifactorial assessment and treatment procedures have become widespread. Nevertheless, it needs to be underscored that, while all multimodal therapists are (technically) eclectic, all eclectic therapists are not multimodal practitioners.

Overall Effectiveness

At present there are Multimodal Therapy Institutes in New York, Illinois, Ohio, Pennsylvania and Virginia. Data obtained from several colleagues at the different institutes plus the findings from my own outcome and follow-up studies have been reliable and reasonably impressive. Multimodal therapy is an approach that endeavors to incorporate state-of-the-art research findings into its framework. It is not intended as yet another 'system' to be added to the hundreds already in existence. The multimodal practitioner tends to scan the field for better assessment and treatment methods and tries to be at the cutting edge of clinical effect-iveness.

A 3-year follow-up of 20 'complex cases' who had completed a course of multimodal therapy (e.g. people suffering from extreme agoraphobia, pervasive anxiety and panic, obsessive–compulsive rituals, or enmeshed family or marital problems) showed that 14 maintained their gains or had made additional progress without further therapy. Moreover, a recent sur-vey of 100 clients who had failed with at least three previous therapists (thereby ruling out the 'placebo reactors' and those mildly disturbed indi-viduals who require little more than a good listener and a touch of em-pathy) revealed that 61 had achieved measurable and unequivocal benefits. For example, there were quantifiable *decreases* in compulsive behaviors, depressive reactions, marital and family disputes, panic attacks, sexual inadequacy and avoidance behaviors. There were corresponding *increases* in assertive responses, work-related achievements and prosocial behaviors. Significantly, many of these clients were regarded by their pre-vious therapists as 'intractable'. In terms of overall statistics, during the past 7 or 8 years, more than 75 per cent of the people who have consult-ed me have achieved their major treatment goals. Data from other multi-modal practitioners are in keeping with my own findings. Failures are minimized by a strong willingness to use teamwork, cross-referrals, and by explicitly seeking second and third opinions when doubts arise.

The populations with whom we have been least effective include drug addicts and substance abusers in general, character disorders, grossly inad-equate personality disorders, a certain number of bipolar depressives (despite the use of lithium in addition to a thorough attempt to traverse the BASIC I.D.), and a number of people with florid psychoses. At times, we have failed because someone in the client's social network managed to sabotage what we were attempting to achieve (Kwee, 1984). There are some clients who appeared to be receiving too many secondary gains for them to relinquish their maladaptive behaviors. (See Lazarus, 1986, for additional details on applications and research.)

In terms of future directions, perhaps the first point of emphasis should be on controlled experimentation. Attempts to receive the necessary funding to test certain propositions have been unsuccessful. Consequently the virtues of employing modality profiles, structural profiles, second-order BASIC I.D. assessments, and the use of tracking modality 'firing orders' are all based on uncontrolled clinical observations. It should be remembered that the multimodal orientation is an open approach, not a closed system. Consequently, its practitioners maintain a vigilant lookout for state-of-the-art assessment and treatment strategies that are readily incorporated into the technically eclectic framework. Thus, depending on what the field at large generates over the next decade, the entire spectrum of multimodal methods may, or may not, undergo extensive changes.

Concluding Comment

I was asked to address a specific issue. I was told:

> With your approach more than most of the others discussed in this book, I have a problem distinguishing between the therapy technology and the therapist who is providing the technology. I have always wondered when reading your work, what proportion of the variance in your effects results from your modalities and strategies per se, and what proportion results from your own unique clinical skills. Furthermore, it is not just Neil Jacobson who has wondered about this. Do you frequently experience frustration with students who may apply the multimodal approach effectively, but get inferior results because they lack your natural clinical skills?

I have been accused, quite justly at times, of being an elitist. This is because I refuse to work closely with students who do not possess 'natural clinical skills'. For me, it is a given that any aspirant multimodal clinician is basically warm, empathic, perceptive, insightful, caring and has a history of having been the confidant and counselor of friends and associates long before entering any professional training program. Given these fundamental attributes, we then teach our students to think more critically, to reason more logically, to become more astute observers (i.e. to be hyper-alert to inconsistencies and anomalies), and to develop courage and boldness in doing what has to be done to serve one's clients best. Thus, I am seldom frustrated by my students' clinical performance. At times, they are inept, but so is virtually any therapist, no matter how skilled and how well trained. Clearly, while practice does not make most things perfect, it usually does enable one to make fewer and fewer blunders. After having practiced therapy for more than a quarter of a century, I have acquired a 'data bank' that not only renders me a lot more effective than I was 10–15 years ago, but also signals when best to quit trying to achieve the impossible. Knowing one's personal limitations as well as the upper limits of existing psychotherapeutic knowledge, saves time and money, and reduces frustration.

A most important point about the multimodal orientation is that it tries to articulate specific procedures that expedite assessment and therapy. In retrospect, the multimodal tradition had its inception in 1963 when, as a visiting assistant professor in the Department of Psychology at Stanford University, I was teaching 'behavior therapy' to graduate students. I made liberal use of one-way mirrors: students would observe me treating numerous clients, and we would subsequently discuss the rationale behind the choice of specific techniques. Frequently, a student would inquire why I had selected one procedure rather than another; how I had deduced certain factors or inferred others. Sometimes, there were reasonably clear-cut and objective reasons, but just as often, I would say that my previous 'clinical experience' or my 'intuition' had led me to pursue (or avoid) a specific issue, or had pointed the way to an effective intervention. They were not impressed. Indeed, they had every right to feel that the didactic virtues of such answers left much to be desired. It is incumbent on a teacher to be able to specify, to articulate and to pinpoint the verbal and non-verbal cues that elicit certain hunches and lead to the selection of particular methods and interventions. Thus, instead of providing glib answers, I really started thinking, 'soul-searching', to discover the precise mechanisms that guided my clinical inventiveness.

For example, it is rarely for capricious reasons that a seasoned veteran says to a client, 'Can you form a *mental image* of that event?' whereas to someone else under seemingly identical circumstances, he or she asks, 'Can you notice a *sensation* somewhere in your body?'. Nevertheless, when asked to explain the precise reasoning behind the particular point of emphasis, the expert may be hard-pressed to do so and might contend that 'clinical experience', 'know-how' and 'intuition' had all played a part. Closer introspection will probably reveal that the therapist was at least subliminally aware that the first client was especially prone to vivid imagery as a potent agent of change, whereas the second one was much more of a 'sensory reactor'. Alternatively, the first client may have been *avoiding* any imagery referents, and thus it was likely that an inquiry into this modality might 'strike oil' (and likewise for the second client who might have been playing down his or her sensory reactions). My novice students, who have learned the tenets of multimodal therapy and are trained to think in BASIC I.D. terms, are told to pay attention to clients' favored modalities and to those they eschew or gloss over, and to zero in on those dimensions when therapy falters. In this way, these novices end up acting like experts.

Many of the multimodal assessment techniques have been formulated to provide beginners with a map, a set of directives and a template with which to design effective interventions. All good, intuitive, experienced therapists use some form of 'bridging' and 'tracking' procedures, but it is my contention that there is much to be gained by writing this into the treatment manuals as explicitly as possible. I have been told by some experts that this has sharpened many of their already well-honed procedures, and beginners have told me that they have gained a sense of direction and confidence from having these tactics spelled out for them. It is towards the foregoing ends that multimodal assessment procedures have been designed.

Acknowledgment

My special thanks to Allen Fay, MD, for his cogent criticisms.

References

ALEXANDER, F. (1932). *The Medical Value of Psychoanalysis*. New York: Norton.

BECK, A.T. (1976). *Cognitive Therapy and the Emotional Disorders*. New York: International Universities Press.

BRUNELL, L.F. and YOUNG, W.T. (Eds) (1982). *A Multimodal Handbook for a Mental Hospital: Designing Specific Treatments for Specific Problems*. New York: Springer.

DAVISON, G.C. (1980). Some views on effective principles of psychotherapy. *Cogn. Ther. Res.* 4, 273.

DiMATTEO, M.R. and DiNICOLA, D.D. (1982). *Achieving Patient Compliance: The Psychology of the Medical Practitioner's Role*. New York: Pergamon.

EDWARDS, S.S. and KLEINE, P.A. (1986). Multimodal consultation: A model for working with gifted adolescents. *J. Counsel. Develop.* 64, 598-601.

ELLIS, A. (1962). *Reason and Emotion in Psychotherapy*. New York: Lyle Stuart.

FAY, A. (1976). The drug modality. In: Lazarus, A.A. (Ed.), *Multimodal Behavior Therapy*. New York: Springer.

FAY, A. and LAZARUS, A.A. (1982). Psychoanalytic resistance and behavioral nonresponsiveness: A dialectical impasse. In: Watchel, P.L. (Ed.), *Resistance: Psychodynamic and Behavioral Approaches*. New York: Plenum.

JACOBSON, N.S. and MARGOLIN, G. (1979). *Marital Therapy: Strategies Based on Social Learning and Behavior Exchange Principles*. New York: Brunner/Mazel.

KAZDIN, A.E. and WILSON, G.T. (1978). *Evaluation of Behavior Therapy: Issues, Evidence, and Research Strategies*. Cambridge, MA: Ballinger.

KEAT, D.B. (1979). *Multimodal Therapy with Children*. New York: Pergamon.

KWEE, M.G.T. (1984). *Klinische Multimodale Gedragstherapie*. Lisse, Holland: Swets & Zeitlinger.

LAZARUS, A.A. (1968). Learning theory and the treatment of depression. *Behav. Res. Ther.* 6, 83-89.

LAZARUS, A.A. (1971). *Behavior Therapy and Beyond*. New York: McGraw-Hill.

LAZARUS, A.A. (1981). *The Practice of Multimodal Therapy*. New York: McGraw-Hill.

LAZARUS, A.A. (1984a). Multimodal therapy. In: Corsini, R.J. (Ed.). *Current Psychotherapies*, 3rd edn. Itasca, IL: F.E. Peacock.

LAZARUS, A.A. (1984b). *In the Mind's Eye: The Power of Imagery for Personal Enrichment*. New York: Guilford.

LAZARUS, A.A. (1985). A brief overview of multimodal therapy. In: Lazarus, A.A. (Ed.), *Casebook of Multimodal Therapy*. New York: Guilford.

LAZARUS, A.A. (1986). Multimodal psychotherapy: Overview and update. *Int. J. Eclectic Psychother.* **5**, 95–103.

LAZARUS, A.A. and FAY, A. (1984). Behavior therapy. In: Karasu, T.B. (Ed.), *The Psychiatric Therapies*. Washington, DC: American Psychiatric Association.

LEIBLUM, S.R. and PERVIN, L.A. (Eds), (1980). *Principles and Practice of Sex Therapy*. New York: Guilford.

LONDON, P. (1964). *The Modes and Morals of Psychotherapy*. New York: Holt, Rinehart & Winston.

MAYS, D.T. and FRANKS, C.M. (Eds), (1985). *Negative Outcome in Psychotherapy and What to Do about it*. New York: Springer.

McFALL, R.M. (1985). Nonbehavioral training for behavioral clinicians. *Behav. Ther.* **8**, 27–30.

MEYER, A. (1915). Objective psychology or psychobiology with subordination of the medically useless contrast of mental and physical. *J. Am. Med. Assoc.* **65**, 860–862.

PEARL, C. and GUARNACCIA, V. (1976). Multimodal therapy and mental retardation. In: Lazarus, A.A. (Ed.), *Multimodal Behavior Therapy*. New York: Springer.

RACHMAN, S.J. and WILSON, G.T. (1980). *The Effects of Psychological Therapy*, 2nd edn. New York: Pergamon.

RIDLEY, C.R. (1984). Clinical treatment of the nondisclosing black client: A therapeutic paradox. *Am. Psychol.* **39**, 1234–1244.

SANK, L.I. (1979). Community disasters: Primary prevention and treatment in a health maintenance organization. *Am. Psychol.* **34**, 334–338.

SCHOFIELD, W. (1964). *Psychotherapy: The Purchase of Friendship*. Englewood Cliffs, NJ: Prentice-Hall.

SHELTON, J.L. and ACKERMAN, J.M. (1974). *Homework in Counseling and Psychotherapy*. Springfield, IL: Charles C. Thomas.

SHELTON, J.L. and LEVY, R.L. (1981). *Behavioral Assignments and Treatment Compliance: A Handbook of Clinical Strategies*. Champaign, IL: Research Press.

SHEVRIN, H. and DICKMAN, S. (1980). The psychological unconscious: A necessary assumption for all psychological theory? *Am. Psychol.* **35**, 421–434.

SLOWINSKI, J.W. (1985). Three multimodal case studies: Two recalcitrant 'Ghetto Clients' and a case of post-traumatic stress. In: Lazarus, A.A. (Ed.), *Casebook of Multimodal Therapy*. New York: Guilford.

STEKETEE, G., FOA, E.B. and GRAYSON, J.B. (1982). Recent advances in the behavioral treatment of obsessive-compulsives. *Arch. Gen. Psychiatr.* **39**, 1365–1371.

WILSON, G.T. (1980). Toward specifying the 'nonspecific' factors in behavior therapy. A social-learning analysis. In: Mahoney, M.J. (Ed.), *Psychotherapy Process: Current Issues and Future Directions*. New York: Plenum.

WILSON, G.T. (1982). Clinical issues and strategies in the practice of behavior therapy. In Franks, C.M., Wilson, G.T., Kendall, P.C. and Brownell, K.D. (Eds), *Annual Review of Behavior Therapy: Theory and Practice*, Vol. 8. New York: Guilford.

WILSON, G.T., FRANKS C.M., BROWNELL, K.D. and KENDALL P.C. (1984). *Annual Review of Behaviour Therapy: Theory and Practice,* Vol. 9. New York: Guilford.

WOLF, S., WOLF, C.M. and SPIELBERG, G. (1980). *The Wolf Counseling Skills Evaluation Handbook*. Omaha, NE: National Publication.

WOLPE, J. (1984). Behavior therapy according to Lazarus. *Am. Psychol.* **39**, 1326–1327.

ZILBERGELD, B. (1982). Bespoke therapy. *Psychol. Today* **16**, 85–86.

Chapter 16
A Multimodal Perspective on Problems of Sexual Desire (1988)

Lazarus has contributed several articles and chapters to the field of sex therapy, and has also been regarded as a pioneer in this area. His chapter on the assessment and treatment of sexual desire disorders affords the reader an opportunity to glean some novel information, as well as being able to appreciate anew how the 'multimodal' orientation ensures comprehensive and yet highly focused, well-targeted therapeutic processes and procedures. Lazarus draws an intriguing distinction between what he terms 'CNS sex' and 'ANS sex' as part of a general 'formula' for resolving desire discrepancies. He also discusses the use of 'time tripping' and offers a successful and an unsuccessful case vignette to underscore the strengths and weaknesses of his position.

Overview: The Kaleidoscopic Heterogeneity of Desire Dysfunctions

Theoretically, problems of sexual desire may be placed on a continuum ranging from hypoactive to hyperactive degrees of intensity. The 'normal' degree of libidinal desire would lie somewhere in the middle of the distribution. Attempts to narrow this global description into clinically precise definitions, diagnoses and descriptions all suffer from the fact that, despite data from statistical surveys and diverse observations, the normal parameters of human sexual behavior have yet to be established. As with height, weight, intelligence and so on, individual differences regarding the intensity of the sexual drive show wide variations, thus rendering it difficult in many instances to distinguish between 'normal' and 'abnormal' tendencies. Nonetheless, for practical purposes, there is sufficient professional consensus to identify extreme and clearly pathological patterns of sexuality. For example, a person who appears to be preoccupied with sex

First published in 1988. Reproduced, with the permission of Guilford Press, from Lazarus, A.A. (1988). A multimodal perspective on problems of sexual desire. In: Leiblum, S.R. and Rosen, R.C. (Eds) *Sexual Desire Disorders*, pp. 145–167. New York: Guilford Press.

and masturbates to orgasm 15 times a day would generally be viewed as sexually hyperactive. An individual who never masturbates, very rarely has sexual thoughts or fantasies, and is attracted to members of neither sex would be regarded as sexually blocked or hypoactive.

Hyperactive sexual desire remains one of the most controversial clinical entities. Kaplan (1979) has stated, 'In my experience, excessive sexual desire is so rare as to constitute a clinical curiosity when it is a primary symptom' (p. 76). She separates 'primary hyperactive sexual desire' from those instances where high levels of sexual activity are due to manic and hypomanic states, extreme anxiety and tension, and obsessions centered on fears of inadequate sexual performance. Basically, very few individuals experience an excessive or constant desire for sex per se; most who are viewed as sexually hyperactive tend to rely on sexual outlets to relieve discomfort (be it tension, insecurity, anxiety or any other negative state of mind).

It would seem that hyperactive sexual desire is very rarely a monistic or discrete clinical entity. Thus, the *Longman Dictionary of Psychology and Psychiatry* (Goldenson, 1984) defines 'nymphomania' as 'a female disorder consisting of an excessive or insatiable desire for sexual stimulation and gratification, due to such factors as denial of homosexual tendencies, attempts to combat or disprove frigidity, a reaction to seduction in childhood, or a response to emotional tension' (pp. 502–503). The same dictionary points out that 'satyriasis' (a male psychosexual disorder consisting of an excessive or insatiable desire for sexual gratification) 'is not due to being "oversexed" in the physiological sense but arises from unconscious emotional needs, such as (a) the need for reassurance of potency, (b) a compensation for failures, frustrations, or a poor self-image, (c) a means of warding off anxiety stemming from emotional conflicts, or (d) an attempt to deny homosexual tendencies' (p. 652). It is a matter for debate whether or not some of the paraphilias are special instances of hyperactive sexual desire. The entire area of 'deviant arousal' is often typified by case histories in which excessive desire figures prominently, and wherein unusual or aggressive sexual appetites predominate (e.g. Barlow and Wincze, 1980).

Practitioners will be consulted by patients complaining about hypoactive sexual desire far more frequently than by those who seek treatment for hypersexuality. Diminished libido, however, is anything but unitary or easily defined. As Friedman and Hogan (1985) have emphasized, 'Although low sexual desire is a topic of current concern for sex therapists, there seems to be little agreement as to what this "syndrome" is, and particularly, how to operationally define it' (p. 422). Patterns of asexual behavior vary widely. Some people may avoid sexual outlets despite feelings of desire; others simply have minimal or virtually no wish for sex. In rare instances, people have been devoid of sexual interest for their entire lives. Such primary sexual apathy carries a negative prognosis. Some patients with primary hypoactive sexual desire whose asexuality is global (rather than person- or situation-specific) may be constitutionally unable to experience endogenous desire. Kinsey, Pomeroy and Martin (1948, p. 209) claimed that some persons 'never were equipped to respond erotically'.

It is more usual to encounter patients who report a loss of sexual drive or interest after a history of moderate to considerable desire and activity. Zilbergeld and Ellison (1980) distinguish between 'desire' and 'arousal': 'Whereas desire refers to how often one wants sex, arousal denotes how high (excited, turned on) one gets during sex' (p. 68). There are those who, despite a lack of sexual drive, can nevertheless perform reflexively if genitally stimulated; others respond to all sexual overtures with nothing but irritation, anger, anxiety or disgust. A low sexual desire can be total or situational (e.g. the person who has no desire for his or her spouse but is highly active with a lover). Regardless, when consulted by a patient whose sexual frequency is low, a crucial consideration is whether the low sexual activity is basically a function of diminished desire, or fear of sex, or of aversion to sex. There is an important difference between 'apathy' and 'inhibition'. Indeed, what Lief (1977) has called 'inhibited sexual desire' (ISD) may be a product of numerous etiological factors.

Prior to the middle to late 1970s, low sexual desire, especially in males, had not been clearly delineated as a discrete problem. Many writers applied the label 'frigidity' to women with virtually any sexual dysfunction, ranging from partial or total impairment of desire, to sexual interest and pleasure without orgasm. Among male disorders, the term 'impotence' included 'premature ejaculation, limited interest in sex, orgasm without experiencing pleasure, coitus without ejaculation, and sexual ability only with prostitutes' (Goldenson, 1984, p. 370). 'Gradually, it was recognized that the sexual response is *not* an indivisible entity, vulnerable to a single pathogen, subject to only one disorder, and amenable to a single treatment regimen' (Kaplan, 1979, p. 4). While Masters and Johnson (1966) proposed a sequential continuum of human responses to effective sexual stimulation – excitement, plateau, orgasm and resolution – desire was not mentioned. Kaplan (1979) has proposed a triphasic concept of human sexuality – desire, excitement and orgasm. I have found it clinically advantageous to think in terms of desire, arousal, stimulation, orgasm, resolution and satisfaction. Each of these phases may present discrete problems:

1. *Desire*: disorders of desire, as already mentioned, are many and varied, but the most common clinical entity is ISD, which is characterized by no or low interest in any form of sexual activity.
2. *Arousal*: arousal deficits refer to the absolute or relative absence of penile tumescence (erection) or of the vaginal lubrication and distension necessary for coitus.

3. *Stimulation*: typical problems that may arise during the stimulation phase include loss of erection, premature ejaculation, cessation of vaginal lubrication, and loss of interest or desire prior to orgasm.
4. *Orgasm*: orgasmic difficulties include anorgasmia, pain, diminished sensation and ejaculation without sensation.
5. *Resolution*: resolution difficulties include such phenomena as extreme postorgasmic lassitude or fatigue, depression, headache, or genital pain or discomfort.
6. *Satisfaction*: difficulties with satisfaction refer to a negative subjective evaluation of the sexual experience, or deficits in the overall level of gratification or fulfillment that flows from the sexual experience.

A wide range of medical illnesses, especially those of a urological or gynecological nature, may result in loss of sexual interest and/or sexual avoidance. Hormonal deficiency, particularly of testosterone, may produce a diminution of sexual interest in men and women. Drugs may attenuate sexual desire, especially certain antihypertensive agents, high doses of alcohol, sedatives and some neuroleptics. Depression tends to compromise the sexual appetite. On the psychological front, the range of factors interfering with sexual desire is wide: Among the most common are various conflicts; anger and hostility; guilt (often associated with a Puritan antisex ethic and other religious prohibitions); or fears about intimacy, vulnerability, responsibility, rejection, pleasure and commitment. Severe stress and situational anxiety are also associated with truncated desire.

When called upon to treat disorders of sexual desire, the practitioner will find that problems are usually defined by a dyadic unit: 'The person with low desire is often perfectly content with his or her own level of desire, and comes to therapy because of pressure from his or her partner' (Friedman and Hogan, 1985, p. 422). It is for the foregoing reasons that the term 'desire discrepancies', proposed by Zilbergeld and Ellison (1980), seems preferable to positing some arbitrary standard of high or low sexual interest. As these authors note, 'It is not that one person has too much desire and another too little on some absolute scale; it is rather a discrepancy in two people's styles or interest' (1980, p. 68). The paradoxes of adopting some putative criterion of high or low sexual desire are readily demonstrated. If a couple has intercourse twice a year, but both partners are entirely content with their sex life, should we intervene, attempt to raise their sexual consciousness, and thus perhaps elevate their coital frequency? Is an unattached person who desires and obtains sex once every 3 or 4 months, and who has no complaints about this frequency, in need of help? If we are treating Mr and Mrs X because he desires sex once every 2 weeks and she craves it at least three times a week, would we regard him as suffering from low desire? Then if Mr and Mrs X get divorced and he marries a woman who wants sex only every couple of months, would we now alter our diagnosis?

Most therapists have tended to focus on the partner who displays the lesser interest of the two, with a view to increasing the sexual appetite of that individual. The implication seems to be that 'more is better' and that a lower level of desire is dysfunctional. Zilbergeld and Ellison (1980) challenge this view and emphasize the necessity to 'attend to both partners, trying to increase the desire of the one while at the same time trying to decrease that of the other' (p. 68). In treating desire discrepancies, the goal is to achieve a satisfactory compromise.

The Multimodal Approach

Multimodal therapy (Lazarus, 1976, 1981, 1985a, 1986 and see Chapter 15) emphasizes the need for a thorough and comprehensive assessment of *B*ehavior, *A*ffect, *S*ensation, *I*magery, *C*ognition, *I*nterpersonal relationships and *B*iological factors. The convenient mnemonic device 'BASIC I.D.' is an acronym derived from the first letters of these discrete yet interactive modalities by changing 'B' (*B*iological) to 'D' (*D*rugs), because most interventions in this area call for neuroleptics, antidepressants, and anxiolytic agents. However, it must be remembered that the 'D' modality addresses *all* issues of physical well-being, such as diet, sleep habits, exercise, central nervous system (CNS) pathology, endocrine disorders and metabolic disorders, in addition to the effects of prescribed medications and recreational drugs.

Multimodal therapy recommends a level of systematic attention devoted to each area of a client's BASIC I.D. that exceeds the thoroughness and diagnostic scrutiny of most other multifactorial, multidimensional, multifaceted, and eclectic orientations. When the assessment template of multimodal therapy is applied to disorders of sexual desire, some salient questions in each modality are immediately apparent.

Behavior

Is the problem that of hyperactivity or hypoactivity? Can specific response deficits or excesses be identified? Are there issues related to sexual skills and performance (e.g. kissing, caressing, massaging and other forms of stimulation)? What are the details concerning oral–genital contact, masturbation and the impact of situational variables?

Affect

Is there evidence of anxiety, and/or guilt, and/or depression, and/or anger? Are there *aversions* to any body parts or functions? Is there love, affection or caring? Are there signs of displaced affect being deflected from a parent onto a partner or spouse? Do there appear to be any specific fears of intimacy?

Sensation

Primarily, are we dealing with pain (e.g. dyspareunia or postcoital discomfort) or the absence of pleasure (e.g. anorgasmia or ejaculation without sensation)? Is self-stimulation unpleasant, neutral, pleasant or non-existent? Is there arousal, but limited or no pleasure?

Imagery

Does the thought of sexual encounters conjure up negative or intrusive images? Are there reports of any spontaneous seductive or erotic mental images? Can specific fantasies increase or decrease sexual desire? What are the frequency and content of erotic dreams (if any)? Do books, pictures or erotic films stimulate any arousal or desire?

Cognition

What connection is there between the client's ethics, morals and religious beliefs, and his or her own sexuality? What are the client's basic sexual outlook and attitudes? Are there definite sex-role expectations? Which 'shoulds', 'oughts' and 'musts' are self-imposed, and which are placed on the partner? Does the person lack sexual information and/or have misinformation?

Interpersonal relationships

How assertive and communicative is the client? Is there a specific relational problem (e.g. lack of attraction to the partner) and/or is there evidence of generalized interpersonal difficulties? What role does power play? Who have served as sexual role models? What are the details vis-à-vis initiation and refusal of sexual activity? Is there any evidence of sexual trauma – rape, coercive incest, parental punishment?

Drugs (biological factors)

What medications or drugs does the client ingest? Are there any urological or gynecological dysfunctions? Have other organic factors been ruled out? Do endocrinological tests seem warranted?

The foregoing questions and issues are by no means complete or exhaustive; they provide the basis for more detailed explorations into the specific areas that may call for elaboration and clarification. The point is that even this preliminary BASIC I.D. inquiry provides an impressive degree of precision and comprehensiveness. It differs from most other multidimensional approaches. For example, Friedman and Hogan (1985) have described 'a multidimensional behavioral treatment model for inhibited sexual desire' (p. 419) that integrates four therapeutic components: (1)

experiential/sensory awareness exercises; (2) insight; (3) cognitive restructuring; and (4) behavioral interventions. In multimodal vernacular, they cover a *trimodal* sequence (sensation, cognition and behavior).

While broad-based eclectic therapists tend to traverse most aspects of the BASIC I.D., they nevertheless leave much to chance and to the individual clinician's perspicacity. There is a difference between an assessment schema that calls deliberate and specific attention to behavior, affect, sensation, imagery, cognition, interpersonal relationships and biological factors, and those diagnostic protocols that gloss over one or more of these modalities or condense them into fewer categories. Thus, in their 'experiential/sensory awareness' component, Friedman and Hogan (1985) include 'fantasy training' as well as 'imaginal recreation of an earlier traumatic experience' (p. 437). It is especially easy for novice therapists and trainees to downplay certain elements unless they are explicitly built into the assessment–therapy sequence, and even experienced clinicians tend to require guideposts or reminders to ensure that they do not bypass or overlook less obvious components. In multimodal therapy, the imagery modality (no less than the other six) is explicitly identified and thoroughly assessed (see Lazarus, 1984).

It is important to underscore the way in which treatment interventions are selected within the multimodal approach. Specifically, when there are deficits or problems in several dimensions of the BASIC I.D., how does the clinician decide when and how to intervene? Usually, the areas to be addressed are decided upon in concert with input from the client. The therapist might say, 'Perhaps we could begin by dealing with your reluctance to be explicit with your wife about your sexual preferences, and also maybe we can explore some of your attitudes about male–female differences. Or are there other issues that you would prefer to include?'. If the client proposes different priorities or additional objectives, the therapist might agree to follow the client's script, unless the therapist has explicit reasons for not doing so. (It would be myopic always to follow the client's predilections. Those with passive–aggressive, manipulative and sabotaging tendencies usually require firm direction.) In this event, a discussion ensues until a mutually agreeable treatment sequence is reached. The therapist then provides a description of the different pathways toward the specified goal. While eschewing push-button panaceas, the aim is to select those methods most likely to prove beneficial: tense people are taught relaxation; dysfunctional beliefs call for the 'correction of misconceptions'; interpersonal skills training is offered to those who are socially inept or unduly reticent. Some individuals prefer to deal with only one problem at a time. Others respond better when working on two or more issues simultaneously. Regardless, the final goal is to insure that no significant problems throughout the BASIC I.D. are bypassed or glossed over.

It is perhaps necessary to underscore the fact that the BASIC I.D. is *not* a 'flat', static, linear representation of human temperament and personality. While it is clinically convenient to divide the reciprocal interactive flux that typifies actual life events into the seemingly separate dimensions of the BASIC I.D., in actuality we are always confronted by a continuous, recursive, multileveled living process. The multimodal approach essentially asks: (1) What are the specific and interrelated problems? (2) Who or what appears to be maintaining these problems? (3) What appears to be the best way in each individual instance of remedying these problems? The BASIC I.D. offers a systematic structure that insures thoroughness and also provides specific methods for identifying idiosyncratic reactions.

A General 'Formula' for Resolving Desire Discrepancies

Before I describe some typical multimodal treatment sequences, it may be useful to place the issue of 'desire discrepancies' and its potential resolution into some overall perspective. Within any dyad, desire discrepancies are inevitable; perfect sexual harmony and synchrony exist only in romantic novels. It is obvious that times will arise when one partner desires sex and the other is not in the mood for it, or when one person is aroused and the other is uninterested. Usually, these differences pose no problem and constitute no threat, and couples adjust to them as they see fit. Problems arise when the discrepant pattern becomes frequent and unpredictable, or when a significant difference in respective sexual 'appetites' seems evident.

The most common complaint within the foregoing context translates into the following: 'I desire sexual relations far more frequently than my spouse [partner], and there is therefore something wrong with him [her].' In my experience, the complainant is usually, but not always, the one who wants more sex; the defendant is often the one who requires less. I have stated the problem legalistically because it is frequently presented in this manner. A major overriding difficulty stems from the fact that the person wanting more sex usually insists on 'complete intercourse' (foreplay that culminates in penile–vaginal stimulation followed by mutual, if not simultaneous, orgasms). Many such individuals subscribe to unfortunate myths: 'If he really loved me, he would want to have sex with me as often as I wish to have it with him'; 'If she was truly turned on to me, she would become aroused as soon as I started kissing and caressing her'. A first step is to challenge the faulty 'if-then' assumptions that many people bring to their sexual encounters. It is also important that the therapist search for implicit or explicit *demands* that undermine sexual activity: 'Before I let my husband make love to me, I must be sure that he wants *me* and not just my body'; 'My wife wanted me to have intercourse with her last night. How could I, when only 3 days ago she accused me of being stingy?' Of course, the astute clinician will be on the alert for possible hidden agendas that lead some people to latch onto virtually any event as an excuse for sexual distance.

It is often especially helpful in resolving desire discrepancies to underscore the similarities between the 'sexual drive' and the 'hunger drive'. The therapist can point out that these 'appetites' show wide individual differences, and that a continuum extends in both areas from compulsive gluttony to total anorexia. The person who always insists on nothing less than a gourmet's epicurean preparation and elegant presentation of delicious cuisine – who will not eat in any place less sumptuous than a four-star restaurant, replete with the best china and crystal, soft music and subdued lights – might go hungry most of the time, become seriously undernourished and feel chronically deprived. Similarly, in matters pertaining to sex, those who insist on delicate intimacy, or passionate intensity, under ideal conditions will find their sexual frequency and enjoyment decidedly curtailed. It is more sensible to enjoy a wide range of options – to have the capacity to appreciate and enjoy sumptuous dining on meticulously prepared victuals, while also remaining open to the delights and pleasures (and nourishment) of a pizza or a quick sandwich. Sexually, the couple who develops the ability to enjoy 'four-star gourmet lovemaking' on some occasions, and 'local pizza parlor fare' on others, will not miss out on those delightful and spontaneous 'quickies' from time to time that tend to promote intimacy, caring and physical relief.

The foregoing analogies translate into the following therapeutic tactics:

● When it is the woman who desires more sex than the man, I point out that no man is capable of willing an erection, and I often provide a brief explanation of the psychophysiology of sexuality, emphasizing that much of it is under the control of the autonomic nervous system (ANS). I also stress that activities such as manual, digital and oral stimulation fall under the domain of the CNS. Therefore, if the woman desires sexual stimulation and relief four times a week to the man's two, I would recommend two 'CNS + ANS' sexual unions (foreplay that culminates in coitus) and two purely 'CNS' encounters (wherein he engages in loving and erotic foreplay, culminating in oral and/or manual stimulation to bring her to orgasm – repeatedly if she so desires). During 'CNS' lovemaking, there is no penile–vaginal stimulation, and the man seeks no sexual gratification for himself unless he becomes erect and sexually excited. I emphasize very strongly that no anticipations and hidden expectations must enter the situation; it is perfectly acceptable for the male to stimulate the female without becoming aroused, and this signals neither the absence of love nor the existence of a sexual problem. (CNS sex is tantamount to a hamburger or a sandwich; ANS sex is at least a three-course meal!)

● When the man desires more sex than the woman, I deliver my psychophysiology lecture by explaining that sexual arousal is autonomically mediated, and that the female cannot control vaginal lubrication and distension any more than the male can will an erection. Nevertheless, 'CNS' lovemaking may include anything from back rubs to fellatio. The primary objective is for the woman to stimulate the man so that he has an orgasm. One difference in the case of a woman engaging in 'CNS sex' is that penile–vaginal stimulation is usually possible, i.e. the man (perhaps with the aid of a lubricating cream) is able to enter the vagina and achieve orgasm. One of my clients stated her position very clearly: 'Hal wants sex virtually every night, whereas I am in the mood two or perhaps three times a week. So when he wants it and I don't, I have no problem with him masturbating inside of me.' In this situation, the problem was that Hal felt insulted and became angry when his wife failed to respond erotically every time he stimulated her, particularly when he entered her. It was necessary to persuade Hal to separate ANS from CNS sexual intercourse and never to confuse the two. I have treated other couples wherein the male had no difficulties receiving CNS sex, but the female objected because she felt 'used'. Here again, considerable 'cognitive restructuring' was required to effect a satisfactory solution.

We have all been successful with couples wherein low sexual desire is due to situational factors: the overly competitive corporate husband or wife is so burned out, or so preoccupied with work, that fun, leisure, sex and other pleasures have been tabled. Certainly, in my experience, it is not difficult, when at least a modicum of attraction and desire is still present within the dyad, to fan the fire so that it crackles away to a heart-warming degree. Another situational factor that usually responds rapidly to professional intervention is the 'desire disorder' that stems from one partner's neglect of basic hygiene. I have had to urge many a spouse to take a bath or a shower before even considering making sexual overtures. Compliance in such cases has usually led to an immediate increase in the formerly reluctant partner's sexual desire.

Recently, a couple consulted me because the wife, who had been sexually responsive for the first 5 years of marriage, had become almost totally unresponsive for the past 3 months. The problem was simply that her mother had come to live with them and the wife was afraid that 'sexual sounds' would carry through the 'flimsy walls'. The solution? The installation of soundproofing tiles in the main bedroom restored a sense of privacy that enabled the wife to return to her uninhibited former self. (I am often astonished how these obvious solutions sometimes prove so elusive!)

Another situationally specific 'low-desire' problem involved a 55-year-old physician and his second wife. He stated that the frequency of sex throughout the 26 years of his first marriage (which ended in divorce) had averaged once or twice a month. For the past 2 years, he had been married to a 36-year-old woman who desired sex at least once a week. 'At first, this was no problem,' the doctor explained, 'as I was very stimulated and excited by her....But now I no longer feel so aroused by her.' We discussed the natural evolution of most relationships and the impact of 'habituation' – the fact that most people, after a while, find that the initial thrills tend to subside if not to disappear altogether. I inquired whether he ever masturbated. 'Occasionally,' he said. I asked, 'Do you use any fantasies while so doing?' He answered, 'Yes. I have quite a vivid imagination.' I inquired, 'Then why not use this "vivid imagination" to good effect while in bed with your wife?' The doctor had two objections to this idea: (1) he viewed it as 'cheating' and (2) he thought it might be considered 'abnormal'. I was able to persuade him that both of these notions were unfounded, whereupon he accepted my 'permission' to season his sex life with the intrinsic powers of erotic imagery. Thereafter, his apparent 'low desire' was no longer an impediment.

It should be re-emphasized that medical/biological factors may play a crucial role in desire disorders. The 'D' modality is particularly relevant when definite endocrinopathy has been established. Nevertheless, as Reckless and Geiger (1975) pointed out, hormone treatment can increase desire without improving performance, and thus can worsen the patient's plight. (At the very least, a bimodal treatment approach – behavioral-biological – would seem indicated even where clear-cut medical interventions are necessary.) It is also interesting that certain patients have demonstrated significant improvement when treated with a placebo (Miller, 1968; Sobotka, 1969).

Having discussed some routine and situationally determined problems, I now focus attention on more complex issues calling for the full spectrum of multimodal methods. The first therapy illustration is a description of a successfully completed case, and the second is a description of a treatment failure.

Case Presentations

A successful case

Description

Lisa, aged 35, and Al, aged 37, had been married 8 years at the time of intake. Lisa stated (and Al agreed) that during their premarital period (approximately 8 months), sex had been frequent and passionate. As soon as they were married Lisa noticed an attenuation in Al's interest, but the frequency and quality of their sexual interactions nevertheless remained satisfactory for about 2 years. At that juncture, Al evidenced erectile difficulties, and he consulted a psychiatrist who attributed the problem to undue work pressures. (Al's responsibilities on the job had intensified, and he felt harassed much of the time.) Soon thereafter, he accepted a new position that removed many of the previous work demands, and his potency was restored – but never to its former level. Over the next 4 years, intermittent problems (erectile difficulties, rapid ejaculation, non-specific prostatitis) progressively undermined Al's sexual interest and desire. For the past year, he reported having no spontaneous sexual desires, and Lisa stated that during this time they had had sex 'less than three or four times at most'.

Al held a master's degree in electrical engineering and had a managerial-cum-technical position with a large company. Lisa had a master's degree in library science, but worked as an advertising representative and freelance copywriter. They had no children, although for the past 2 years Lisa had felt that a final decision had to be reached, because her 'biological clock' was running out. Al seemed highly ambivalent in this regard.

Al's background

Al had a sister 3 years his junior with whom he had fought 'like cats and dogs' and from whom he felt 'disconnected'. He described his father as 'passive', and called his mother 'a battle-ax'. He said, 'She was often on the warpath, and at an early age I learned how to keep out of her way'. When asked whether he had felt loved as a child and whether he had been shown affection and warmth, he stated that, despite his father's passivity and his mother's aggressiveness, he had received adequate love and attention from both parents. He regarded them as sexually inhibited – the subject was never discussed in the home. He had learned the facts of life from peers when he was about 11, at which time he started masturbating. At age 16 he started dating, and although he engaged in heavy petting on dates, his first intercourse was at age 20 with a prostitute. Over the next 8 years he had several 'serious relationships', but it was only when he met Lisa, when he was almost 29, that he considered marriage for the first time. 'I had never seemed to see eye-to-eye so closely with anyone....We laughed at the same things and agreed about everything from agnosticism to our taste in art.'

Lisa's background

Lisa had a sister 9 years her senior, to whom she had always felt very close. Lisa excelled academically and was favored by her father. Her parents tolerated each other, and the home atmosphere was one of 'serenity but no real joy'. Her mother often voiced the view that wives have to 'second-guess' their husbands and see to it that they (the wives) remain in control. When Lisa was about 14, her mother received a small inheritance, which 'through cunning and some luck, she managed to turn into a large sum of money'. Her mother's financial independence seemed to drive a wedge between her parents. When she was 19, Lisa's mother confided in her that the father was having a clandestine love affair – a fact that her mother seemed to find amusing rather than threatening or annoying. 'During my junior year at college, my parents got divorced and, during my senior year, they each remarried.'

She was popular in college and dated frequently, 'but I hung onto my virginity until the end of my senior year'. Soon after graduating, at age 21, she married a man 10 years her senior. 'He was super-brilliant, and I was attracted to his intellect.' Nevertheless, they had few common interests; Lisa never found him physically attractive, and within 2 years they had grown so far apart that they 'simply drifted into a divorce'. Thereafter, while she dated several men, it was not until meeting Al that she 'fell in love'. She described him as 'brilliant like my first husband, but infinitely more attractive and sexy'.

The multimodal assessment

The foregoing information is a summary of the more salient points that emerged from two intake interviews with the couple. At the end of the initial interview, Lisa and Al were each asked to fill out a Multimodal Life History Questionnaire* and to return it at the second meeting. This instrument covers the BASIC I.D. in some detail and usually enables the therapist to determine in which particular areas the chief problems reside.

It seemed that Al's background had rendered him especially sensitive to aggression (real or imagined) from women. He reacted to Lisa, who thought of herself as 'assertive', as a person who was extremely 'controlling and aggressive'. In describing Lisa on the Multimodal Life History Questionnaire, Al had written: 'She treats me like a moron. One would assume that I lacked the intelligence to compose a business letter or remember simple everyday things.' Lisa, in turn, had written: 'Al is just too laid back at times, and I think he views any affectionate nudging as a critical attack.' During the fourth conjoint session, Lisa stated, 'Look here, you two, I want answers and I want them now. I think I've been patient far too long!' I asked Lisa whether this was an example of her 'affectionate nudging'. I also inquired whether or not it represented her usual style when frustrated. At the end of the session, the following points of agreement had been reached: (1) in general, Lisa was inclined to 'come on strong'; (2) Al tended to overreact and was needlessly hypersensitive to real or imagined slights from most people, especially from women, and most of

---

*The Multimodal Life History Questionnaire is obtainable from Research Press, Box 3177, Champaign, IL 61821, USA.

all from Lisa; (3) when feeling under attack, Al, instead of asserting himself, almost always withdrew (thereby adhering to tactics that had functional validity as a child, but no longer served him as an adult).

Al alleged that Lisa had been openly derisive and hypercritical of his sexual inadequacies. 'When I first had that problem with impotence about 6 years ago, you should have heard the things she said to me!' Lisa retorted, 'That was over 6 years ago! Have I said anything since then?' Lisa turned to me and said, 'That's his main problem; he's so damn negative. Al's forever reading aspersions and contempt into just about everything I say or do.' Al responded by saying, 'Lisa, I may be way too sensitive, but I'm by no means alone in regarding you as very pushy and too damn controlling. Your own sister remarked that even as a kid you liked to take charge, to be in command, to dish out orders. And didn't Sue, and Phyllis, and your whole tennis group call you the Great Dictator? And how many times has Gordon [her boss] been on the verge of firing you for insubordination? It's not all in my head. Sure, I may be too touchy, but you're one hell of a tough cookie'. I interjected, 'Just like your mother?' to which Al responded, 'Yeah, but at least I could get away from her.' I said, 'Al, I think you and I should meet alone a few times, man to man, so that we can more closely examine your withdrawal tendencies, your wish to get away from tough situations instead of facing them and beating them. And Lisa, I would like to meet with you individually for a while to see if you might benefit by acquiring a different interpersonal style. Al, Lisa, how does this one-on-one idea grab you?' They both replied, 'Fine'.

Before embarking on individual sessions with me, the couple was asked to employ sensate focus twice a week. I strongly impressed upon them that these encounters were to be relaxed, affectionate, unhurried sensual massages that excluded the involvement of breasts and genitals, and explicitly did not include any coitus or orgasms. I ascertained that Lisa particularly enjoyed receiving foot massages, whereas Al enjoyed back rubs, and I obtained a firm agreement that they would pleasure each other in this manner twice weekly. Separate individual sessions with Al and Lisa were scheduled for the following week.

Individual sessions with Al

Prior to seeing Al individually, I had drawn up the following modality profile:

Behavior:	Withdrawal tendencies
Affect:	Anxiety (over attaining an erection)
	Anger (mostly unexpressed)
Sensation:	Tension (mainly in jaws, shoulders and neck)
	Discomfort in scrotum (during bouts of prostatitis)
Imagery:	Pictures (vivid memories) of negative sexual experiences

Cognition:	Perfectionistic tendencies
	'I can't stand criticism'
	Performance concerns and expectations
	Conflicted about becoming a father
Interpersonal relationships:	Communication dysfunction
	(does not state sexual preferences explicitly)
	Unassertive (especially in expressing anger)
	Overreacts to aggression, especially from women
Drugs/biological factors:	Recurrent bouts of non-specific prostatitis.

Al read through the profile and agreed that it pinpointed his main areas of difficulty. After discussing a logical starting point, we agreed on the following: (1) Al would read, most thoroughly, the first chapter of Zilbergeld's (1978) *Male Sexuality* (which deals with significant myths about sexuality and helps men modify unrealistic expectations). (2) We would address his withdrawal tendencies and his basic lack of assertiveness. (3) He would be taught specific relaxation procedures and given cassettes for home use.

Assertiveness training commenced with the usual behavior rehearsal and role-playing procedures, but soon uncovered a host of subjective dangers that characterized Al's perceptions about adopting an assertive stance in life. To Al's way of thinking, it was safer to withdraw, to remain silent, and (if necessary) to retaliate in a passive–aggressive manner when criticized or when placed in any compromising position. The basis of this pattern appeared to be a consequence of contending with his aggressive mother while at the same time identifying with his passive father.

Accordingly, 'time-tripping imagery' (Lazarus, 1984) was employed as follows: while reclining on a comfortable chair, Al was given standard relaxation instructions and then asked to close his eyes and imagine a scene in which he, as an adult, stepped into a 'time machine' and went back in time to significant encounters with his mother. The following dialogue (taken from a slightly edited transcript of the session) ensued:

Therapist: You can stop the time machine and enter your life at any time in the past. Can you imagine that clearly?

Client: Yes. [Pause] I remember a time, oh, I was about 5 or 6, and I had done something to enrage my mother, I forget what, but I was playing with some toys in the den and she came in, kicked the toys all over the room, and yelled at me.

Therapist: OK, now you enter the picture at age 37. You step out of the time machine and into the den. See and hear your mother yelling. [Pause] Look at 5- or 6-year old Al. [Pause] What's happening?

Client: My mother and little Al don't seem to be aware of me, they don't notice me.

Therapist: Well, can you make your presence felt? How would you like to gain their attention?

Client: By strangling my mother! [Chuckles]

Therapist: Can you picture yourself handling the situation *assertively*? You are 37. Little Al is 5 or 6. How old is your mother?

Client: She's about 28 or 29.

Therapist: Fine. Now there's no point in telling her who you are, that you are 37-year-old Al on a visit back from the future. Instead, how about simply telling her that she is mistreating 5-year-old Al?

Client   [A 30- or 40-second pause]: Yes, I can put her in her place.

Therapist: Good. In a few moments, let's discuss what transpired. But before you leave that scene, can you say something to little Al?

Client: [Pause]: I really don't know what to say to him.

Therapist: Why not reassure him? Tell him that he's a good kid, and explain to him that his mother's a bit unstable, but that he shouldn't take it to heart when she flies off the handle.

Client   [Pause]: Okay. In retrospect, I can tell little Al, 'The battle-ax means no harm'.

Therapist: Excellent. Now are you ready to step into the time machine and return back here?

The foregoing imagery excursion was then discussed, and Al was asked to practice similar scenes at his leisure several times a day, wherein he went back in time to comfort his young alter ego and upbraid his mother (assertively, not aggressively). In subsequent sessions, time tripping was employed to encourage his (passive) father to stand up to his mother. Instead, the client preferred not to try to modify his father's behavior, but to inform him that from now on he (Al) was going to be a very different (more assertive) individual. (It seemed that he was seeking permission to stop identifying with his father, and to become his own person.) In my experience, when clients employ these imagery exercises conscientiously, salubrious effects usually accrue. Al was one of those clients who found these imagery exercises 'ego-syntonic' and whose treatment gains coincided with their application.

In tandem with the imagery exercises, each item on Al's modality profile was addressed. Thus, a non-performance outlook on sex was underscored; approach responses rather than avoidance behaviors were encouraged; his anger, instead of being suppressed, was to be appropriately vented; relaxation skills were provided to offset his tensions; images of positive and erotic sexual fantasies were to be practiced in place of his negative imagery; a strong antiperfectionistic philosophy of life was advocated; role-playing was employed to enhance communication (e.g. stating sexual preferences explicitly); and behavior rehearsal was used to contend with criticism and aggression. The foregoing required 8 weekly sessions, at the end of which time significant changes had accrued. (By the fifth session, Al mentioned that during the preceding week, the sensate focus assignments had turned into 'passionate lovemaking' on two occasions. Sensate focus procedures thus became their 'new version of foreplay', and sexual intercourse occurred twice or three times a week thereafter.) Because Al still espoused certain sexual and marital myths, he was encouraged to reread Zilbergeld (1978), paying particular attention to the myths outlined therein; I also gave him a copy of my book *Marital Myths* (Lazarus, 1985b), suggesting that we might profitably discuss his reactions at the next session. One area that had not been specifically addressed was his ambivalence about parenthood, and it was recommended that we might focus on this issue during some further conjoint sessions.

Individual sessions with Lisa

One of the significant features of the multimodal approach is its flexibility. Lisa was negatively disposed to any systematic BASIC I.D. exploration, but preferred to address the issues of self-blame and low self-esteem. (A modality profile was constructed from her Multimodal Life History Questionnaire for my own enlightenment.) Lisa's penchant for self-abnegation seemed to stimulate acutely defensive and overcompensatory (aggressive, hypercritical) responses. The origin of her self-blame remained a mystery (she did not have the usual condemnatory, overcritical parents so often found in cases of this kind). Attempts, through imagery, to determine whether there were more subtle cues that had rendered her so vulnerable, met with no success. Unlike Al, Lisa was unresponsive to mental imagery excursions. Consequently, the mainstay of therapy was focused on 'cognitive restructuring', which endeavored to modify her dysfunctional beliefs (Beck, 1976; Ellis and Bernard, 1985).

Lisa was seen six times over a 9-week interval. In addition to cognitive therapy, her interpersonal style was a major focus for discussion in each of the meetings. It was impressed upon her that Al would always remain hypersensitive to actual or implied criticism, which he would tend to construe as an assault. I said, 'I am trying to attenuate this sensitive zone, but I know of no method that will eliminate it'. Role-playing was employed to teach Lisa an essentially supportive, non-pejorative, non-critical way of talking, disagreeing, questioning and making requests. The virtues of positive reinforcement were underscored; when in doubt, she was counseled to fall back on a principle of positive connotation (i.e. to search for the potentially caring, unselfish and prosocial motives behind others' actions). 'If you ever want to sabotage your marriage, just go ahead and criticize Al strongly, put him down as a man, and cast aspersions on his sexuality.' The sexual area per se required very little attention. Lisa stated that she was easily brought to orgasm, described herself as 'sensual and uninhibited', and reported 'no hang-ups in this area'. She was cautioned again to beware of 'coming on strong', of being critical and of making demands instead of stating her preferences. I inquired, 'Is this unfair? Are you being asked to do things or avoid things that are simply impossible in the long run?' 'Not if I want this marriage to succeed', she answered.

Conjoint sessions

Three additional meetings with the couple consolidated their gains and also addressed the question of whether they should consider having a child. Al summarized it as follows: 'I am still uncertain, but I think that's because I want guarantees. But I'm willing for us to stop using contraceptives for the next few months and see what happens.'

Follow-up

At the time of writing (11 months after terminating therapy), Al and Lisa have maintained their gains, and Lisa is in her final weeks of pregnancy. Amniocentesis showed that they can look forward to having a girl. Al described his feelings as 'terrified and thrilled'.

Commentary

It is always a pleasure to work with intelligent, motivated individuals who are not extremely disturbed. While the treatment of Al and Lisa called for no heroic, extremely innovative or intriguing tactics, it nevertheless illustrates the *technically eclectic* multimodal approach quite well. Let us now turn to a case in which my most ardent efforts and ministrations proved utterly futile.

An unsuccessful case

Description and background

Ed, aged 39, the president of a very successful manufacturing company, and Pam, aged 32, a former teacher but full-time homemaker, had been married 4 years and had a 1-year-old son. This was Ed's second marriage. His first marriage, which had lasted almost 5 years, had ended when he discovered that his wife had been having extramarital relations with one of his associates. Ed contended that premarital sex with his first wife had been 'fiery and passionate', but that soon after the wedding, his sexual interests had waned: 'I shut down sexually, not only to my wife, but to everyone.' Ed added, 'It's as if when I married, I took on the cloak of righteousness and ultrarespectability'. He described his sexual activity as confined to nocturnal emissions and very occasional masturbation (to images of lascivious women). 'The day my divorce was finally granted, I came to life sexually again and almost made up for lost time.' Ed claimed that during the course of the next 3 years, he dated many different women and was very active sexually. After he met Pam, they dated for 2 years and enjoyed 'passionate sex'. (According to Pam, while sex with Ed was 'just fine', it was never what she would term 'really passionate'. She explained, 'I always felt that Ed was holding back to some degree'.) Immediately after Ed and Pam married, the same pattern that had occurred with his first wife re-emerged – Ed's sexual desire rapidly disappeared.

Ed had been raised as a Roman Catholic and had thought of becoming a priest. Instead, he joined the Air Force, obtained a college degree and opened his own company. He was an energetic, tall, commanding individual; it was not surprising that within 5 years his company had grown into a successful enterprise. An only child, he described himself as having been 'close' to his mother and 'distant' from his father. When leaving home for the first time at age 18 to join the Air Force, he realized that he had experienced his mother as 'cloying and suffocating'. He added, 'Actually, time and distance led me to realize how much I hated her, what a totally self-centered, neurotic woman she always was, and how she had used me for her own ends and played me against my father'. Discussions concerning his hostility to his mother were unproductive. My attempts to mitigate his antipathy (compare Bloomfield and Felder, 1983) also proved futile. Ed insisted that while he was antagonistic toward his mother, he did not feel this way towards Pam or about women in general.

Pam, highly active in various fund-raising groups and extramural activities for women, was extremely successful in her own right. Most people regarded her as beautiful, elegant, refined, cultivated, sensitive and sexy. She claimed to be deeply in love with Ed, but stated that her patience was beginning to wear thin. She said that there had been no sexual contact whatsoever since she had become pregnant (a period of approximately 21 months). 'I don't know if I am doing something wrong, or if there is a deep-seated problem in Ed, or both.' Certainly, during two individual sessions with Pam followed by two conjoint meetings, I was unable to discern any untoward attitudes or behaviors emanating from Pam – except perhaps for (what I viewed as) her unusual tolerance and forbearance.

Treatment

I embarked on a course of systematic desensitization with Ed and soon reached the point in the hierarchy where he could envision having intercourse with Pam while feeling comfortable. I then recommended a series of sensate focus exercises. 'The drive's just not there, Doc!' I suggested that the couple rent an X-rated videotape and watch it together. Ed refused. 'I just wouldn't feel right watching something like that with Pam.' Perhaps he would view it alone and then, if sexually stimulated, have sex with Pam. He agreed, but instead of having sex with Pam, he masturbated. At this juncture, Ed was scheduled to attend a convention at a well-known holiday resort. Pam accompanied him in the hope that the ambience would 'turn him on'. They did in fact have sex on one occasion, but there was no carry-through.

I again examined to what extent Ed had performance anxiety, and I recommended Janson's (1981) book *Sexual Pleasure Sharing*. In exquisite detail, I discussed with Ed and Pam a variety of tactile practices in which they might engage and how they could do so in a completely relaxed and non-demanding manner. Initially, I thought we were on the verge of a breakthrough. For 3 weeks, they enjoyed several 'pleasure-sharing sessions', with Pam achieving orgasm each time orally or manually, and on three occasions they had intercourse. Nevertheless, Ed reverted to his former level – zero contact. 'I was pushing myself, Doc. I thought that perhaps if I bit the bullet I would get back the urge. To tell you the truth, I love Pam but she just doesn't make me the least bit horny.'

Ed's modality profile contained considerable problematic material in the cognitive and interpersonal areas. Consequently, I decided to switch from behavioral prescriptions and to dwell more heavily on his entire developmental history, to examine the formation of his values and attitudes, and to explore his obvious Madonna–whore complex. I even enlisted the aid of an extremely well-informed and enlightened Catholic priest who met first with Ed, and then with the couple, and endeavored to impart a non-moralistic outlook on sex. Shortly after the priest's interventions. Pam called to tell me that Ed had approached her two nights in a row and they had had 'excellent lovemaking'. Thereafter, it was back to base zero! Ed's reasoning? 'I really don't know, Doc. There's just something holding me back. I have no turn-off, I just don't have the desire for Pam.'

Pam scheduled an appointment with me. 'I want you to see Ed more often', she said, whereupon she focused on some of her own problems – the fact that 'there's an obedient little girl aspect to me', 'I want always to please people' and the realization that 'Ed is simply not turned on to me'. She mentioned that Ed was talking about having more children, an idea that was for her 'out of the question unless we function like a normal couple'. Pam underscored that the therapy had rendered Ed 'softer, kindlier, and able to apologize and admit when he is wrong'. However, there was virtually no improvement on the sexual front after 2 years of therapy. I then referred Ed to a colleague whose orientation is entirely different from my own. He is still in therapy at the time of writing. I referred Pam to a female therapist, whom I believe is assisting her in 'raising her consciousness'. A few days ago I saw Pam in a supermarket. She mentioned, en passant, that she is of the opinion that 'Ed is delighted that he was able to defeat you so completely'.

Commentary

Usually, when one is analysing unsuccessful cases, the benefits of retrospective wisdom enable one to distil clues pertaining to clinical omissions and commissions that might have made a difference. Second thoughts about the treatment format often lead to speculations about the reasons for failure and point to modifications or interventions that could have changed the outcome. At the very least, one emerges with some sense of specific interactive factors in the therapist-patient relationship or couple relationship that could account for the lack of significant change. With regard to Ed and Pam, considerable analysis and introspection have provided no leads, no clues, no post hoc indications that shed any light on this most frustrating case.

In general, unsuccessfully treated cases of sexual desire disorders display subtle (or blatant) internecine power struggles, encrusted hostility, gross incompatibility, malignant distrust or extreme demandingness (e.g. individuals who insist on penile-vaginal intercourse and refuse to consider what I have termed 'CNS lovemaking'). Successful cases are those in which the partners are willing to negotiate and compromise, and to expend mutual effort in developing an acceptable way of life.

Conclusion

The major strength of the BASIC I.D. approach for treating desire disorders is its thorough and systematic format. The multimodal emphasis on problem specification is in keeping with current psychiatric practice, in that it augments cognitive mastery, behavioral regulation and affective experiencing (Karasu, 1986). This orientation encompasses (1) specification of goals and problems; (2) specification of treatment techniques to achieve these goals and remedy these problems; and (3) systematic measurement of the relative success of these techniques. It is noteworthy that therapists with differing backgrounds and training have reported that multimodal assessment yields significant gains in diagnostic accuracy and enhances clinical creativity (Lazarus, 1985a).

Acknowledgment

In addition to the editors, I thank Allen Fay, MD, for providing critical comments and constructive suggestions.

References

BARLOW, D.H. and WINCZE, J.P. (1980). Treatment of sexual deviations. In: Leiblum, S.R. and Pervin, L.A. (Eds), *Principles and Practice of Sex Therapy*. New York: Guilford Press.

BECK, A.T. (1976). *Cognitive Therapy and the Emotional Disorders*. New York: International Universities Press.

BLOOMFIELD, H.H. and FELDER, L. (1983). *Making Peace with Your Parents*. New York: Random House.

ELLIS, A. and BERNARD, M.E. (Eds) (1985). *Clinical Applications of Rational-Emotive Therapy*. New York: Plenum.

FRIEDMAN, J.M. and HOGAN, D.R. (1985). Sexual dysfunction: Low sexual desire. In: Barlow, D.H. (Ed.), *Clinical Handbook of Psychological Disorders*. New York: Guilford Press.

GOLDENSON, R.M. (Ed.) (1984). *Longman Dictionary of Psychology and Psychiatry*. New York: Longman.

JANSON, W.J. (1981). *Sexual Pleasure Sharing*. Jaffrey, NH: Human Development.

KAPLAN, H.S. (1979). *Disorders of Sexual Desire*. New York: Simon & Schuster.

KARASU, T.B. (1986). The specificity versus nonspecificity dilemma: Toward identifying therapeutic change agents. *Am. J. Psychiatr.* **143**, 687–695.

KINSEY, A.C., POMEROY, W.B. and MARTIN, C.E. (1948). *Sexual Behavior in the Human Male*. Philadelphia: W.B. Saunders.

LAZARUS, A.A. (1976). *Multimodal Behavior Therapy*. New York: Springer.

LAZARUS, A.A. (1981). *The Practice of Multimodal Therapy*. New York: McGraw-Hill.

LAZARUS, A.A. (1984). *In the Mind's Eye*. New York: Guilford Press.

LAZARUS, A.A. (Ed.) (1985a). *Casebook of Multimodal Therapy*. New York: Guilford Press.

LAZARUS, A.A. (1985b). *Marital Myths*. San Luis Obispo, CA: Impact.

LAZARUS, A.A. (1986). Multimodal therapy. In: Norcross, J.C. (Ed.), *Handbook of Eclectic Psychotherapy*. New York: Brunner/Mazel.

LIEF, H.I. (1977). What's new in sex research? Inhibited sexual desire. *Med. Asp. Human Sex.* **2**(7), 94–95.

MASTERS, W.H. and JOHNSON, V.E. (1966). *Human Sexual Response*. Boston: Little, Brown.

MILLER, W.W. (1968). Afrodex in the treatment of impotence: A double-blind cross over study. *Curr. Therapeut. Res.* **10**, 354–359.

RECKLESS, J. and GEIGER, N. (1975). Impotence as a practical problem. In: Dowling, H.F. (Ed.), *Disease-a-month*. Chicago: Year Book Medical.

SOBOTKA, J.J. (1969). An evaluation of Afrodex in the management of male potency: A double blind cross over study. *Curr. Therapeut. Res.* **11**, 87–94.

ZILBERGELD, B. (1978). *Male Sexuality*. New York: Bantam.

ZILBERGELD, B. and ELLISON, C.R. (1980). Desire discrepancies and arousal problems in sex therapy. In: Leiblum, S.R. and Pervin, L.A. (Eds), *Principles and Practice of Sex Therapy*. New York: Guilford Press.

Chapter 17
Why I am an Eclectic (Not an Integrationist) (1989)

Issues revolving around the concepts of eclecticism and integration have become the mainstay of Lazarus's professional concerns. Since first publishing his brief remarks about the virtues of 'technical eclecticism' (see Chapter 7), Lazarus has written extensively on the subject. He has cautioned against 'unsystematic eclectics' who resort to hybrid coalitions of incompatible notions. He has endeavoured to explain that those who see eclecticism as the subjective selection of bits and pieces from divergent systems only add confusion to the equation. His emphasis on systematic, technical eclecticism, and his objections to theoretical integration, are clearly stated in this next chapter. He stresses that technical eclecticism is neither antitheoretical nor atheoretical – a view that many thinkers have mistakenly embraced.

Overview

Definitional and descriptive grounds may determine whether one favors eclecticism over integrationism, or vice versa. Beitman (1989) claims that eclectics merely gather bits of data, eschew general principles, advocate a conceptually limited stance, provide no model for therapeutic change processes, ignore the individual personality of the therapist, emphasize strict adherence to prescribed therapist behaviors in place of clinical flexibility and, in the final analysis, only administer simple or complex rote techniques. If any of these assertions were true, I would be a vociferous opponent of eclecticism.

The first point to be underscored is that eclecticism is not a single edifice or a unitary construct (Lazarus, 1988). Some eclectics wish to achieve a synthesis of seemingly divergent approaches; others may aspire to find synergistic combinations of various principles and procedures. Norcross

First published in 1989. Reproduced, with permission of Hobsons Publishing plc, from Lazarus, A.A. (1989). Why I am an eclectic (not an integrationist). *British Journal of Guidance and Counselling*, **17**, 248–258.

(1986) has shown that eclecticism is a complex set of structures and conceptions, comprising, among others, a transtheoretical stance, an atheoretical position, a synthetic integration, a structural–phenomenological approach, and one that is governed by a preferred theory but also borrows techniques from other orientations (*technical eclecticism*). Nevertheless, there is still a widespread and persistent tendency to regard 'eclecticism' as a single entity. Thus, Eysenck (1986, p. 378) stated that 'an eclectic point of view by definition means an anti-scientific point of view: eclecticism has always been the enemy of scientific understanding'. This misguided conclusion stems from the refusal to recognize that convergence, rapprochement, and data-based eclecticism can rest on the bedrock of rigorous scientific inquiry.

Haphazard, idiosyncratic eclecticism, wherein clinicians and theorists incorporate various ideas and methods on the basis of subjective appeal, should not be bracketed with systematic eclecticism which is based on years of painstaking research and clinical work (Lazarus, 1988). Unsystematic eclecticism is practiced by therapists who require neither a coherent rationale nor empirical validation for the methods they employ. Beitman (1989) contends that the form of integration selected, plus the strategies and tactics embraced, are largely determined by the individual personality of the therapist. But systematic prescriptive (technical) eclectics do not simply choose 'whatever feels right'. They base their endeavors on data from the three-fold impact of patient qualities, clinical skills and specific techniques (Chapter 15).

It may be helpful to distinguish between *eclecticism* and *fusionism* (Lazarus, 1988). Fusionists tend to blend what they regard as the most helpful notions and ingredients from two seemingly disparate orientations. Starting with a paper by French (1933), the proposed fusion that has received the greatest attention is the attempted consolidation of behavior therapy and psychoanalysis (e.g. Wachtel, 1977; Marmor and Woods, 1980; Goldfried, 1982; Arkowitz and Messer, 1984). More recent fusionists propose to integrate cognitive–behavior therapy and gestalt therapy (Fodor, 1987), and systems and psychodynamic methods (Kirschner and Kirschner, 1986). Any bimodal melding strikes me as arbitrary and capricious. If this trend proliferates, we can anticipate any number of strange bedfellows – Adlerian/Morita; Jungian/rational–emotive; primal/existential (the list is almost endless).

When a therapist identifies his or her orientation as 'eclectic', this conveys nothing of meaning or substance. Differences among various eclectics may surpass even rigid school adherents. The entire field of psychotherapy, I believe, needs to drop generic labels – eclectic, psychodynamic, behavioral, humanistic etc. – to be replaced by consensus on the specification of goals and problems, the specification of strategies to achieve these goals and remedy these problems, and the systematic measurement of the relative success of these different techniques and processes (Lazarus, 1989). If and when the foregoing have been achieved, we will be in a position to move toward integration. At this stage of our development, integrationism seems to me premature and strongly ill-advised.

My Main Objections to Integrationism

In their attempt to avoid ideological rigidity, integrationists try to meld disparate ideas and conflicting schools into a cooperative and harmonious whole. While the field of psychotherapy is in need of a unified theory – a superordinate umbrella that will reconcile divergent points of emphasis and blend multiple concepts and techniques into a coherent framework – the pre-paradigmatic level at which we presently function is far from this ideal. Meanwhile, to my way of thinking, it is a mistake to blend seemingly compatible theories from different schools in the hope of harnessing greater energy from each. The main problem here is that, upon close scrutiny, what seems to be interchangeable among different theories, often turns out to be totally irreconcilable. As Messer and Winokur (1981) have shown, 'in many instances what appears at first glance as commonality becomes, on closer inspection, so basic a difference that we wonder on what grounds therapists of different theoretical persuasions can meet' (p. 1547). In their search for common components, integrationists are apt to emphasize insignificant similarities and gloss over significant differences.

Hence my emphasis on *technical eclecticism* (e.g. Lazarus, 1967, 1971, 1989 and see Chapter 15), which looks mainly to social and cognitive learning theory (Bandura, 1986) for explanatory constructs, because its tenets are grounded in research and are open to verification and disproof. By operating from a consistent, testable, theoretical base, and then drawing on useful techniques from any discipline without necessarily subscribing to the theoretical underpinnings that gave rise to the techniques in question, one avoids the jumble, the melange and the subjective bias of theoretical eclecticism or integrationism. As London (1964) observed: 'However interesting, plausible, and appealing a theory may be, it is techniques, not theories, that are actually used on people. Study of the effects of psychotherapy, therefore, is always the study of the effectiveness of techniques' (p. 33). Technical eclectics regard the therapeutic relationship as the soil that enables the techniques to take root (Lazarus and Fay, 1984).

It is most important to bear in mind that one remains theoretically consistent when practicing technical eclecticism (compare Dryden, 1987). Moreover, while techniques are strongly emphasized, this is not to the detriment of a conceptual and theoretical appreciation of the issues at stake. Technical eclecticism, as many have erroneously assumed, is not antitheoretical or atheoretical. Unfortunately, some who call themselves technical eclectics have tended to select methods and styles that *they* individually consider appropriate, based on guiding principles that are at best questionable.

Thus, although I see technical eclecticism as an evolutionary step towards eventual integrationism, I maintain that it is extremely premature to embark on 'the conceptual synthesis of diverse theoretical systems' (Beitman, Goldfried and Norcross, 1989, p. 139). I fear that many of our current theories will suffer the same fate as Gall and Spurzheim's studies on phrenology. Their work on physiognomy and craniology was based on the most advanced neurology, physiology and psychology of their day, and their theories of personality were acclaimed by scientists, scholars, and professionals in France, Germany, Switzerland, Scotland, England, Ireland and North America. In 1823, *The British Phrenological Journal* was launched and, in 1838, the New York Institute of Phrenology founded *The American Phrenological Journal* which finally ceased publication in 1911 after its 124th volume. The theory and practice of phrenology enjoyed its greatest popularity in the 1850s. Today it is but a roost for charlatans.

Similarly, I predict that most of Freud's ideas about the unconscious will fall into total disrepute. So when integrationists start borrowing and blending psychoanalytic tenets with behavioral constructs, to which they may add ingredients from any number of additional systems, it seems to me that they emerge with a confused and confusing farrago, thus taking the field aeons away from the coherent super-organizing theory to which they aspire. And in place of the superstructure under whose umbrella theoretical differences can be subsumed and reconciled, we will be handed nothing but syncretistic muddles.

Is Technical Eclecticism Merely a Collection of Techniques?

Let it be understood that I am in favor of striving towards eventual integrationism. The fragmented, disparate methods and theories which presently characterize our field need to be replaced by a coherent, unified and consolidated body of knowledge. But, as already mentioned, I believe that premature integrationism will only defeat these ends. Can technical eclecticism point the way?

For me, the seeds of technical eclecticism were sown in 1964 at the Veterans Administration Hospital in Palo Alto, California, where I had treated three patients behind a one-way mirror for approximately 3 months. The audience comprised a wide array of professionals and graduate students from the Bay area who were interested in seeing the new methods and techniques of behavior therapy in action. It was the heyday of my behavioristic zeal, and I demonstrated the use of systematic desensitization based on relaxation, assertiveness training, homework assignments (especially graded in vivo excursions), stimulus control and various ancillary procedures. All three patients had proved unresponsive to traditional psychotherapy. One of them was bulimic and the excessive binging and purging presented a problem of considerable clinical urgency. My use of 'behavior therapy' resulted in a dramatic remission within 3 months – the patient was eating normally, gained much-needed weight and was discharged from the hospital. Improvement in the other two patients, though less dramatic, was also quite apparent. My colleagues who had observed the entire course of treatment were asked whether they could specify the processes to which the therapeutic benefits might be ascribed.

No agreement could be reached concerning the reasons for the undisputed gains. My own views at that time leaned heavily upon notions of counterconditioning and extinction. The views of my colleagues, however, were as different from my own as they were from one another's. Rich varieties of theoretical opinions were offered and sometimes generated heated arguments. It was obvious that the many (often divergent) theoretical positions could not all be correct. But it was possible that every theoretical explanation, including my own, could be false. Thus, I became convinced of the futility of post hoc theorizing, and felt that genuine progress would ensue if therapists were willing and able to spell out precisely what operations they perform with various patients. It then seemed logical to assume that all therapies may succeed, in so far as they do, for reasons other than the causal factors specified in their theories. This paved the way to accepting all empirically valid techniques without having to subscribe to their underlying theories, and a brief statement on technical eclecticism (Lazarus, 1967) was offered and subsequently elaborated (e.g. Lazarus, 1971 and see Chapter 15).

It is important to underscore that technical eclecticism is not merely a collection of techniques but operates within a consistent theoretical base, and endeavors to pinpoint various processes and principles. For example, one may start with Pavlovian conditioning and inquire whether 'associations and relations among events' (Rescorla, 1988) adequately explain the factors that shape and maintain human behavior. In accounting for the variance, it will soon be necessary to add additional concepts such as 'modeling and imitation', 'non-conscious processes', 'defensive reactions', 'idiosyncratic perceptions', 'metacommunications' and 'physiological thresholds' (non-conscious processes should not be confused with the reified unconscious mind, and defensive reactions are not synonymous with the mechanisms of defense – see Lazarus, 1989).

The point at issue is that a technically eclectic stance endeavors to use effective techniques from any persuasion, while also searching for guiding principles and concepts, and tries to avoid the needless addition or multiplication of explanatory principles. Unfortunately, most therapists are guided by selective perception and personal preference. The hallmark of technical eclecticism is the use of prescriptive treatments based on empirical evidence and client need, rather than theoretical and personal predisposition (Beitman, Goldfried and Norcross, 1989; Frances, Clarkin and Perry, 1984; Karasu, 1989). As Norcross (1986, p. 11) has noted: 'the promise of eclecticism is the development of a comprehensive psychotherapy based on a unified and empirical body of work'. I concur and would point out that, if technical eclecticism amounted to no more than a grab-bag of techniques, this objective would never be achieved.

Additional Problems with Integrationism

It is unfortunate that 'when instructed to select the type of integration that they practice, the majority of eclectics – 61% and 65% – chose theoretical integration' (Norcross and Grencavage, 1989). There is a seductive quality to the notion of being able to select the best elements from the different schools of therapy. As I have tried to emphasize, counselors who mingle techniques, while mixing theories and formats across various schools of thought, merely breed confusion worse confounded. But integrationism (as opposed to eclecticism) seems to fall into several other traps.

Semantic baggage and ill-defined labels

My form of technical eclecticism avoids vague terms and labels and strives for operational and quantifiable descriptions. For example, terms such as 'avoidance behavior', 'tachycardia' and 'negative self-statements' are preferred to 'neurosis' or even 'anxiety'. A *problem-focused approach* to therapy is favoured, one that expedites clinical decision-making and sidesteps the quagmire of putative complexes and other untestable intrapsychic entities. In the field of organic medicine, Weed (1968) was among the first to underscore the advantages of developing a problem-oriented record approach in place of the usual diagnostic labels. This emphasis upon problem specification was introduced into psychiatry by Hayes-Roth, Longabaugh and Ryback (1972).

But integrationists, even when discussing strategies, tend to converse at a level of meaningless abstraction. I refer you to Table 2 in Norcross and Grencavage (1989). One integrationist may state: 'I select my tactics from an interpersonal and humanistic perspective.' Another might say: 'I use a combination of systems and behavioral strategies.' It is my contention that these labels convey no clear meanings whatsoever. Some 'humanists' are very 'behavioral'. Some 'systems' theorists are 'cognitive', whereas others are 'psychoanalytic' or 'interpersonal'. Continued use of nebulous labels seriously hinders our efforts to achieve open inquiry, informed pluralism and intellectual relativism. In the final analysis, unless therapists stop hiding behind labels, and are able and willing to state precisely what they do, and don't do, to and with their clients at specific choice points (Lazarus and Messer, 1988), psychotherapy will continue to be guided by faith rather than fact.

The equality-of-outcomes myth

One of the spearheads of integrationism is the 'everybody has won' conclusion (Luborsky, Singer and Luborsky, 1975) which asserts that all psychotherapies are equally effective and that there are negligible differences among the different treatment methods. The work of Smith, Glass and Miller (1980) on meta-analysis has bolstered this idea, but it has been shown that the conclusions of meta-analysis can be extremely misleading (Wilson, 1982, 1985; Wilson and Rachman, 1983; Kendall, 1987). Wilson (1987) points out that despite numerous flaws and inaccuracies in Smith, Glass and Miller's (1980) study, its conclusions are widely cited in the literature. In fact, when selecting 'well-controlled' studies, Smith, Glass and Miller found behavior therapy to be significantly superior to psychodynamic and other verbal therapies. Subsequent meta-analyses (e.g. Andrews, Moran and Hall, 1983; Shapiro and Shapiro, 1983) have consistently concluded that behavior therapy is superior to all other forms of psychological treatment. This is not surprising because the range of techniques employed by present-day cognitive–behavioral therapists suggests that most are technically eclectic (Kendall, 1987). Yet Beitman, Goldfried and Norcross (1989) and Norcross and Grencavage (1989) insist that it has not been shown that one therapeutic approach is superior to another.

There are indeed many mildly or even moderately disturbed individuals who will probably respond equally well to any non-noxious therapy and therapist, and here, the equivalence conclusion will most probably be upheld. It is also probable that minimal outcome differences will emerge in a large sample of unselected patients which included: a fair number of pervasively anxious individuals; schizophrenics; substance abusers; sociopathic, antisocial and borderline personalities; encrusted obsessive–compulsive sufferers; impulse control and dissociative disorders; and various undifferentiated somatoform disorders.

But Beitman, Goldfried and Norcross's (1989, p. 140) statement that 'with few exceptions, there is little compelling evidence to recommend the use of one form of psychotherapy over another in the treatment of specific problems' flies in the face of the facts. There *are* specific treatments for specific problems and specific strategies for specific syndromes (Kazdin and Wilson, 1978; Lazarus, 1984). For example, the clinical reports on the use of specific techniques for overcoming sexual inadequacy provided by Wolpe and Lazarus (1966) were confirmed and amplified by Masters and Johnson (1970), and further refined by subsequent research (e.g. LoPiccolo and LoPiccolo, 1978; Leiblum and Pervin, 1980; Leiblum and Rosen, 1988). It is almost a quarter of a century since Paul

(1966), in treating public-speaking anxieties, showed significantly superior effectiveness for systematic desensitization compared to insight therapy and an attention–placebo group. With regard to the treatment of phobic disorders, Bandura (1986) cites numerous studies that show various modeling and exposure techniques to be superior to other treatments. But apart from phobias, tics, enuresis and habit disorders, there are also data pertaining to specific treatments of choice for certain anxiety and depressive disorders, stress-related difficulties, social skill deficits, obsessive-compulsive disorders, pain and other aspects of behavioral medicine (see Rachman and Wilson, 1980; Woolfolk and Lehrer, 1984; Hersen and Bellack, 1985; Barlow, 1988).

In treating agoraphobia, for instance, both flooding and exposure have been shown to be more effective than alternative psychological methods (Chambless, 1985; O'Leary and Wilson, 1987). In the psychological treatment of panic disorders, the methods of choice appear to be exposure combined with cognitive restructuring, and respiratory control training (Barlow, 1988; Clark, Salkovskis and Chalkley, 1985). (Biological psychiatrists tend to favor the use of antidepressant drugs and other psychotropic medications for the treatment of panic, but I am concerned about untoward side effects, and am unimpressed with the follow-up data once the drugs are discontinued.)

There are many other specific treatment effects that can be mentioned. Blackburn et al. (1981) confirmed the finding that cognitive therapy is superior to antidepressant medication for depressed outpatients (Rush et al, 1977). Exposure and response prevention have proved consistently effective in eliminating compulsive rituals (Grayson, Foa and Steketee, 1985; Mills et al, 1973). In the treatment of bulimia nervosa, there is much evidence to recommend the specific use of cognitive–behavioral procedures (e.g. Wilson and Smith, 1987; Fairburn, 1988). Additional examples can be cited, but perhaps the foregoing will suffice to challenge the notion that there are only a few instances in which one treatment can be recommended over another for specific problems.

In essence, technical efficacy is likely to suffer when one's attention is focused on the amalgamation of diverse ideologies. One good theory and a panoply of techniques can accomplish much more than the fusion and melding of different theories. In this regard, Beutler (1989) has marshaled cogent arguments against looking for or finding a suitably relevant and accepted integrated theory, and he presents a compelling case in favor of technical eclecticism.

Conclusion

To a large extent, this entire debate is an exercise in sophistry. As mentioned at the beginning of this chapter, so much hinges on conceptual, definitional, and semantic issues, that the positions reflected and advocated by Norcross and Grencavage, Beitman, Messer and myself, can be regarded as somewhat specious. In place of conceptual and terminological debates, I have tried to provide a systematic, comprehensive psychotherapeutic structure that pragmatically combines techniques, strategies and modalities, and addresses specific assessment and treatment operations. I have called this approach 'multimodal therapy' (Lazarus, 1976, 1985, 1989 and see Chapter 15) and offer it as a heuristic for diagnosing and treating discrete and interactive problems within and among each vector of 'personality'. It addresses such factors as 'client readiness' (compare Prochaska and DiClemente, 1986; Howard, Nance and Myers, 1987); spells out when to treat family systems rather than individuals, and vice versa; and emphasizes *goodness of fit* in terms of the patient's expectancies, therapist–patient compatibility and the selection of appropriate techniques. In essence, the multimodal orientation asserts that patients are usually troubled by a multitude of specific problems that should be dealt with by a similar multitude of specific treatments. Each area of a client's BASIC I.D. is addressed (B = *B*ehavior, A = *A*ffect, S = *S*ensation, I = *I*magery, C = *C*ognition, I = *I*nterpersonal relationships, D = *D*rugs/biological factors). It matters little whether we label the foregoing 'eclecticism' or 'integrationism'. Perhaps we can all agree that we need more rational and empirical bases in place of purely notional and speculative conceptualizations, and that more clearly operationalized and concretized therapist decision-making processes need to be articulated. To step out of the field of theology and enter the realm of science, psychotherapy must replace hermeneutic abstractions with testable operations.

References

ANDREWS, G., MORAN, C. and HALL, W. (1983). Agoraphobia: A meta-analysis of treatment outcome studies. Unpublished manuscript, University of New South Wales Medical School, Australia.

ARKOWITZ, H. and MESSER, S.B. (Eds) (1984). *Psychoanalytic Therapy and Behavior Therapy: Is Integration Possible?* New York: Plenum.

BANDURA, A. (1986). *Social Foundations of Thought and Action: A Social Cognitive Theory*. Englewood Cliffs, NJ: Prentice-Hall.

BARLOW, D.H. (1988). *Anxiety and its Disorders: The Nature and Treatment of Anxiety and Panic*. New York: Guilford.

BEITMAN, B.D. (1989). Why I am an integrationist (not an eclectic). *Br. J. Guid. Counsel.* **17**, 259-273.

BEITMAN, B.D., GOLDFRIED, M.R. and NORCROSS, J.C. (1989). The movement toward integrating the psychotherapies: an overview. *Am. J. Psychiatr.* **146**, 138-147.

BEUTLER, L.E. (1989). Differential treatment selection: The role of diagnosis in psychotherapy. *Psychotherapy* **26**, 271-281.

BLACKBURN, I.M., BISHOP, S., GLEN, A.I.M., WHALLY, L.J. and CHRISTIE, J.E. (1981). The efficacy of cognitive therapy in depression: A treatment trial using cognitive therapy and pharmacotherapy, each alone and in combination. *Br. J. Psychiatr.* **139**, 181-189.

CHAMBLESS, D.L. (1985). Agoraphobia. In: Hersen, M. and Bellack, A.S. (Eds), *Handbook of Clinical Behavior Therapy with Adults*. New York: Plenum.

CLARK, D.M., SALKOVSKIS, P.M. and CHALKLEY, A.J. (1985). Respiratory control as a treatment for panic attacks. *J. Behav. Ther. Exp. Psychiatr.* **16**, 23–30.

DRYDEN, W. (1987). Theoretically consistent eclecticism: Humanizing a computer 'addict'. In: Norcross, J.C. (Ed.), *Casebook of Eclectic Psychotherapy*. New York: Brunner/Mazel.

EYSENCK, H.J. (1986). Consensus and controversy: Two types of science. In: Modgil, S. and Modgil, C. (Eds) *Hans Eysenck: Consensus and Controversy*. London: Falmer.

FAIRBURN, C.G. (1988). The current status of the psychological treatments for bulimia nervosa. *J. Psychosom. Res.* **32**, 635–645.

FODOR, I.G. (1987). Moving beyond cognitive behavior therapy: Integrating gestalt therapy to facilitate personal and inter-personal awareness. In: Jacobson, N.S. (Ed.) *Psychotherapists in Clinical Practice*. New York: Guilford.

FRANCES, A., CLARKIN, J. and PERRY, S. (1984). *Differential Therapeutics in Psychiatry*. New York: Brunner/Mazel.

FRENCH, T.M. (1933). Interrelations between psychoanalysis and the experimental work of Pavlov. *Am. J. Psychiatr.* **89**, 1165–1203.

GOLDFRIED, M.R. (1982). *Converging Themes in Psychotherapy*. New York: Springer.

GRAYSON, J.B., FOA, E.B. and STEKETEE, G. (1985). Obsessive–compulsive disorder. In: Hersen, M. and Bellack, A.S. (Eds) *Handbook of Clinical Behavior Therapy with Adults*. New York: Plenum.

HAYES-ROTH, F., LONGABAUGH, R. and RYBACK, R. (1972). The problem-oriented medical record and psychiatry. *Br. J. Psychiatr.* **121**, pp. 27–34.

HERSEN, M. and BELLACK, A.S. (Eds) (1985). *Handbook of Clinical Behavior Therapy with Adults*. New York: Plenum.

HOWARD, G.S., NANCE, D.W. and MYERS, P. (1987). *Adaptive Counseling and Therapy*. San Francisco: Jossey-Bass.

KARASU, T.B. (1989). New frontiers in psychotherapy. *J. Clin. Psychiatr.* **50**, 46–52.

KAZDIN, A.E. and WILSON, G.T. (1978). *Evaluation of Behavior Therapy: Issues, Evidence and Research Strategies*. Cambridge, MA: Ballinger.

KENDALL, P.C. (1987). Cognitive processes and procedures in behavior therapy. In: Wilson, G.T., Franks, C.M., Kendall, P.C. and Foreyt, J.P. (Eds) *Review of Behavior Therapy: Theory and Practice*, Volume 11. New York: Guilford.

KIRSCHNER, D.A. and KIRSCHNER, S. (1986). *Comprehensive Family Therapy: An Integration of Systemic and Psychodynamic Treatment Models*. New York: Brunner/Mazel.

LAZARUS, A.A. (1967). In support of technical eclecticism. *Psychol. Rep.* **21**, 415–416.

LAZARUS, A.A. (1971). *Behavior Therapy and Beyond*. New York: McGraw-Hill.

LAZARUS, A.A. (1976). *Multimodal Behavior Therapy*. New York: Springer.

LAZARUS, A.A. (1984). The specificity factor in psychotherapy. *Psychother. Private Pract.* **2**, 43–48.

LAZARUS, A.A. (Ed.) (1985). *Casebook of Multimodal Therapy*. New York: Guilford.

LAZARUS, A.A. (1988). Eclecticism in behaviour therapy. In: Emmelkamp, P.M.G., Everaerd, W.T.A.M., Kraaimaat, F. and van Son, M.J.M. (Eds) (1988). *Advances in Theory and Practice in Behaviour Therapy*. Amsterdam: Swets & Zeitlinger.

LAZARUS, A.A. (1989). *The Practice of Multimodal Therapy*. Baltimore: Johns Hopkins University Press (updated paperback edition).

LAZARUS, A.A. and FAY, A. (1984). Behavior therapy. In: Karasu, T.B. (Ed.) *The Psychiatric Therapies*. Washington, DC: American Psychiatric Association.

LAZARUS, A.A. and MESSER, S.B. (1988). Clinical choice points: Behavioral versus psycho-analytic interventions. *Psychotherapy* **25**, 59-70.

LEIBLUM, S.R. and PERVIN, L.A. (Eds) (1980). *Principles and Practice of Sex Therapy*. New York: Guilford.

LEIBLUM, S.R. and ROSEN, R.C. (Eds) (1988). *Sexual Desire Disorders*. New York: Guilford.

LONDON, P. (1964). *The Modes and Morals of Psychotherapy*. New York: Holt, Rinehart & Winston.

LoPICCOLO, J. and LoPICCOLO, L. (Eds) (1978). *Handbook of Sex Therapy*. New York: Plenum.

LUBORSKY, L., SINGER, B. and LUBORSKY, L. (1975). Comparative studies of psychotherapies: Is it true that 'everybody has won and all must have prizes'? *Arch. Gen. Psychiatr.* **32**, 995-1008.

MARMOR, J. and WOODS, S.M. (Eds) (1980). *The Interface between the Psychodynamic and Behavioral Therapies*. New York: Plenum.

MASTERS, W.H. and JOHNSON, V.E. (1970). *Human Sexual Inadequacy*. Boston: Little, Brown.

MESSER, S.B. and WINOKUR, M. (1981). Therapeutic change principles: Are commonalities more apparent than real? *Am. Psychol.* **36**, 1547-1548.

MILLS, H.L., AGRAS, W.S., BARLOW, D.H. and MILLS, J.R. (1973). Compulsive rituals treated by response prevention. *Arch. Gen. Psychiatr.* **28**, 524-529.

NORCROSS, J.C. (Ed.) (1986). *Handbook of Eclectic Psychotherapy*. New York: Brunner/Mazel.

NORCROSS, J.C. and GRENCAVAGE, L.M. (1989). Eclecticism and integration in counselling and psychotherapy: Major themes and obstacles. *Br. J. Guid. Counsel.* **17**, 227-247.

O'LEARY, K.D. and WILSON, G.T. (1987). *Behavior Therapy: Application and Outcome*, 2nd edn. Englewood Cliffs, NJ: Prentice-Hall.

PAUL, G.L. (1966). *Insight versus Desensitization in Psychotherapy*. Stanford: Stanford University Press.

PROCHASKA, J.O. and DiCLEMENTE, C.C. (1986). The transtheoretical approach. In: Norcross, J.C. (Ed.) *Handbook of Eclectic Psychotherapy*. New York: Brunner/Mazel.

RACHMAN, S.J. and WILSON, G.T. (1980). *The Effects of Psychological Therapy*, 2nd edn. Oxford: Pergamon.

RESCORLA, R.A. (1988). Pavlovian conditioning: It's not what you think it is. *Am. Psychol.* **43**, 151-160.

RUSH, A.J., BECK, A.T., KOVACS, M. and HOLLON, S. (1977). Comparative efficacy of cognitive therapy and imipramine in the treatment of depressed outpatients. *Cogn. Ther. Res.* **1**, 17-37.

SHAPIRO, D.A. and SHAPIRO, D. (1983). Comparative therapy outcome research: Method-ological implications of meta-analysis. *J. Consult. Clin. Psychol.* **51**, 42-53.

SMITH, M.L., GLASS, G.V. and MILLER, T.I. (1980). *The Benefits of Psychotherapy*. Baltimore: Johns Hopkins University Press.

WACHTEL, P.L. (1977). *Psychoanalysis and Behavior Therapy: Toward an Integration*. New York: Basic Books.

WEED, L.L. (1968). Medical records that guide and teach. *N. Engl. J. Med.* **278**, 593-600.

WILSON, G.T. (1982). How useful is meta-analysis in evaluating the effects of different psychological therapies? *Behav. Psychother.* **10**, 221-231.

WILSON, G.T. (1985). Limitations of meta-analysis in the evaluation of the effects of psy-chological therapy. *Clin. Psychol. Rev.* **5**, 35-47.

WILSON, G.T. (1987). Clinical issues and strategies in the practice of behavior therapy.

In: Wilson, G.T., Franks, C.M., Kendall, P.C. and Foreyt, J.P. (Eds) *Review of Behavior Therapy*, vol. 11. New York: Guilford.

WILSON, G.T. and RACHMAN, S.J. (1983). Meta-analysis and the evaluation of psychotherapy outcome: Limitations and liabilities. *J. Consult. Clin. Psychol.* **51**, 54-64.

WILSON, G.T. and SMITH, D. (1987). Cognitive-behavioral treatment of bulimia nervosa. *Ann. Behav. Med.* **9**, 12-17.

WOLPE, J. and LAZARUS, A.A. (1966). *Behavior Therapy Techniques*. New York: Pergamon.

WOOLFOLK, R.L. and LEHRER, P.M. (Eds) (1984). *Principles and Practice of Stress Management*. New York: Guilford.

Chapter 18
The Case of George (1989)

Lazarus's multimodal approach to therapy is illustrated in the following case study. 'George', whose major complaint was agoraphobia and a host of attendant anxieties, was anything but 'easy'. He had consulted eight therapists before seeing Dr Lazarus, who claims that he did nothing especially noteworthy or in the least spectacular in his dealings with George. 'It was simply a matter of being willing to work really hard', he said. Nevertheless, this chapter neatly captures and conveys some interesting philosophies, and highlights Lazarus's interpersonal flexibility, inventiveness and dedication.

George was 32 years old when he first consulted me. A sallow, ungainly, overweight man, with reddish-brown hair that he nervously pushed from his forehead from time to time, George slouched in the chair and conveyed an aura of helplessness and hopelessness. His tattered sneakers, baggy corduroy pants and faded shirt helped to round out the picture of a most unhappy individual. The man made virtually no eye contact. His cousin, one of my colleagues, described him as 'a basket case, an emotional cripple'. His mother, with whom he lived, accompanied him to the first session and explained that 'George is very nervous and has always been delicate'. As family systems theorists would express it, mother and son were 'enmeshed'.

George complained of multiple fears, generalized anxiety, panic attacks, obsessions and compulsions, and many somatic difficulties, adding 'I guess I'm a bit of a hypochondriac'. He was agoraphobic and would not leave the house unless accompanied by his mother. He had 'panic attacks' when he attempted to do so. He had specific phobias of illness and death, as well as compulsive washing and cleaning rituals related to germ phobias. He traced the beginning of his major fears to age 17, when he had completed high school and was about to leave for college. 'But come to think of it', he added, 'I've sort of been afraid all my life.'

First published in 1989. Reproduced, with permission of F. E. Peacock, from Lazarus, A.A. (1989). The case of George. In: Wedding, D. and Corsini, R.J. (Eds) *Case Studies in Psychotherapy*, pp. 227–238. Itasca, IL: Peacock.

George was the only child of an alcoholic and abusive father and an exceedingly overprotective mother. As he was growing up, he felt alienated from his father and assumed the role of his mother's protector, often interceding when his father became nasty to her. His mother frequently said, 'I don't know what I'd do without you'. At age 17 he was in a quandary. He wished to go to college, but how could he abandon his mother? The eruption of his pervasive feelings of anxiety led his mother to collude with him. He was 'too sick to leave home'. Thus, the stage was set for a paradoxical relationship in which he functioned as his mother's protector while nurturing an infantile dependency on her. He managed to take courses in a community college near his home and almost earned a BA degree. It was about this time that he developed his agoraphobia.

When George was 20 his father died of a coronary thrombosis. His mother's widowed sister moved into the home, and George now assumed the role of a 'double protector'. He was the 'man of the house' who looked after his aunt and mother, even though he never left the house without his mother. He began complaining of numerous physical ailments and, together with his mother, made the rounds of various specialists who subjected him to extensive medical tests and examinations. When he was 21, his internist referred him to a psychoanalyst.

George was analyzed several times a week for over 6 years, at which point he concluded that he was not being helped. He was as fearful, phobic, compulsive and hypochondriacal as ever. His family situation remained unaltered; he had no friends, no independence, no mobility. He stayed at home, watched television, played cards with his aunt, went grocery shopping with his mother and spent many hours preoccupied with bathroom rituals. He then consulted a 'behavior therapist'. George liked this therapist and together they embarked on a course of in vivo desensitization, thought-stopping and progressive relaxation training. After 2 months George was able to go to and from the supermarket without his mother. On one of his excursions, he had what he called 'a panic attack'. (Careful questioning revealed that he did not suffer from a classic panic disorder but would generate high levels of anxiety.) Thereafter, he retreated back into the home, and terminated behavior therapy. Over the next few years his situation deteriorated. Frequent nightmares of dying added to his burdens. His compulsions increased in number, as did his psychosomatic complaints. He became prone to temper outbursts directed at his mother. By the time George was referred to me, he had received – in addition to his 6 years of psychoanalysis and his brief exposure to behavior therapy – drug therapy, electroconvulsive therapy, primal therapy, transactional analysis, transcendental meditation and existential therapy. He still continued to suffer from anxiety, panic, withdrawal, hypochondriasis, agoraphobia, other phobias, nightmares, temper tantrums, bathroom rituals and obsessive–compulsive habits.

An Indictment of the Field?

Before discussing the specifics of the multimodal approach that was employed with this client, let us first ask: What is happening here? Is this a 'resistant patient' who does not want to get better and who will fight desperately to maintain his status quo? Is he a 'therapist killer' who will continue making the rounds of various therapists and therapies to 'defeat' them and add more and more therapists and systems to his collection of 'trophies'? Is he a 'therapist shopper' whose way of life now requires him to 'be in therapy'?

Significantly, in his search for help, the client avoided the lunatic fringe. He consulted only reputable internists, psychiatrists, a most highly respected psychoanalyst and licensed clinical psychologists. Why then did he experience no relief from his suffering? How can his first therapist justify charging approximately $50 000 while prescribing more and more of the same over a period of 6 years, without any evidence of results? Since it is claimed that primal therapy is the only cure, which renders all other psychologic theories obsolete and invalid, we are entitled to ask why George was not cured by primal therapy. Similarly, did he just happen to see a poorly trained transactional analyst, a half-baked existentialist, an unqualified behavior therapist and so forth?

Some theorists and therapists stress commonalities among divergent therapeutic approaches. They seek similarities and point out where different systems and methods overlap. But to ignore differences is to overlook significant factors that may account for critical variance. Multimodal therapy obviously has much in common with many other psychotherapeutic approaches. Is there anything unique about it? Do multimodal therapists do anything that differs from what other psychotherapists do?

Proceeding Multimodally: How and Where to Intervene

By the time George consulted me, his morale was low. He was anxious, depressed and skeptical about embarking on yet another futile endeavor. Since his cousin, whom he respected, had recommended me so highly, he was willing to give me a try. Clearly, the challenge was to achieve his compliance and establish a liaison that would succeed where so many others had failed.

It requires considerable skill to motivate patients, to augment compliance and to diminish resistance. In the psychotherapeutic arena, innumerable clinicians have stressed the need to 'talk the patient's language', and to establish a level of rapport that transforms a respectful 'working alliance' into a truly cooperative venture. The importance of achieving and maintaining flexibility and versatility has been widely recognized, and it is well known that the manner in which specific techniques are explained and presented to clients will determine whether or not they are put to good use. Nevertheless, despite a vigilant lookout for individual and personalistic entry points, if the therapist's personality and approach do not mesh with the client's fundamental expectancies, compliance is unlikely to occur. In these cases, it seems best to refer the client to a more compatible resource rather than try to 'work through' the differences.

Although the points discussed in the foregoing paragraph all fall under the rubric of 'commonsense', they are often violated in clinical practice. Too many therapists are apt to approach patients in a stylized manner that may appeal to some and alienate others. Following Gordon Paul's admonition to determine, as precisely as possible, who or what is best for each individual, the major question was how to gain George's cooperation and compliance, especially in view of his many treatment failures. To smoke out possible oppositional tendencies, I asked him if he could visualize himself cooperating with me. 'What happens', I asked, 'if I say to you that there is a new rhythmic breathing exercise that I want to teach you in order to diminish certain feelings of anxiety? Can you picture yourself allowing me to teach it to you and then can you see yourself applying it, or do you see yourself opposing me?'. George said that he would probably be cooperative. I immediately stressed that 'probably' was not good enough and asked if I could depend on a 100 per cent level of cooperation for four sessions. 'By that time I will know if you will work with me or against me', I said.

I asked George to complete the Multimodal Life History Questionnaire and bring it to his second session. Thereafter, the modality profile shown in Figure 18.1 was drawn up.

This cursory profile lists some of George's main problems and provides a flexible 'blueprint' for establishing treatment goals and evaluating progress. After examining the profile and rereading his Multimodal Life History Questionnaire, it seemed best to start with his biological modality. I shared my reasoning with George by pointing out that he was obviously physically unfit, overweight, and that he spent most of his time sitting around the house and got very little exercise. I stressed the mind–body connection and pointed out that an immediate objective was to have him attain a higher level of physical fitness. I emphasized that someone who is in top physical shape was less likely to feel anxious, or suffer from psychosomatic afflictions and low self-confidence. We discussed the role of good nutrition and I underscored how George's current eating habits could have contributed to his emotional problems. He was informed: 'Step number one in your therapy therefore is going to have to be a vigorous physical training regimen. I also want you to put yourself in the hands of a qualified nutritionist.' When asked how he felt about the idea George said, 'It makes sense'.

Behavior	Avoidance
	Playing sick role
	Absence of mobility or involvement
	Bathroom rituals and other obsessive-compulsive acts
Affect:	Fear
	Panic
	Anxiety
	Impetuous anger
	Discouraged/depressed
Sensation:	Dizziness, palpitations
	Tremors
	Aches/pains
	etc.
Imagery:	Poor self-image
	Feuding parents
	Teasing from sadistic teacher
Cognition:	'Other people see me as odd and peculiar'
	'No woman would ever want to get close to me'
	Contamination notions
	Musts and shoulds
Interpersonal:	Timid, inept, hermit-like
Drugs/biology:	Regularly takes Valium (diazepam) 10 mg three times daily
	Eats junk foods
	Flabby, unfit, overweight

Figure 18.1. George's modality profile

I insisted that he undergo a medical checkup including a stress electro-cardiogram. 'I want to be sure there are no physical defects', I said, 'because I am going to push you like a coach or a trainer getting an athlete or a fighter ready for a big event.' It was evident from his responses on the Multimodal Life History Questionnaire that George very much wanted someone to 'take charge'. There are those therapists who would see this as a reason to maintain distance to avoid fostering his dependency. I regard this as a common error. If we are to gain compliance, it is usually necessary to respond in ways that match the client's expectancies. I was willing to take charge *initially* in order to mobilize adaptive behaviors.

For George, the image of an athlete being trained to win the 'big event' had metaphorical overtones that matched his needs and perceptions. On the Multimodal Life History Questionnaire, in response to the question, 'How do you think a therapist should interact with his or her clients?' George had stated that an effective therapist would be like a hard-driving Army sergeant who is very demanding, acts tough with his men, but who, deep down, has a soft spot for them. (His father had been 'an Army man' but was a *bad sergeant* – irresponsible and abusive without the redeeming virtue of basic compassion.) Upon inquiry, I learned that the least effective therapists were those who played a warm, avuncular role with him, and who were unconditionally supportive and empathic. It was obvious that if I was to gain George's cooperation, I would have to 'come on strong', or my 'multimodal therapy' would be as ineffective as his previous treatments to date.

The medical examinations revealed slightly elevated levels of cholesterol and triglycerides, and mild hypertension which reinforced the need for a change in his dietary and exercise habits. He joined his local YMCA and, while his mother knitted in the lobby, George started walking and then jogging around the track, and gradually added swimming and body-building exercises to his regimen. Cognitive relabeling was deliberately emphasized. Instead of viewing heart palpitations with alarm and terror, his new association was to be in terms of cardiac output, collateral circulation and cardiovascular activity.

Concurrently with his physical training and nutritional changes, he and I embarked on a systematic program of *exercises in coping imagery*. One of my fundamental assumptions is that, before people are capable of doing certain things in reality, they first need to rehearse them in imagery. If people cannot picture themselves performing an act, they will probably not be able to do it in real life. George had to cultivate pictures of himself moving about, dealing with people, having gainful employment, developing and maintaining friendships, dining in a restaurant, being at a party, making love to a woman and, of course, leaving his mother to her own devices.

We constructed a hierarchy of situations, starting with some simple desensitization images (walking half a block from his home and gradually increasing the distance until he could visualize himself driving to the supermarket without his mother, driving to the YMCA alone, and so forth), and then I added imaginary social situations (picnics, cocktail parties, formal dinners etc.). I had recommended group therapy as an adjunct to his individual therapy, but he remained opposed to this idea and I decided not to insist, as I was already requiring a great deal from him.

Within a few weeks George started looking trimmer and his jogging time and distance had increased. He still complained of endless pains, aches and imaginary afflictions. I consistently ignored these to avoid reinforcing his hypochondriacal tendencies. At times, I resorted to my 'tough sergeant' position and said: 'The next time I hear anything about your aches and pains, I will insist that you run around the track three times carrying 20 lb dumbbells!'

It was emphasized that he would invariably have 'anxiety attacks' from time to time, and that this would not mean that he or his therapy were failing. Rather, it was necessary to find a method of containing, checking and eliminating these attacks. In multimodal assessment, we use a method known as *tracking*. This consists of identifying the modality firing order, or sequence, that usually precedes negative affective reactions. George began to see that his anxiety attacks usually followed an S-I-C-B-C sequence. First, he would become aware of some minor *sensation* (a slightly rapid heartbeat, some facial tension), which would produce frightening *images* (fleeting scenes of operating rooms and intravenous drips), whereupon his *cognitions* would signal 'danger' and add a 'what if' to the equation (generally 'what if I become catastrophically ill?'), whereupon he would retreat *behaviorally* and intensify the vicious circle by dwelling on further *cognitions* ('something must be dreadfully wrong with me'). Having identified the order of events, effective measures could be prescribed. As soon as George experienced a negative sensation, he was instructed to use differential relaxation plus the breathing techniques he had been taught. He was then to switch to various success and coping images, while subvocally chanting, 'Keep cool, keep calm and cut the crap!'. He was told: 'Instead of retreating, withdrawing, and running away, hang in there and use your sequential antidotes.' (In therapy, 'talking a client's language' often adds up to tracking his or her modality firing order – identifying sequential proclivities – and intervening in the relevant modalities. An A-B-S-C sequence calls for a different treatment from a B-C-S-A or a C-S-A-B sequence, and so forth. *Tracking* is an important feature of multimodal assessment and therapy.)

George's cognitive modality was addressed first by stressing the unfortunate consequences of living by categorical imperatives (what Karen Horney called 'the tyranny of the shoulds', a point that Albert Ellis has elaborated on to offset abolustistic thinking). We also devoted several hours to general discussions such as the virtues of 'long-range hedonism' and his entitlements as a human being. A variety of techniques were employed including self-monitoring, imaginal and in vivo desensitization, thought-stopping, mental imagery exercises, role-playing, assertiveness training and the empty chair technique (mainly to complete 'unfinished business' with his late father).

George's bathroom rituals called for response-prevention (or response attenuation) because outcome data suggest that compulsive habits typically do not respond to other methods. Consequently, we agreed that instead of his spending 4 hours in the bathroom performing his rituals, George would reduce this time by half or forfeit watching his favorite TV shows for an entire week. Thereafter, bathroom time was systematically reduced from 2 hours to less than 45 minutes. (When the going got tough, George typically suggested that it might be better for us to explore the meanings behind his symptoms. I would react, using my 'tough army sergeant stance' by pointing out that he had devoted 6 years of his life to exploring meanings and dynamics to no avail.)

In addition to our individual sessions, I also had family therapy sessions with George and his mother and, on two occasions, I worked with George, his mother and his aunt. The two women, especially his mother, seemed to have vested interests in infantalizing George and in maintaining his dependence. Significantly, when George managed to come to his sessions without his mother (after therapy had been ongoing for about a year) her attitude towards me and the therapy became extremely antagonistic. She refused to have any further family meetings, nor would she meet with me individually. She went out of her way to persuade her son to terminate therapy.

One of George's major anxieties revolved around the theme of being alone in a strange city and becoming ill. I suggested that if this occurred he could go to the nearest hospital emergency room and see the physician on duty. I wanted George to realize that the world is full of benevolent others, better trained and more capable than his mother of ministering to him. Accordingly, I presented the following image: 'Imagine that you are all alone in Chicago. You become ill and are admitted to a hospital. . . . Now imagine the scene in the hospital. . . . The doctors are standing around your bed, talking to each other, helping you, curing you . . . .' At this point the client started hyperventilating, sobbing, retching and panicking.

This image had elicited a 'forgotten memory' that evoked a full-blown abreaction. When he finally calmed down, George recounted vivid memories of an event that took place when he was 7 years old. He was in a hospital after a tonsillectomy and was coming out of the anesthetic and could barely make out some people hovering around his bed. His mother was talking to someone about his frail and sickly make-up. 'I hope he lives to see 21!' she declared. I asked him why his mother labeled him 'frail and sickly', and he replied that perhaps it was because he was prone to infections and high fevers as a child, which is why the doctor had recommended a tonsillectomy. But his mother's alleged postoperative commentary about the delicate state of his health – 'I hope he lives to see 21!' – had left an indelible impression.

As we explored the repercussions of his mother's appraisals at subsequent sessions, it seemed probable that George's somatic and psychosomatic tendencies were related to her attitudes. His mother's alleged pronouncement as he was coming out of the anesthesia seemed to play a central etiological role. He had been (1) in a semiconscious, perhaps highly suggestible, postoperative (traumatic) condition, when (2) an authority (his mother) proclaimed him to be frail and sickly, which, in turn, (3) centered on self-deficiency as a focal guiding concept. There could be little doubt that these messages had predated and followed the incident in question.

Regardless of the accuracy of this brief analysis, George was obviously upset by these real or imagined events, and something had to be done to alleviate his distress. My initial entry point was to emphasize that *benevolent intent* on his mother's part lay behind all her actions, but that we were concerned with the consequences. Since in multimodal therapy, we try to cover the entire BASIC I.D. whenever feasible, the 'antidotes' listed in Figure 18.2 were prescribed.

As these recommendations were discussed and applied, other feelings and associations emerged. For example, George raised his ongoing fears about death, and he discussed his ambivalence, particularly his antagonistic feelings, towards his mother. (Incidentally, his preoccupation with death seemed to abate after a most fatuous discussion. George was born in 1942. I asked him where he had been in 1941. He answered, 'I wasn't born until 1942'. I then said, 'Oh, so you weren't alive in 1941 . . . . In other words, if you were not alive in 1941 or 1931 or 1921, it means that

Affect:	Try to generate anger or indignation in place of anxiety
Sensation:	Use 'directed muscular activity' – pound a pillow to assist with anger arousal
Imagery:	Picture yourself going back in a 'time machine' so that you, at age 32, can appear 'out of the future' to reassure yourself, at age 7, in that hospital bed. That little boy (you in the past) senses something special about that 32-year-old man (you at present) reassuring the child that he is not frail and sickly
Cognition:	Understand that your mother was projecting her own hypochondriacal and anxious feelings. There was no 'objective reality' to her remarks
Interpersonal:	Discuss your recollection of this event with your mother. Be confrontative, but do not attack or blame
Biology/drugs:	Keep working at improving physical fitness, and ask your doctor to gradually phase out the Valium

Figure 18.2 Multimodal recommendations for George

you were dead during those years. Tell me George, was 1941 or 1906 or 1873 a particularly bad year for you? Do you remember suffering and being dreadfully unhappy in 1920? So when you die, it will be back to 1941 or 1901 or 1899 for you. What's the big deal?')

One of the coping images that called for repeated rehearsal and role-playing was the scene in which George pictured his mother begging him not to leave home, not to desert her. By the time these issues were receiving attention, therapy had been continuing for about 15 months. Behaviorally, George had made impressive gains. He was willing and able to travel alone, and his numerous fears, avoidance, compulsions and generalized anxiety had diminished significantly. Nevertheless, George became discouraged by setbacks from time to time. I found that he remained unresponsive to reassurance, morale-building and empathic encouragement, but tended to snap out of his depression when I used paradoxical statements. For instance, I would say: 'Well, as everybody knows, you are frail and sicky, weak, defective, about to fall apart, living on borrowed time, inferior, contaminated, deficient. . . .' He would invariably laugh, utter some expletive, and therapy would proceed in a positive direction.

After 20 months of therapy, despite the improvements already mentioned, George was still living with his mother and her sister; he had not looked for gainful employment, and he had not gone out on a date (What remained of the father's life insurance policy and his army pension, plus the mother's and aunt's social security checks were the family's sole means of financial support.) Getting George to move out of his mother's home, to find a job and to start socializing with women proved extremely difficult. One of my many tactics was the use of 'coercive persuasion'. I painted an ugly verbal picture of him as a bewildered, nervous and incompetent recluse who would lapse into his pervasively neurotic ways if he refused to risk taking three essential steps: (1) gaining employment, (2) leaving home and (3) dating women. His mother did not make the task easy. She played on George's sense of obligation and managed to ignite his residual doubts and fears on several occasions. I was more persuasive and George prevailed. He moved into an apartment, obtained a job with a company that was willing to give him managerial training, started dating one of the secretaries, and finally lost his virginity at age 34.

Our meetings had tapered off at this stage and we met once every 6 or 7 weeks for 'booster' sessions. George suffered needless discouragement following minor episodes of anxiety, but was soon back on track. A year later, he had changed his job (he was earning a good salary plus commission from selling life insurance), had moved to a better apartment, was enjoying 'plenty of sex', had become an excellent squash player and was taking up horseback riding. On the negative side, he remained somewhat phobic – he avoided crowded places and insisted on having the aisle seat in a theatre. George still seemed overconcerned about his health and, while he looked remarkably trim and fit, seemed to be overly invested in health foods and jogging.

At a 4-year follow-up George's progress had been maintained. He was water-skiing and had made two trips to Acapulco. He was thinking about 'settling down and getting married'. He had won an award as 'insurance salesman of the year' and, during the follow-up interview, had the audacity to attempt to sell me life insurance! He was in training for the New York marathon and was 'trying out vegetarianism'. While he still reported some discomfort in crowded places, he claimed to be less claustrophobic. Interestingly, his mother's view of the treatment outcome was that her son had been corrupted. He overheard her telling someone that he used to be 'such a good boy', but by the time an 'awful psychologist' got through with him, he started running around with women and had picked up other bad behaviors. As for his relationship with his mother, he said: 'We get along just fine because she has learned to keep away from certain subjects.'

About 3 years later, I received a wedding invitation with a cursory note to the effect that he had moved to the midwest to assume a 'high powered' managerial position.

Discussion

It seems evident that certain constructive objectives were achieved. Some might argue, however, that these benefits may have come about with or without multimodal therapy. Others may even claim that positive gains had occurred in spite of therapy. When I first presented this case at a professional meeting shortly before George and I had terminated therapy, a psychoanalyst claimed that the treatment was 'superficial' and predicted that George had an inability to form mature attachments, and that this deficit would lead him to become seriously depressed within 3-5 years. But the client had undergone 6 years of psychoanalytic therapy with no discernible improvement!

Perhaps this client needed 6 years of psychoanalysis, plus behavior therapy, plus drug therapy, electroconvulsive therapy, primal therapy, transactional analysis, transcendental meditation and existentialism – all of which merely primed him to respond to whatever brand of therapy happened to be number nine. Would he have done as well if he had not received any previous treatment? How long would it have taken to achieve the noted improvements if he had initially received multimodal therapy? Had his previous therapy rendered George more accessible to multimodal therapy? On the contrary, I believe that more 'unlearning' was required to correct impressions that he had acquired from previous therapists, because similar cases who received no previous treatment have tended to respond rapidly to multimodal methods.

Reaching people whose excesses and deficits across the BASIC I.D. are rigid, encrusted and pervasive requires hard work, sensitivity, wisdom and talent. In most instances, the patient–therapist relationship provides the soil that enables the specific techniques to take root. I believe that the case of George exemplifies the way in which the 'right' relationship blended with the 'correct' techniques to produce a salubrious result.

Chapter 19
Emotions: A Multimodal Therapy Perspective (1990)

Arnold Lazarus and his son Clifford Lazarus co-authored this chapter when Lazarus Junior was completing his PhD in clinical psychology. It re-emphasises the main multimodal tenets but also puts them into a clearer perspective. The emphasis on affect or emotion, as a consequence of the reciprocal interactions among one's salient behaviours, sensations, images, cognitions, interpersonal relationships and biological inputs, points explicitly to necessary assessment and treatment processes. Their brief account of where they differ from theories of emotion, put forth by Freud, Wolpe and Ellis, enables one to understand clearly their multimodal viewpoint (whether or not one agrees or disagrees with it).

Introduction

According to the *Encyclopedia of Psychology* (Corsini, 1984), 'Emotions are a basic component of human experience, but their exact nature has been elusive and difficult to specify' (p. 427). *Webster's Ninth New Collegiate Dictionary* (1984) defines emotion as 'a psychic and physical reaction (as anger or fear) subjectively experienced as strong feeling and physiologically involving changes that prepare the body for immediate vigorous action'. Plutchik (1980a) listed 28 definitions of the word *emotion*. The psychological literature usually refers to three interlocking components that constitute emotion: (1) the subjective experience, (2) the physiological responses, and (3) the overt or expressive reactions. Lang (1977) proposed a tripartite conception of *fear* consisting of verbal, physiological and behavioral components, these three modes being only loosely correlated. In other words, reports of fear, visceral reactions and avoidance behaviors may converge, diverge or remain independent of each other.

Written with Clifford Lazarus and first published in 1990. Reproduced with permission from Lazarus, A.A. and Lazarus, C.N. (1990). Emotions: A multimodal perspective. In: Plutchik, R. and Kellerman, H. (Eds) *Emotion: Theory, Research and Experience*, vol. 5, *Emotion, Psychopathology and Psychotherapy*, pp. 195–208. © 1990, New York: Academic Press.

Emotions provide much leeway for different patterns of action, physiology and thought: there appears to be no predetermined linkage across all conditions.

The wide ranges, forms, intensities and varieties of emotion make classification extremely difficult. While no universal agreement on any single classificatory schema exists, Plutchik (1980a,b) has provided a model that is perhaps the most widely accepted. In essence, he has postulated eight primary emotions – fear, surprise, sadness, disgust, anger, anticipation, joy and acceptance – with each one varying in intensity. Thus, fear can range from mild apprehension to pervasive terror; sadness extends from pensiveness to abject grief. Plutchik also considers the positive-to-negative spectrum of emotions, as well as mixed emotions (e.g. disappointment may be considered a mixture of sadness and surprise).

In discussing the vicissitudes of emotion, the present chapter will first examine the debate between Zajonc and R.S. Lazarus regarding the relation between cognition and emotion, followed by the multimodal viewpoint of affective processes as a product of the reciprocal interaction of six 'modalities'. Thereafter, the main features of multimodal assessments and diagnostic processes will be reviewed. Finally, the modification of affect will be addressed, and the multimodal position will be compared with behavioral and cognitive–behavioral perspectives.

The Cognition–Emotion Debate

Over the last century, psychologists have debated how physiological (autonomic) arousal interacts with emotion-provoking events to produce the subjective reactions we call 'affective responses'. To this very day, the theories of William James (1890) and Carl Lange (1887) are cited, and the virtues and limitations of the James–Lange theory of emotion still receive prominent coverage, even in modern and sophisticated introductory textbooks (e.g. Crider et al., 1986). James contended that bodily changes precede the feeling state. His sequencing of events was perception–bodily changes–action–feeling. As Plutchik (1985) points out, 'this chicken-and-egg problem posed by William James has never been fully resolved' (p. 197). Nevertheless, the psychotherapeutic implications of this theory are that a combination of cognitive therapy (perception), biofeedback (sensation) and behavior therapy (action) is necessary for the thorough treatment of emotional disturbance. This point will be expanded in the sections dealing with multimodal assessment and therapy.

More recently, the relation between cognition and emotion has been hotly debated in the literature (R.S. Lazarus, 1982; Zajonc, 1980). Zajonc asserts that cognition and emotion are under the control of separate and partially independent psychological systems, and that emotions can occur prior to and independently of cognitive processes. R.S. Lazarus contends that all emotional responses are preceded by some basic cognitive processing (appraisal), and he implies that emotions are postcognitive.

Zajonc (1980) implies that emotional responses are synonymous with irrational, automatic and uncontrollable behaviors. He stated: 'People do not get married or divorced, commit murder or suicide, or lay down their lives for freedom upon a detailed analysis of the pros and cons of their actions' (p. 1972). It seems therefore that his view of cognitions is that they are necessarily rational, deliberate and controllable. In arguing for the primacy of affect, Zajonc appears to have overlooked the difference between cognitive content and cognitive process. The latter operates outside of awareness (Nisbett and Wilson, 1977). In essence, cognitive psychologists have demonstrated that personal meaning (semantic knowledge) influences perception, that the larger cognitive structure of semantic–network associations may be divided into subcomponents (schemas), and that the activation of schematic processing is automatic and uncontrollable (compare Collins and Loftus, 1975; Bower, 1981); and furthermore, the cognitive domain includes both explicit and implicit learning. Implicit learning is the acquisition and usage of formal rules through exposure to examples without being able to verbalize them.

More recently, Zajonc (1984) has suggested that emotional reactions are directly triggered by pure sensory inputs. With respect to this supposition, Bandura (1986) remarked: 'The notion that emotional reactions are triggered directly by pure sensory input requires decisive evidence that sensory experiences undergo no interpretation whatsoever. People select and process sensory information, rather than simply react to whatever impinges on their sense organs' (p. 198). To a large extent, it can be argued that the debate between Zajonc and R.S. Lazarus is partially a question of semantics, and that they both embrace limited definitions of cognition and emotion (compare Watts, 1983). Nevertheless, from a clinical standpoint, Zajonc's (1980) assertion that people cannot voluntarily control the emergence of emotion in response to affectively valent stimuli casts a pall on the psychotherapeutic endeavor. If this were indeed the case, how could even the most skilful therapists ever hope to alleviate depression or eliminate phobic responses? Zajonc's claim is essentially that once an object or situation (automatically and holistically) elicits an affective response (e.g. anxiety) it will always do so. In the face of such compelling evidence directly supporting the effectiveness of specific therapies in treating affective disturbances such as anxiety (e.g. Bandura, 1977, 1986) and depression (e.g. Rush et al., 1977), Zajonc's supposition of emotional inescapability is highly suspect.

A more serious problem for the clinician is posed by Zajonc's (1980) claim that 'affective judgments tend to be irrevocable' (p. 157). Again, by virtue of the unquestionable success of specific treatment techniques in remediating emotional disturbance – such as guided exposure (Matthews,

Gelder and Johnston, 1981) and participant modeling (Bandura, Adams and Beyer, 1977) for anxiety – Zajonc's assertion does not appear to be correct. By and large, the literature (e.g. Gordon and Holyoak, 1983; Bandura, 1986) tends to support R.S. Lazarus's position. As Plutchik (1985) underscored:

> One can put an electrode into the brain of a cat, or of a human being, and produce emotional reactions without a cognitive evaluation of an external event, and even without arousal. In such unusual cases, cognitive events are not primary, but such cases rarely occur in the course of life.... When emotions are conceptualized as complex chains of events with feedback loops, it is obviously possible to focus attention on any of the elements of the chain. One can then produce theories that emphasize, for example, the primacy of arousal, or the primacy of expressive behavior.
>
> (p. 199)

Psychotherapy and Emotion

In the clinical arena, each therapist's conceptualization of emotion will dictate the particular subset of the client's past and present activities that are viewed as significant and relevant, or as incidental and unimportant. Whereas current theory suggests that emotional phenomena are a product of complex interactions among several organismic systems – cognitive, behavioral, perceptual and neurophysiological/biochemical – few therapists are apt to invoke each of the foregoing in their understanding or treatment of emotional disturbance. Evidence of bias and selectivity is clearly apparent in the psychoanalytic, narrow behavioral and rational–emotive perspectives. A brief critique of each will be presented.

The psychoanalytic model of emotion had its origins in the 'cathartic technique' developed by Breuer and Freud (1895/1955), which led them to postulate that neurotic symptoms are based on buried conflictual feelings. In this context, affect was associated with the resurrection of traumatic memories; therapeutic reminiscences usually resulted in some emotional release. However, as Nichols and Efran (1985) pointed out, Freud 'was never really an emotivist – he was a seeker after memories, who saw affect as a signal that critical memories were being uncovered' (p. 48).

The earlier Freudian view of emotions had a distinctly hydraulic flavor. Feelings were conceptualized as entities that could be stored up and then drained off. Subsequently, in revising his theories, Freud presented affective responses in a totally different light. They were regarded as dispositions to action, calling for recognition and appropriate expression. Freud (1912/1959) emphasized that buried feelings must be made manifest, so that they could be dealt with directly (see 'Modifying Affect'). These views have permeated the entire field of psychodynamic thinking. Thus, Davanloo (1980) in his modern, short-term dynamic psychotherapy, places primary importance on 'releasing hidden feelings by actively working on and interpreting resistance or defenses' (p. 45).

The linguistic construction of psychoanalytic or psychodynamic viewpoints seems to eschew operational definitions, so we are provided with no specific ingredients that point to the essence of affective processes. All we have are generalizations to the effect that human behavior and feelings are motivated from within by various drives, impulses, needs and instincts. Moreover, the interplay of these dynamic forces usually operates below the level of consciousness. Thus, the closest one can get to a definition of emotion is that it is somehow associated with blocked drives. In short, circular explanations abound within this model. For example, a hostile impulse is inferred from the individual's overt (irascible) behavior and thereupon attributed to the influence of an underlying hostile impulse. Basically, the main criticism of this type of theorizing is that its 'explanations' have no predictive value and end up being pseudo-explanations at best (Bandura, 1986).

The kinds of techniques employed by different schools of therapy are usually consistent with their specific or implicit theories of emotion. Thus, for Wolpe (1958, 1982), anxiety (sympathetic nervous arousal) is the cornerstone of 'unadaptive behavior' and the therapist's primary task is to ferret out the stimuli to which needless fear has been conditioned and, subsequently, to break the stimulus–response connection by 'reciprocal inhibition' or counterconditioning at the level of the autonomic nervous system. In this system, cognitive factors are regarded as secondary, if not irrelevant, to the understanding and treatment of anxiety. By contrast, rational-emotive therapy (Ellis, 1962; Ellis and Bernard, 1985) regards thought and emotion as inextricably intertwined, with *thinking* as the trigger of emotional states. Without denying the biochemical or physiological substrate, Ellis regards virtually all emoting as the result of the individual's internal monologue of his or her beliefs: 'Much of our emoting takes the form of self-talk or internalized sentences....Then for all practical purposes the phrases and sentences that we keep telling ourselves frequently *are* or *become* our thoughts and emotions' (Ellis, 1962, p. 50).

The Affective Modality: The Multimodal View

We have alluded to the current viewpoint that emotional phenomena rest upon complex interactions among cognitive, behavioral, phenomenological, perceptual, biochemical and neurophysiological functions. We have also stated that few approaches to psychotherapy invoke each of the foregoing in understanding or treating emotional disturbance. The multimodal approach (e.g. Brunell and Young, 1982; A.A. Lazarus, 1976, 1985, 1986, 1989a,b and see Chapter 15) endeavors to cover this entire spectrum in assessment, and in treatment if indicated.

For example, to generate the emotion of anxiety most effectively (powerfully), you would do something, act in a certain way (behavior); you would conjure up negative thoughts and images pertaining to yourself (cognition and imagery) and to significant others (interpersonal); you would observe various unpleasant sensory concomitants (sensation); and all of this would, of course, rest on the substrate of your neurophysiological and biochemical processes (biology). For illustrative purposes, we have confined ourselves to one negative emotion, anxiety, but the same holds for any emotional reaction (affective response). Hence: 'The multimodal position is that *affect is the product of the reciprocal interaction of behavior, sensation, imagery, cognitive factors, and biological inputs, usually within an interpersonal context*' (A.A. Lazarus, 1986, p. 68). Of course, not all behaviors, sensations, images and cognitions produce emotions. As Plutchik (1985) stated, 'The whole complex process begins with a significant stimulus in the life of the individual' (p. 198). R.S. Lazarus (1982) ties emotion into a transaction between the individual and the environment that involves a cognitive evaluation about central life agendas related to survival.

Multimodal assessment employs the mnemonic BASIC I.D. as a template to ensure thoroughness and comprehensiveness by serving as a constant reminder that each of the seven modalities calls for equal attention during the diagnostic process: B = behavior, A = affect, S = sensation, I = imagery, C = cognition, I.= interpersonal and D. = drugs–biology. The acronym BASIC I.B. is less compelling than BASIC I.D. and, because most psychiatric interventions in the biological modality involve the use of *drugs* (mainly neuroleptics, antidepressants and anxiolytic agents), neurophysiological-biochemical processes are subsumed under the convenient 'drugs–biology' rubric. Nevertheless, it cannot be overemphasized that the 'D.' modality addresses *all* medical–physiological issues such as diet, sleep habits, exercise, central nervous system (CNS) pathology, and endocrine and metabolic disorders, in addition to the use of prescribed medications and recreational drugs.

A Brief Description of the BASIC I.D.

1. *Behavior* refers mainly to overt responses, acts, habits, gestures and reactions that are observable and measurable.
2. *Affect* refers to emotions, moods and strong feelings.
3. *Sensation* simply covers the five basic senses – seeing, hearing, touching, tasting and smelling. (Clinically, we are usually required to correct negative sensations – tension, dizziness, pain, blushing etc.)
4. *Imagery* includes dreams, fantasies and vivid memories; mental pictures; and the way people view themselves (self-image). 'Auditory images', recurring tunes or sounds, also fall into this category.

5. *Cognition* refers to attitudes, values, opinions and ideas (self-talk). (Clinically, in this modality, the main task is to identify and modify dysfunctional beliefs.)
6. *Interpersonal relationships* include all significant interactions with other people (relatives, friends, lovers, acquaintances etc.).
7. *Drugs-biology* includes drugs (self- or physician prescribed) in addition to nutrition, hygiene, exercise, and all basic physiological and pathological inputs. It involves the panoply of neurophysiological–biochemical factors that affect personality.

In addition to providing a template for comprehensive assessment, the BASIC I.D. represents the fundamental vectors of personality just as ABCDEFG represent the notes in music. Combinations of ABCDEFG (with some sharps and flats) will yield everything from 'Chopsticks' to Beethoven. Or consider the primary colors (red, yellow and blue) and how secondary colors (green, purple, orange etc.) are derived from various combinations thereof. Thus, our hypothesis is that virtually every human condition can be related to the BASIC I.D. – love, faith, ambition, hope, joy, optimism, pessimism, anticipation, disappointment, surprise, failure, awe, boredom, ecstasy, grief, assertiveness and so on. Let us discuss, for instance, how pessimism would be characterized multimodally.

Pessimism tends to result in restricted, somewhat withdrawn behaviors, similar to that often seen when depression is present. Sensations that feed into an aura of pessimism include muscle tension and many of the responses associated with anxiety, suggesting that pessimism combines certain aspects of anxiety and depression. (When depression predominates, hope is all but abandoned, whereas pessimism implies that hope has merely been attenuated.) The imagery modality clearly reveals a spate of pictures involving disappointment, failure or significant loss, which ties into negative cognitive appraisals, often typified by approach–avoidance conflicts. When the pessimism involves interpersonal reactions, these will be characterized by reluctance, hesitancy and the manifestations of discouragement. At the biological level, pessimism would be indistinguishable from mild anxiety and minor mood disturbances.

Clinically speaking, patients seek therapy because of disturbances in one or more areas of their BASIC I.D. Presenting complaints may be confined to one modality: 'I want to stop the bad habit of biting my nails' (behavior) or 'I feel depressed' (affect). The stated problem may involve two or more modalities: 'My shoulders and jaws feel tense' (sensation) and 'I also have these recurring nightmares and fantasies' (imagery); 'I can't decide what to do about my marriage' (cognitive and interpersonal) and 'My diabetes is out of control' (biological). Regardless of the entry point(s), the multimodal therapist will conduct a thorough assessment of the discrete yet interactive aspects of the entire BASIC I.D. While it is clinically expedient to divide the reciprocal interactive flux which typifies actual life events into the seemingly separate dimensions of the BASIC I.D., it must be underscored that we are always confronted by a recursive, continuous, multileveled living process. What we have outlined should not be viewed as a flat, static, linear representation.

By viewing *affect* as involving reciprocal interactions of behavior, sensation, imagery, cognition, interpersonal factors and biological processes, the multimodal clinician invokes a systematic and interactive way of working. For example, a patient states, 'I am anxious'. Most scientifically minded therapists would thereupon endeavor to obtain specific information about the so-called anxiety. What exactly is the patient experiencing? What appears to trigger these reactions? When did the problem start? What are the most relevant antecedents? What are the main physiological and behavioral concomitants? Who or what appears to be reinforcing (maintaining) the problem? What solutions have been sought? What has helped to ameliorate the problem? What is apt to exacerbate it? What are its main consequences?

A multimodal assessment would be more comprehensive than the foregoing. It would examine a wider range of the salient behaviors that seem to precipitate, accompany and follow the affective state. Moreover, apart from the presenting complaint (anxiety), a systematic and detailed inquiry would be conducted into other emotional reactions that may also be playing a role (e.g. depression, guilt and anger). The accompanying sensory responses would receive detailed attention (e.g. tension triggers and palpitations), as would the associated imagery and cognitive factors. The interpersonal network (e.g. family systems) would be closely scrutinized to determine to what extent the patient's significant others were deliberately or inadvertently nurturing the problem, and to what extent there were social-skill deficits. The 'D' modality (medicine–physiology) is, of course, fundamental. Indeed, in certain instances, most of the variance vis-à-vis a given individual's complaint of anxiety, depression or rage may be a function of a space-occupying intracranial lesion, endocrinological imbalance, simple caffeinism or a host of other medical disorders. Nevertheless, the multimodal position is that since we are unified dynamic entities, the entire BASIC I.D. is implicated in almost every situation.

The modality profile of a patient who complains of depression might contain the following interactive items:

1. *Behavior*: inertia, statements of self-denigration, fitful sleep pattern, and weepy and tearful.
2. *Affect*: depression (the presenting complaint), guilt and self-hate.
3. *Sensation*: diminished pleasure from food, sex and other sensory inputs; various somatic discomforts (aches and pains); easy fatigability.
4. *Imagery*: pictures of gloom and doom (past, present and future).

5. *Cognition*: considers self unworthy and deficient globally and particularly in specific areas (negative self-appraisal), anticipates indefinite suffering.
6. *Interpersonal*: sullen and uncommunicative.
7. *Drugs–biology*: fatigue possibly related to anemia or hypothyroidism (many medical conditions can result in depression, and a complete physical examination is recommended prior to the possible administration of antidepressants or other drug treatments).

Even when the diagnosis is predominantly organic, a multimodal inquiry will traverse the entire spectrum of the BASIC I.D. lest some crucial 'stone' be left unturned. Let us assume that a man is informed by his physician that he has diabetes and will require a special diet as well as injections of insulin. A multimodal practitioner would not simply let it go at that but would ask the following questions:

1. *Behavior*: How is this going to change his day-to-day activities? What will he do more of and less of? What will he stop doing? What will he start doing?
2. *Affect*: What affective impact will this have on him? Will he become anxious, depressed or angry?
3. *Sensation*: Will his sensory pleasures be compromised, especially when having to avoid foods that he had enjoyed and looked forward to in the past?
4. *Imagery*: Will his self-image or his body-image change significantly? What sorts of fantasies will he entertain about his bodily functioning? Will he dwell on images pertaining to his premature demise?
5. *Cognition*: How much factual information should he acquire about diabetes and its management? What implications will he apply to himself? What sorts of inferences will he draw? Will he be concerned about his potency?
6. *Interpersonal*: Will his interpersonal interactions be affected? Will others accept his condition? Will he become more gregarious, more withdrawn, or will there be no interpersonal consequences?
7. *Drugs–biology*: Will he comply with his doctor's prescriptions vis-à-vis his dietary habits, insulin injections, exercise regimen, rest and relaxation, and so forth?

The first published report of multimodal therapy (A.A. Lazarus, 1973; Chapter 9) argued that in the treatment of schizophrenia, once the florid symptoms are controlled by medication, the other six modalities should be addressed. The case history of a woman with a diagnosis of chronic undifferentiated schizophrenia was presented. Thirty-one interrelated problems were treated by the same number of specific techniques. It is hypothesized that, in addition to biological treatments, unless all significant problems in behavior, sensation, imagery, cognition and the interpersonal sphere are remedied, optimal recovery and durability of change are unlikely. Compliance with the medical regimen itself is likely to be compromised unless the other modalities are addressed (Fay, 1976). This is the essence of the multimodal treatment rationale and leads to an important question: How can one deal *directly* with affects or emotions?

Modifying Affect

Wilson (1984), in commenting on Rachman's (1981) paper on the primacy of affect, stated: 'If the affective or emotional system is largely inaccessible to cognitive influences, then means must be found for modifying affect directly' (p. 114). *We submit that one cannot deal with affects or emotions directly; this modality can be worked with only indirectly*. If asked to deal directly with behavior, we can readily show someone how to act, what to say, what to do, what not to do, and so on. The sensory modality is also open to direct stimulation – hear that, see this, touch that, smell this, taste that. In the interpersonal modality, direct interventions such as imitation, role-playing and modeling are among the most common. The biological modality lends itself to numerous direct interventions, drugs and surgery being the most obvious. Even inferred constructs such as cognitions and images are amenable to direct intervention: 'Think about it this way', 'Dispute that false belief', 'Imagine yourself sitting on a sandy beach', and 'Picture a big tiger running through the jungle'. But affect can only be reached through behavior, sensation, imagery, cognition, interpersonal relationships and biological processes.

One therapist declared: 'I arouse emotions directly by getting my patients to get in touch with their childhood agonies and then scream out loud.' Our answer was that loud screaming (behavior) coupled with painful memories (images and cognitions) could probably stimulate affective responses in many people, but that this was still a matter of generating emotion via the other modalities. Another therapist stated that she evoked powerful emotional reactions by encouraging her patients to pound foam rubber cushions while yelling at the top of their lungs. We pointed out that pounding and yelling are specific behaviors, not emotions. Even if emotions are specifically generated by electrodes implanted into the brain, this is still *indirect* (i.e. via stimulation at the biological level). While many people seek the counsel of professional psychotherapists because they *feel* bad (i.e. they are experiencing negative affective states such as anxiety, depression and guilt), the multimodal position is that the most elegant and thorough way of reducing anxiety, lifting depression and assuaging guilt is to eliminate the specific and interrelated dysfunctional patterns of behavior, sensation, imagery, cognition, interpersonal relationships and possible biological processes.

Final Commentary

As alluded to earlier in this chapter, each therapist's explicit or implicit theory of emotions will determine which methods and techniques he or she employs in clinical practice. Carl Rogers did not regard emotion as the reciprocal interaction of the six modalities specified throughout this chapter, and his treatment arsenal rested exclusively upon a single technique – genuine, concrete, empathic reflection of the client's affective reactions and emotionally charged statements. This stands in sharp contrast to the training, shaping, modeling, rehearsing, disputing and restructuring that typifies most multimodal interventions or, for that matter, the more limited cognitive–behavioral strategies.

To cite another example, Eysenck (1986), in the face of all evidence to the contrary, insists that 'Pavlovian conditioning... is the principal causal factor in neurotic disorders, and that Pavlovian extinction is the basis of all curative efforts' (p. 378). Thus, by downplaying cognitive factors while underscoring the role of hypothalamic, subcortical reflexes, he subsequently claims that 'flooding and response prevention' (Rachman and Hodgson, 1980) achieve an 80–90 per cent cure in people suffering from compulsive handwashing. Follow-up data are not provided. Indeed, our own follow-ups suggest that unimodal treatment is seldom durable. While response prevention and flooding may be necessary treatments for compulsive handwashers, we find that they are often insufficient and are best supplemented with additional interventions that tend to prevent relapse (e.g. family-systems interventions and communication training, the modification of dysfunctional beliefs, the acquisition of sensory skills – such as relaxation – to offset future stresses, coping imagery techniques to enhance a sense of self-confidence and social-skills training whenever specific person-to-person deficits are in evidence).

To reiterate a significant point, even if certain conditions (e.g. some schizophrenias and depressive conditions) tend to emanate primarily from the genetic diathesis and fall under the rubric of neurophysiological–biochemical processes, the multimodal position on emotion is that an assessment of behavior, sensation, imagery, cognition and interpersonal relationships will nevertheless play an integral role in any holistic understanding and therapy of the afflicted individual. Emotional pain and dysfunction are likely to be durably assuaged and improved to the extent that salient problems in each discrete but interactive modality are addressed.

This is the essence of the multimodal position vis-à-vis emotions and the resolution of emotional dysfunction. It stands in marked contrast to the more limited views espoused by Freud, Wolpe, Ellis, Rogers and Eysenck.

Its major hypothesis is that durable results are in direct proportion to the number of specific modalities deliberately invoked by any therapeutic system. Thus, in pointing to the necessary and sufficient conditions for stable treatment outcomes, the major thesis is that comprehensive therapy at the very least calls for the correction of irrational beliefs, deviant behaviors, unpleasant feelings, intrusive images, stressful relationships, negative sensations and possible biochemical imbalance. To the extent that problem identification (diagnosis–assessment) systematically explores each of these modalities, whereupon therapeutic intervention remedies whatever deficits and maladaptive patterns emerge, treatment outcomes will be positive and long lasting.

Acknowledgments

We appreciate the incisive criticisms of Dr Windy Dryden, Dr Allen Fay and Dr Robert Plutchik.

References

BANDURA, A. (1977). *Social Learning Theory*. Englewood Cliffs, NJ: Prentice-Hall.

BANDURA, A. (1986). *Social Foundations of Thought and Action: A Social Cognitive Theory*. Englewood Cliffs, NJ: Prentice-Hall

BANDURA, A., ADAMS, N.E. and BEYER, J. (1977). Cognitive processes mediating behavioral change. *J. Personal. Soc. Psychol.* **35**, 125–139.

BOWER, G.H. (1981). Mood and memory. *Am. Psychol.* **36**, 129–148.

BREUER, J. and FREUD, S. (1955). Studies on hysteria. In J. Strachey (Ed. and Trans.), *The Standard Edition of the Complete Works of Sigmund Freud*, vol. 2. London: Hogarth Press. (Original work published 1895.)

BRUNELL, L.F. and YOUNG, W.T. (Eds) (1982). *Multimodal Handbook for a Mental Hospital: Designing Specific Treatments for Specific Problems*. New York: Springer.

COLLINS, A.M. and LOFTUS, E.F. (1975). A spreading-activation theory of semantic processing. *Psychol. Rev.* **82**, 407–428.

CORSINI, R.J. (Ed.) (1984). *Encyclopedia of Psychology*. New York: Wiley.

CRIDER, A.B., GOETHALS, G.R., KAVANAUGH, R.D. and SOLOMON, P.R. (1986). *Psychology*, 2nd edn. Glenview, IL: Scott, Foresman.

DAVANLOO, H. (1980). A method of short-term dynamic psychotherapy. In: H. Davanloo (Ed.). *Short-term Dynamic Psychotherapy*. New York: Jason Aronson.

ELLIS, A. (1962). *Reason and Emotion in Psychotherapy*. Secaucus, NJ: Lyle Stuart.

ELLIS, A. and BERNARD, M.E. (Eds) (1985). *Clinical Applications of Rational-Emotive Therapy*. New York: Plenum.

EYSENCK, H.J. (1986). Consensus and controversy: Two types of science. In: Modgil, S. and Modgil, C. (Eds). *Hans Eysenck: Consensus and Controversy*, pp. 375–398. London: Falmer.

FAY, A. (1976). The drug modality. In: Lazarus, A.A. (Ed.). *Multimodal Behavior Therapy*, pp. 65–85. New York: Springer.

FREUD, S. (1959). The dynamics of transference. In: Riviere, J. (Ed.). *Collected Papers*,

Vol. 2. New York: Basic Books. (Original work published 1912).

GORDON, P.C. and HOLYOAK, K.J. (1983). Implicit learning and generalization of the 'mere exposure' effect. *J. Personal. Soc. Psychol.* **45**, 492–500.

JAMES, W. (1890). *Principles of Psychology*. New York: Holt.

LANG, P.J. (1977). Physiological assessment of anxiety and fear. In: Cone, J.D. and Hawkins, R.P. (Eds) *Behavioral Assessment: New Directions in Clinical Psychology*, pp. 178–195. New York: Brunner/Mazel.

LANGE, C. (1887). *Uber Gemutsbewegungen: Eine Psycho-physiologische Studie*. Leipzig: Thomas.

LAZARUS, A.A. (1973). Multimodal behavior therapy: Treating the BASIC ID. *J. Nerv. Mental Dis.* **156**, 404–411.

LAZARUS, A.A. (1976). *Multimodal Behavior Therapy*. New York: Springer.

LAZARUS, A.A. (Ed.) (1985). *Casebook of Multimodal Therapy*. New York: Guilford Press.

LAZARUS, A.A. (1986). Multimodal therapy. In: Norcross, J.C. (Ed.), *Handbook of Eclectic Psychotherapy*, pp. 65–93. New York: Brunner/Mazel.

LAZARUS, A.A. (1989a). *The Practice of Multimodal Therapy*. Baltimore: The Johns Hopkins University Press.

LAZARUS, A.A. (1989b). Multimodal therapy. In Corsini, R.J. and Wedding, D. (Eds). *Current Psychotherapies*, pp.a 503–544. Itasca, IL: Peacock.

LAZARUS, R.S. (1982). Thoughts on the relation between emotion and cognition. *Am. Psychol.* **37**, 1019–1024.

MATTHEWS, A.M., GELDER, M.G. and JOHNSTON, D.W. (1981). *Agoraphobia: Nature and Treatment*. New York: Guilford Press.

NICHOLS, M.P. and EFRAN, J.S. (1985). Catharsis in psychotherapy. A new perspective. *Psychotherapy* **22**, 46–58.

NISBETT, R.E. and WILSON, T.D. (1977). Telling more than we can know: Verbal reports on mental processes. *Psychol. Rev.* **84**, 231–259.

PLUTCHIK, R. (1980a). *Emotion: A Psycho-evolutionary Synthesis*. New York: Harper & Row.

PLUTCHIK, R. (1980b). A language for the emotions. *Psychol. Today* 68–78.

PLUTCHIK, R. (1985). On emotion: The chicken-and-egg problem revisited. *Motiva. Emotion* **9**, 197–200.

RACHMAN, S.J. (1981). The primacy of affect: Some theoretical implications. *Behav. Res. Ther.* **19**, 279–290.

RACHMAN, S.J. and HODGSON, R. (1980). *Obsessions and Compulsions*. Englewood Cliffs, NJ: Prentice-Hall.

RUSH, A.J., BECK, A.T., KOVACS, M. and HOLLON, S.D. (1977). Comparative efficacy of cognitive therapy and pharmacotherapy in the treatment of depressed outpatients. *Cogn. Ther. Res.* **1**, 17–31.

WATTS, F.N. (1983). Affective cognition: A sequel to Zajonc and Rachman. *Behav. Res. Ther.* **21**, 89–90.

WILSON, G.T. (1984). Fear reduction and the treatment of anxiety disorders. In: Wilson, G.T., Franks, C.M., Brownell, K.D. and Kendall, P.C. (Eds), *Annual Review of Behavior Therapy*, Vol. 9, pp. 95–131. New York: Guilford Press.

WOLPE, J. (1958). *Psychotherapy by Reciprocal Inhibition*. Stanford, CA: Stanford University Press.

WOLPE, J. (1982). *The Practice of Behavior Therapy*, 3rd edn. New York: Pergamon.

ZAJONC, R.B. (1980). Feeling and thinking: Preferences need no inferences. *Am. Psychol.* **35**, 151–175.

ZAJONC, R.B. (1984). On the primacy of affect. *Am. Psychol.* **39**, 117–123.

Chapter 20
Can Psychotherapists Transcend the Shackles of Their Training and Superstitions? (1990)

We end with a stimulating, provocative, amusing and insightful article that captures 'the essential Arnold Lazarus' as he challenges the psychotherapy establishment. Some of his personal and professional values emerge more fully than in any of his other writings. 'I expected to receive a lot of heat when this article was published', he said, 'but to my surprise I received a large number of requests for reprints, and I received congratulatory letters from many colleagues and from students here and abroad.' His views of how counsellors and therapists should be supervised and trained will hit home in many quarters.

In 1960, shortly after obtaining my PhD, I was introduced to a man a few years my senior with whom I soon became close friends. He was a remarkable fellow – extremely bright, thoughtful, personable, warm, caring, quick witted, with a great sense of humor. The man was multi-talented. He acted in plays and even directed some; he sang, played the clarinet, and conducted choirs; he was well-read, a mine of information and a great raconteur. He was athletic and played a mean game of tennis. He was very much a family man. His wife was a musician and an elementary school teacher, and their four children (who ranged in age from 12 to 2 when I first met them) were clearly the beneficiaries of a loving home life. Professionally, the man of whom I speak was a dentist. The fact that he found the time to conduct a busy dental practice in addition to all the foregoing activities was quite remarkable.

What has this to do with the subject of this paper? Please bear with me. The friend about whom I am writing was an absolute natural when it came to understanding people and showing genuine warmth, wisdom and empathy. He was, in fact, an incredibly excellent therapist. As his wife

First published in 1990. Reproduced with permission from Lazarus, A.A. (1990). Can psychotherapists transcend the shackles of their training and superstitions? *Journal of Clinical Psychology*, 46, 351–358. © 1990, Clinical Psychology Publishing Co. Inc., Brandon, Vermont, USA. It is based on an invited address delivered to the Annual Convention of the American Psychological Association in New Orleans, August 1989.

once pointed out, 'Everyone comes to him with their troubles. He should have been a psychologist'. For 5 or 6 years, he was very much my friend, confidant and, at times, my 'therapist'. Discussing problems with my friend was amazingly therapeutic. When a close relative of mine needed therapy, I advised her to speak to my friend rather than seek the counsel of a professional therapist. Looking at me askance, she said: 'You want me to go to a dentist?' and, then, in my opinion, she made the mistake of consulting a well-known psychiatrist.

Around 1965, my friend started taking various psychology courses for credit, and by the late-1970s he had obtained a PhD in social and clinical psychology. He quipped: 'Now when a patient comes to me I ask, "Is your problem mental or dental?".' But getting to the main point of this paper, as my friend learned more and more psychology, as he took more and more readings and courses in assessment, diagnosis and treatment, it seemed to me that his natural skills eroded. I have not forgotten the shock I felt when, shortly after my mother had died, I was opening my heart to him, to this naturally great therapist. By this time, he had collected many credits in abnormal psychology, assessment, counseling methods and personality development. Instead of the deep understanding, support, empathy and basic caring that I had come to expect, I received a string of platitudes and labels.

The formal psychology and psychotherapy courses he had received were tantamount to taking a can of spray-paint to an artistic masterpiece. In my estimation, he never regained those special and natural relationship skills that were so prominent before he underwent formal psychotherapeutic training and, although today he is actively engaged in psychological research, especially that which pertains to pain management, and teaches psychology courses on the faculty of a school of medicine and dentistry, I continue to regard him as a prime example of someone who remains mutilated by his training and attendant superstitions.

The impact of my friend's professional trajectory led me to ponder whether formal training causes most of us to undergo a similar truncation of our helpful inborn capacities. What about me? How much deadwood, superstition, plain rubbish and stylized professionalism had I incorporated from all my readings, professors and supervisors? Plenty! I arrived at that conclusion after a good deal of introspection and self-monitoring. In an effort to free myself from the shackles and superstitions of my own professional background and training, I developed a systematic, eclectic and integrated approach that I call 'multimodal therapy' (see Lazarus, 1989). But let me not get ahead of myself.

We like to think that our backgrounds in psychology, our understanding of learning theory, personality dynamics, group processes, tests and measurements, cognitive assessment, our many hours of research, supervision and personal therapy, will enable us to develop penetrating insights, a great fund of knowledge and a broad repertoire of effective methods. And this should be so. Our professional training should enhance the caring attitudes, humanistic respect and the accurate perceptions that probably attracted us to a career in psychological therapy in the first place. I submit that more than not, however, this is wishful thinking.

I have been a psychotherapy trainer for more than 25 years. How many naturals have I damaged or destroyed? What is there in the way we train our students that could possibly undermine rather than enhance their intuitive skills? One answer is obvious. If we teach them to stop behaving like human beings, like 'menschen', and instead adopt the trappings of professionalism, we will have rendered a great disservice.

In a book entitled *Becoming Psychiatrists*, Light (1980), a bright and perceptive sociologist, provided 'An inside account of the psychiatric residency with implications for both the profession and the patient' (p. x). Dr Light sat in, observed and reported. He provided verbatim dialogues in which trainees were taught to be combative, sarcastic and aggressive to their patients and made pejorative interpretations. Residents in psychiatry saw their mentors being highly critical, often ridiculing their patients. Light observed that, 'the residents and psychiatrists observed were surprisingly unaware of their own personality and its effects on others, despite the great attention to this very phenomenon' (p. 173). I know several treatment settings in which therapists are taught to use an attack mode in the name of 'therapeutic banter'. Therapeutic for whom?

I think that one of the main shackles under which many therapists labor comes from the almost endless list of proscriptions that we are handed. The word 'boundary' is often touted in this context. Going back to my internship, I remember accepting a client's kind offer to drive me to the nearest bus stop (which was not out of his way) because I did not have my car that day. When this came to my supervisor's attention, I was given a very long lecture on the need to recognize boundary issues and to realize that what I had done would diminish my therapeutic power. He was wrong. Please let it be understood that I fully realize that there are some clients from whom one would not accept a handshake and to whom one would not give the time of day. But, on the other hand, I can point to clients for whom breaking bread, taking walks, going to concerts, or playing tennis had a most salubrious impact. Indeed, on occasion, I have obtained cogent information on a tennis court, or at a dinner party, that probably never would have come to light in my consulting room. With most of our clients, it is unfortunate that we have time to see them only within the confines of our offices and seldom gain first-hand information about their behaviors in other settings.

My teachers handed me a long list of do's and don'ts – actually many more don'ts than do's. I think I have broken all the rules with excellent results. However, I strongly subscribe to some absolute don'ts. I do not think that sexual contact with clients can be constructive, and any form of exploitation and humiliation cannot be condoned.

I am put out by supervisors who give strong negative feedback to trainees. 'That was a mistake!' 'You should have waited for the patient to talk about her mother before you started addressing her sibling rivalry.' In such matters, how can anyone be so sure what the right thing is? I like to provide my students with various options, without labeling them correct or incorrect. I don't think we can argue too strongly for humility and tentativeness given the current state of our basic knowledge. Organic medicine has at least a 300-year jump on us. Let's see what the most prominent doctors believed and practiced in the seventeenth century. An illuminating example is found in the treatment given to King Charles II. At 8 o'clock on Monday morning, February 2, 1685, King Charles was being shaved in his bedroom. With a sudden cry he fell backward and had a violent convulsion. Fourteen physicians were called in to treat the king. 'As the first step in treatment the king was bled to the extent of a pint from a vein in his right arm. Next his shoulder was cut into and the incised area "cupped" to suck out an additional eight ounces of blood. After this homicidal onslaught the drugging began. An emetic and a purgative were administered, and soon after a second purgative. This was followed by an enema . . . repeated in two hours. . . For external treatment a plaster of Burgundy pitch and pigeon dung was applied to the king's feet' (Brown, 1934, p. 9). Seventeenth century medicine added several additional exotic remedies including 'forty drops of extract of human skull', 'dissolved pearls' and 'bezoar stone'. When 'his serene majesty's strength seemed exhausted', a mixture of 'Raleigh's antidote, pearl julep, and ammonia was forced down the throat of the dying king' (Brown, 1934, p. 10).

I think that, in years to come, people will regard many of our present-day psychotherapeutic methods, ideas, theories, strategies and procedures in the same way that we now view medical practice in the seventeenth century. I must admit that I have already come across many current psychotherapeutic practices that have the same impact on me as reading about poor King Charles.

One of the major shackles, I believe, is that graduate students soon find themselves being socialized into one or another school of thought. Most graduate programs usually embody a dominant school or ideology. Even at Rutgers University, where our course catalogues tout the clinical PsyD program as decidedly eclectic, about 90 per cent of students gravitate to 'the psychodynamic track', whereas in our clinical PhD program, over 90 per cent of students are 'behavioral'. Apart from the schism that exists within our own Psychology Building, a rather different set of skills is being taught some 200 yards away at the Medical School. And if you cross the Raritan River, you will find the School of Social Work, where over 300 MSWs are ground out each year, most of whom hang up a shingle and practice 'psychotherapy' according to yet another drummer. And in yet another facility, Rutgers also turns out EdDs who can obtain a state license to practice their brand of psychotherapy.

Over the years, I have pointed out that when somebody decides to become a Jungian analyst, or a gestalt therapist, or a devotee of transactional analysis, or any other delimited school of thought, this is entirely due to subjective factors. It is not because the person has carefully studied scores of therapeutic systems and found the one that has the best outcome and follow-up statistics. 'I am a Jungian, or a Freudian, or an Adlerian either because this is what was taught to me; or this orientation helped me personally; or this rings the right bells for me.' Personally, I have no objection to strict school adherence if the practitioner knows when to refer out. 'I am an existential analyst, but since you need assertiveness training and desensitization, I recommend that you see Dr X.T. Smitherton, who is a first rate cognitive–behavior therapist.' In the real world, the foregoing scenario has two chances – both happen to be zero!

Colby (1964) opened his chapter on 'Psychotherapeutic processes' for the *Annual Review of Psychology* with two words: 'Chaos prevails'. Frank (1971) expressed similar sentiments in the *American Journal of Psychotherapy*. What is our profession like today? Do we now have greater consensus and agreement, more order, convergence, integration, rapprochement, and data-based treatments of choice? Colby and Frank, in 1964 and 1971, respectively, considered the field chaotic at a time when the melange of family systems proponents had yet to be fully heard (e.g. Minuchin, 1974; Whitaker, 1975; Bowen, 1978; Framo, 1982). The term 'chaotic' was used even before the psychoanalysts realized that they had to shorten their act, which yielded 'Time Limited Therapy' (Mann and Goldman, 1982); 'Short Term Dynamic Psychotherapy' (Malan, 1976; Davanloo, 1980); 'Short-term Psychotherapy' (Sifneos, 1979); and 'Time Limited Dynamic Psychotherapy' (Strupp and Binder, 1984). Moreover, the respective Colby and Frank surveys appeared quite a number of years before the demise of Milton Erickson and his subsequent deification. I won't even attempt to reference the innumerable writings that deal with Ericksonian hypnosis, strategic and paradoxical interventions, metaphors and third ear abstractions. Suffice it to say that when Erickson (1964) wrote about 'The confusion technique in hypnosis' he little realized how his followers would lend new impetus to the meaning of confusion if not bewilderment.

Herink (1980) published a book that addresses more than 250 different therapies, and Corsini (1981) edited 'a disciplined, authoritative, concise, and readable account of 64 major innovative approaches to psychotherapy in current use'. These 64 major innovative approaches were drawn from a list of more than 240 different systems of psychotherapy. If I were asked to write a review of the current psychotherapeutic scene, I would find the words 'chaos prevails' far too euphemistic, and I probably would add terms such as 'confusion', 'derangement', 'turmoil' and 'bedlam'. Have you ever really listened to a debate between two or more therapists who are strongly committed to a particular orientation? Meaningful discourse and intelligent communication between and among them does not seem possible. It is like asking a fundamentalist who understands only English to debate with a nuclear physicist who understands only Chinese (see Fay and Lazarus, 1982).

Of the hundreds of psychotherapeutic schools in existence, not to mention the army of eclectics and integrationists who have formed innumerable additional treatment melanges, no school, method, system or orientation is clearly superior. With many problems and conditions, the results are roughly equal whether you ask your clients to lie on a couch, jump up and down, scream, meditate, examine their dreams, use guided imagery, challenge their faulty thinking, be more assertive, delve into their past or contemplate their navel.

It is widely known that many people who suffer from physical, emotional or psychological complaints recover without treatment. Some problems remit spontaneously. The simple passage of time takes care of several types of depressions, specific fears, conflicts and uncertainties. Changes in the environment (fortuitous events) can turn one's life around. Thus, some people go through a difficult phase in which they feel conflicted, confused, frustrated and unhappy, but within a few weeks, or after a couple of months, they manage to come to terms with their problems and feel better. Meanwhile, they may have consulted a therapist, changed their eating habits or joined a health club, and they will most probably give credit for their improvement to these events. In fact, the events may have had little or nothing to do with it.

Unfortunately, virtually anyone can invent a form of therapy, give it a name, apply it to people, and find that some appear to derive benefit. Let's say that someone decides to recommend back rubs, followed by rhythmic breathing combined with loving thoughts about humanity and calls it 'biolove therapy'. According to several scientific predictions, approximately 40 per cent of neurotic patients who undergo this or almost any other regimen will report beneficial results. Unless a therapist works with very difficult problems (e.g. sociopathy, schizophrenia, severe depression, rigid obsessions, extreme impulse control disorders), he or she is likely to find that at least 40 per cent of patients will be measurably improved after 10-12 sessions. Thus, even unskilful therapists are guaranteed a fair amount of gratification if they wish to take credit for these gains. And this is where much of the superstition seems to come from. It appears that the 40 per cent of people who respond positively to whatever form of psychotherapy they receive have made life difficult for the 60 per cent who require highly specific, focused and systematic treatment.

Howarth (1989), a British psychologist, recently stated: 'Psycho-therapists do not know what they are doing and cannot train others to do it, whatever it is' (p. 152). But I think there is a way for psychotherapists to know pretty much what they are doing and to train others to do it quite effectively.

First, let me stress that even some of our leading figures in research and therapy have drawn false conclusions from meta-analytic studies (e.g. Smith, Glass and Miller, 1980) and have concluded incorrectly that few specific techniques are uniquely effective in treating particular disorders. There is in fact a wide array of specific treatments for specific problems. In treating bipolar disorders, therapists who rely entirely on insight, desensitization, hypnosis, psychodrama, sensory retraining, body aware-ness and do not recommend a trial of lithium carbonate are probably open to a serious malpractice suit. Compulsive rituals seem to respond best to response prevention and exposure-based treatments (Grayson, Foa and Steketee, 1985), and just about everything else probably will prove as effective as the enemas that King Charles received. There are specific treatments of choice for certain anxiety and depressive disorders, stress-related difficulties, phobias, bulimia nervosa, social skill deficits, pain and other aspects of health psychology (e.g. Woolfolk and Lehrer, 1984; Bandura, 1986; Wilson and Smith, 1987; Barlow, 1988; Fairburn, 1988).

It is interesting just how specific one can get. For starters, let's take a widespread and seemingly innocuous technique – relaxation training. Relaxation training can make certain asthmatics worse. Relaxation tends to decrease sympathetic autonomic nervous activity. Therefore, asthmatics with small airway obstruction are likely to find the effects of relaxation countertherapeutic because these airways tend to dilate in response to sympathetic autonomic nervous stimulation. Relaxation is indicated only for those asthmatic patients with large airway obstruction (see Lehrer et al., 1986).

Another area in which the use of certain relaxation therapies must be monitored carefully is diseases of the gastrointestinal tract. Instances of bleeding and hyperacidity have been cited, and it has been shown that sud-den changes in autonomic activity, especially decreases in sympathetic tone via muscular relaxation, can lead to a phenomenon known as 'parasympa-thetic rebound', which causes nausea and headaches (DeGood and Williams, 1982). Back in the 1960s (Lazarus, 1965), I published a paper that underscored the negative effects that some people have when they are undergoing relaxation therapy, and almost 20 years later, Heide and Borkovec (1983) coined the term 'RIA' – relaxation-induced anxiety (see Lazarus and Mayne (1990) for an account of methods for overcoming RIA).

The point that I am emphasizing, however, is that there are some high-ly specific, technical facts of which all practicing therapists should be cog-nizant. In the same way that any physician worthy of his or her license would not prescribe tomato juice rather than an antibiotic for a streptococcus infection, I think that psychotherapists of all persuasions first need to be able to agree on specific treatments of choice for particular problems, and they need to stop offering weak and ineffective methods when powerful and effective procedures are available.

Next comes a much-needed awareness that we are still in the dark ages and cannot afford to shut out any potentially useful methods or ideas. And yet I think it is a dreadful mistake to try to blend the best ideas from humanistic theories with psychoanalytic theories, existential theories, trait theories, and so on. As a member of SEPI (Society for the Exploration of Psychotherapy Integration), I am most interested in sifting through compatible and incompatible theories and techniques, in search of a responsible and systematic eclecticism and eventual integrationism. I have tried to provide a framework, a template, that can facilitate a systematic way of deciding who or what is best for each individual client (Lazarus, 1989).

In recent years, a distinctive point of departure has become evident. There is a vast difference between exploring problems and treating them. As I perceive it, greater emphasis needs to be placed upon the process of solution rather than the origin of problems. Let me emphasize again that such problems as phobias, tics, habit disorders, compulsions, obsessions, chronic pain, pervasive anxiety, panic, depression, sexual dysfunctions, eating disorders and stress-related difficulties call for specific methods of learning, unlearning and relearning, as well as biologically based interventions at times. They usually will not respond to introspection, even in the hands of a most astute observer with boundless empathy, genuineness and concern. The quest is to enable clients to develop a variety of life skills. The focus of my own professional endeavors has been to develop a multimodal, systematic, comprehensive and technically eclectic model to achieve these objectives.

I'd like to end this paper with a quote from Karl Popper (1985):

> What we should do, I suggest, is to give up the idea of ultimate sources of knowledge, and admit that all human knowledge is human: that it is mixed with our errors, our prejudices, our dreams, and our hopes: that all we can do is to grope for truth even though it is beyond our reach. We may admit that our groping is often inspired, but we must be on our guard against the belief, however deeply felt, that our inspiration carries any authority, divine or otherwise.　(p. 57)

References

BANDURA, A. (1986). *Social Foundations of Thought and Action: A Social Cognitive Theory*. New York: Holt, Rinehart & Winston.

BARLOW, D.H. (1988). *Anxiety and its Disorders: The Nature and Treatment of Anxiety and Panic*. New York: Guilford Press.

BOWEN, M. (1978). *Family Therapy in Clinical Practice*. New York: Jason Aronson.

BROWN, E.G. (1934). *Milton's Blindness*. New York: Columbia University Press.

COLBY, K.M. (1964). Psychotherapeutic processes. *Annu. Rev. Psychol.* **15**, 347-370.

CORSINI, R.J. (Ed.) (1981). *Handbook of Innovative Psychotherapies*. New York: John Wiley.

DAVANLOO, H. (1980). A method of short-term dynamic psychotherapy. In: Davanloo, H. (Ed.), *Short-term Dynamic Psychotherapy*, pp. 43-71. New York: Jason Aronson.

DeGOOD, D.E. and WILLIAMS, E.M. (1982). Parasympathetic rebound following EMG biofeedback training: A case study. *Biofeedback Self-Regul.* **7**, 461-465.

ERICKSON, M.H. (1964). The confusion technique in hypnosis. *Am. J. Clin. Hypnos.* **6**, 183-207.

FAIRBURN, C.G. (1988). The current status of the psychological treatment for bulimia nervosa. *J. Psychosom. Res.* **32**, 635-645.

FAY, A. and LAZARUS, A.A. (1982). Psychoanalytic resistance and behavioral nonresponsiveness: A dialectical impasse. In: Wachtel, P.L. (Ed.), *Resistance: Psychodynamic and Behavioral Approaches*, pp. 219-231. New York: Plenum Press.

FRAMO, J. (1982). *Family Interaction: A Dialogue between Family Therapists and Family Researchers*. New York: Springer.

FRANK, J.D. (1971). Therapeutic factors in psychotherapy. *Am. J. Psychother.* **25**, 350-361.

GRAYSON, J.B., FOA, E.B. and STEKETEE, G. (1985). Obsessive–compulsive disorder. In: Hersen, M. and Bellack, A.S. (Eds), *Handbook of Clinical Behavior Therapy with Adults*, pp. 133-165. New York: Plenum Press.

HEIDE, F.J. and BORKOVEC, T.D. (1983). Relaxation-induced anxiety: Paradoxical anxiety enhancement due to relaxation training. *J. Consult. Clin. Psychol.* **51**, 171-182.

HERINK, R. (1980). *The Psychotherapy Handbook: The A-Z Guide to More than 250 Different Therapies in Use Today*. New York: New American Library.

HOWARTH, I. (1989). Psychotherapy: Who benefits? *Psychologist* **2**, 150-152.

LAZARUS, A.A. (1965). A preliminary report on the use of directed muscular activity in counter-conditioning. *Behav. Res. Ther.* **2**, 301-303.

LAZARUS, A.A. (1989). *The Practice of Multimodal Therapy* (updated). Baltimore: Johns Hopkins University Press.

LAZARUS, A.A. and MAYNE, T.J. (1990). Relaxation: Some limitations, side-effects, and proposed solutions. *Psychotherapy* **27**, 261-266.

LEHRER, P.M., HOCHRON, S.M., McCANN, B., SWARTZMAN, L. and REBA, P. (1986). Relaxation decreases large-airway but not small-airway asthma. *J. Psychosom. Res.* **30**, 13-25.

LIGHT, D. (1980). *Becoming Psychiatrists*. New York: Norton.

MALAN, D.H. (1976). *The Frontier of Brief Psychotherapy*. New York: Plenum Press.

MANN, J. (1973). *Time-limited Psychotherapy*. Cambridge, MA: Harvard University Press.

MANN, J. and GOLDMAN, R. (1982). *A Casebook in Time-limited Psychotherapy*. New York: McGraw-Hill.

MINUCHIN, S. (1974). *Families and Family Therapy*. Cambridge, MA: Harvard University Press.

POPPER, K.R. (1985). *Popper Selections*. Princeton, NJ: Princeton University Press.

SIFNEOS, P. (1979). *Short-term Psychotherapy and Emotional Crisis*. Cambridge, MA: Harvard University Press.

SMITH, M.L., GLASS, G.V. and MILLER, T.I. (1980). *The Benefits of Psychotherapy*. Baltimore: Johns Hopkins University Press.

STRUPP, H.H. and BINDER, J.L. (1984). *Psychotherapy in a New Key: A Guide to Time-limited Dynamic Psychotherapy*. New York: Basic Books.

WHITAKER, C. (1975). Psychotherapy of the absurd: With a special emphasis on the psychotherapy of aggression. *Family Proc.* 14, 1–16.

WILSON, G.T. and SMITH, D. (1987). Cognitive–behavioral treatment of bulimia nervosa. *Ann. Behav. Med.* 9, 12–17.

WOOLFOLK, R.L. and LEHRER, P.M. (Eds) (1984). *Principles and Practice of Stress Management*. New York: Guilford Press.

Books by Arnold Lazarus

1966   WOLPE, J. and LAZARUS, A.A. (1966). *Behavior Therapy Techniques*. Oxford: Pergamon Press.

1971   LAZARUS, A.A. (1971). *Behavior Therapy and Beyond*. New York: McGraw-Hill.

1971   RUBIN, R.D., FENSTERHEIM, H., LAZARUS, A.A. and FRANKS, C.M. (Eds) (1971). *Advances in Behavior Therapy*. New York: Academic Press.

1972   LAZARUS, A.A. (Ed.) (1972). *Clinical Behavior Therapy*. New York: Brunner/Mazel.

1975   LAZARUS, A.A. and FAY, A. (1975). *I Can If I Want To*. New York: Morrow. (New York: Warner Books, Paperback, 1977.)

1976   LAZARUS, A.A. (1976). *Multimodal Behavior Therapy*. New York: Springer (with contributors).

1978   LAZARUS, A.A. (1978). *In The Mind's Eye: The Power of Imagery for Personal Enrichment*. New York: Rawson. (New York: Guilford Press, Soft Cover, 1984.)

1981   LAZARUS, A.A. (1981). *The Practice of Multimodal Therapy*. New York: McGraw-Hill.

1985   LAZARUS, A.A. (Ed.) (1985). *Casebook of Multimodal Therapy*. New York: Guilford Press.

1985   LAZARUS, A.A. (1985). *Marital Myths*. San Luis Obispo, California: Impact Publishers.

1987   ZILBERGELD, B. and LAZARUS, A.A. (1987). *Mind Power*. Boston: Little, Brown. (New York: Ivy Books, Paperback, 1988.)

1989   LAZARUS, A.A. (1989). *The Practice of Multimodal Therapy*, updated paperback edition. Baltimore: The Johns Hopkins University Press.

Author Index

Abramovitz, A., 95
Ackerman, J.M., 136
Adams, N.E., 208
Adler, Alfred, 95
Alexander, F., 132
Andersen, B.L., 91
Andrew, B.V., 60
Andrews, G., 187
Ansbacher, H., 95
Ansbacher, R.R., 95
Arkowitz, H., 182
Arnold, M., 75, 76

Ban, T.Z., 53
Bandler, R., 95
Bandura, A., 17, 37, 38, 40, 45, 66, 75, 76, 83, 95, 183, 188, 207-209 *passim*, 224
Barlow, D.H., 160, 188, 224
Beck, A.T., 139, 140, 175
Beitman, B.D., 181, 184-189 *passim*
Bellack, A.S., 188
Bergin, A.E., 63, 91, 92
Bernard, M.E., 175, 209
Beutler, L.E., 188
Beyer, J., 208
Binder, J.L., 222
Blackburn, I.M., 188
Blake, B.G., 64
Blinder, M.G., 53
Bloomfield, H.H., 177
Bookbinder, L.J., 37
Borkovec, T.D., 224
Bowen, M., 222
Bower, G.H., 207
Bozarth, J.D., 94
Brentano, F. 65
Breuer, J., 208
Brewer, W.F., 83, 84
Brown, E.G., 221
Broz, W., 6
Brunell, L.F., 153, 209
Bugelski, B.R., 9

Campbell, D., 74
Chalkley, A.J., 188
Chambers, F.T. (Jr), 4
Chambless, D.L., 188
Clark, D.M., 188
Clarkin, J., 186
Colby, K.M., 64, 89, 95, 222
Coleman, J., 38
Collins, A.M., 207
Corsini, R.J., 19, 205, 222
Crider, A.B., 206
Curran, D., 28

Davanloo, H., 208, 222
Davison, G.C., 78, 80, 95, 104, 122, 138
DeGood, D.E., 224
Dengrove, E., 55
Dickman, S., 121
DiClemente, C.C., 189
DiMatteo, M.R., 134
DiNicola, D.D., 134
Dollard, J., 38, 82
Dryden, W., 183
Duncan, G.M., 54, 56

Edwards, S.S., 153
Efran, J.S., 208
Ellis, A., 51, 68, 75, 76, 78, 83, 139, 140, 175, 199, 209
Ellison, C.R., 161-163 *passim*
English, A.C., 75
English, H.B., 75
Erickson, Milton, 222
Evans, I.M., 94, 104
Eysenck, H.J., 9, 16, 28, 36-40 *passim*, 73, 74, 81, 90, 182, 215

Fairburn, C.G., 188, 224
Fay, Allen, 98, 107, 128, 141, 149, 183, 214, 223
Feather, B.W., 108
Felder, L., 177

Feldman, P., 48
Fenichel, O., 100
Ferster, C.B., 54, 55
Fisch, R., 84, 104
Fisher, R.A., 25
Foa, E.B., 117, 136, 145, 188, 224
Franco, J., 222
Frances, A., 186
Frank, J.D., 64, 71, 92, 94, 95, 222
Franks, C.M., 81, 111, 145
French, T.M., 82, 182
Freud, S., 55, 184, 208
Friedman, J.M., 160, 162, 164, 165
Friedman, P., 36

Garfield, S.L., 91
Geiger, N., 169
Gelder, M.G., 208
Gesell, A., 82
Gillespie, R.D., 28
Glass, G.V., 187, 224
Goldenson, R.M., 160, 161
Goldfield, M.R., 80, 95, 182, 184, 186, 187
Goldman, R., 222
Goldstein, A.P., 95, 106
Gomes-Schwartz, B., 92
Gordon, P.C., 208
Grayson, H., 85
Grayson, J.B., 117, 136, 145, 188, 224
Grencavage, L.M., 186, 187, 189
Grinder, J.E., 95
Grinker, R.R., 74
Guarnaccia, V., 153
Guthrie, E.R., 82

Hadley, S.W., 92
Haley, J., 81, 82, 104, 117
Hall, W., 187
Hampton, P.J., 5
Harper, R.A., 50, 51
Hathaway, S.R., 53
Hayes-Roth, F., 68, 186
Heide, F.J., 224
Heiman, J., 91
Heller, K., 106
Henderson, D., 28
Herink, R., 114, 222
Hersen, M., 188
Hodgson, R., 91, 117, 215
Hogan, D.R., 160, 162, 164, 165
Holden, E.M., 114
Holmes, F.B., 30
Holsopple, J.Q., 12
Holyoak, K.J., 208
Horney, Karen, 199
Howard, G.S., 189
Howarth, I., 224
Hull, C.L., 82

Jacobson, E., 12, 19, 38, 39, 51
Jacobson, N.S., 145

James, William, 206
Janson, W.J., 178
Jellinek, E.M., 5
Jerrelmalm, A., 116
Jersild, A.T., 30
Johansson, J., 116
Johnson, D.W., 104
Johnson, H.K., 40
Johnson, V.E., 66, 91, 161, 187
Johnston, D.W., 208
Jones, H.G., 37
Jones, M.C., 30, 82
Jourard, S.M., 51

Kanfer, F.H., 67, 81
Kaplan, H.S., 160, 161
Karasu, T.B., 179, 186
Kazdin, A.E., 90, 91, 141, 187
Keat, D.B., 153
Kelly, G.A., 78
Kendall, P.C., 187
Kinsey, A.C., 161
Kirschner, D.A., 182
Kirschner, S., 182
Kleine, P.A., 153
Kolle, K., 3
Kora, T., 60
Krasner, L., 81, 83
Krasnogorski, N.I., 74
Krauft, C.C., 94
Kretschmer, E., 82
Kubie, L.S., 82
Kwee, M.G.T., 154

Lambert, M.J., 92
Lang, P.J., 44, 205
Lange, Carl, 206
Laverty, S.G., 74
Lazarus, A.A., 9, 27, 28, 31, 36, 37, 40–42
    passim, 44, 51, 55, 64, 66, 70, 76, 81, 84,
    86, 91, 93, 107, 115, 116, 122, 123, 128,
    138, 142, 143, 149, 153, 155, 163, 165,
    173, 175, 179, 181–189 passim, 209, 210,
    213, 219, 223–225 passim
Lazarus, C.N., 205
Lazarus, R.S., 206–210 passim
Lazovik, A.D., 44
Lehrer, P.M., 188, 224
Leiblum, S.R., 145, 187
Lemere, F., 6
Lesse, S., 64
Levy, L.H., 40
Levy, R.L., 134, 136
Lief, H.I., 161
Light, D., 220
Locke, E.A., 80
Loew, C.A., 85
Loew, G.H., 85
Loftus, E.F., 207
London, P., 51, 78, 82, 144, 183
Longabaugh, R., 68, 186

LoPiccolo, J., 91, 187
LoPiccolo, L., 91, 187
Louccas, K.P., 60
Lowen, A., 66
Luborsky, L., 90, 187

McCulloch, M., 44
McFall, R.M., 144
McKinley, J.C., 51
Maddison, D., 54, 56
Mahoney, M.J., 83
Malan, D.H., 82, 222
Mann, J., 222
Margolin, G., 145
Marks, I.M., 75, 117
Marmor, J., 182
Martin, C.E., 161
Martin, I., 35
Maslow, A.H., 28
Masters, W.H., 66, 91, 161, 187
Mather, M.D., 40, 41
Matross, R.P., 104
Matthews, A.M., 207–208
Mayer-Gross, W., 28
Mayne, T.J., 224
Mays, D.T., 145
Meichenbaum, D.H., 78
Messer, S.B., 182, 183, 187, 189
Meyer, A., 120
Miale, F.R., 12
Milby, J.B., 117
Miller, N.E., 38, 74, 82
Miller, T.I., 187, 224
Miller, W.W., 169
Mills, H.L., 188
Minuchin, S., 82, 222
Mitchell, K.M., 94
Mittelmann, B., 28
Modgil, C., 73
Modgil, S., 73
Moran, C., 187
Mowrer, O.H., 114
Murray, H.A., 12
Myers, P., 189

Nance, D.W., 189
Nichols, M.P., 208
Nisbett, R.E., 207
Norcross, J.C., 181–189 *passim*

O'Leary, K.D., 80, 188
Öst, L-G., 116

Partridge, M., 28
Paul, G.L., 44, 90, 116
Pearl, C., 153
Perls, F.S., 70
Perry, S., 186
Pervin, L.A., 145, 187
Plutchik, R., 205, 206, 208, 210
Pomeroy, W.B., 161

Popper, Karl, 225
Porterfield, A.L., 91
Prochaska, J.O., 189

Rachlin, H., 83
Rachman, S., 9, 10, 16, 28, 36, 40, 74, 75, 84, 91, 117, 133, 187, 188, 214, 215
Rayner, R., 74
Razran, G.H.S., 84
Reckless, J., 169
Redd, W.H., 91
Reisman, J.M., 63
Rescorla, R.A., 185
Rhoades, J.M., 108
Ridley, C.R., 153
Rogers, Carl, 81, 215
Rokeach, M., 75
Rosen, R.C., 187
Roth, M., 28
Rush, A.J., 188, 207
Ryback, R., 68, 186

Salkovskis, P.M., 188
Salter, A., 4, 8, 13, 40, 51, 103
Sanderson, R.E., 74
Sank, L.I., 153
Saslow, G., 67
Schofield, W., 95, 145
Sechrest, L.B., 106
Seitz, P.F.D., 39
Shapiro, D., 187
Shapiro, D.A., 187
Shaw, F., 82
Shelton, J.L., 134, 136
Sherman, M.H., 107
Shevrin, H., 121
Sifneos, P., 222
Singer, B., 90, 187
Skinner, B.F., 54
Slater, E., 28
Slowinski, J.W., 153
Smith, D., 188, 224
Smith, M.L., 187, 224
Sobotka, J.J., 169
Spiegal, J.P., 74
Spielberg, G., 147, 148
Stafford-Clark, D., 60
Steketee, G., 117, 136, 145, 188, 224
Stenstedt, A., 53
Strecker, E.A., 4
Strupp, H., 81, 92, 222
Sturm, I.E., 44, 48

Turner, R.M., 117

Ullmann, L.P., 81

Valins, S., 78
Voegtlin, W.L., 6

Wachtel, P.L., 182

Walters, R.H., 37, 40
Walton, D., 40, 41
Watson, J.B., 74
Watzlawick, P., 84, 104
Weakland, J., 84, 104
Weed, L.L., 68, 186
Wells, H.K., 40
Whitaker, C., 222
Wilkins, W., 94
Williams, E.M., 224
Williams, T.A., 82
Willoughby, R., 11
Wilson, G.T., 80, 81, 90, 91, 94, 95, 104, 111, 133, 141, 187, 188, 214, 224
Wilson, T.D., 207
Wincze, J.P., 160
Winokur, M., 183
Wohlgemuth, A., 40

Wolberg, L.R., 22
Wolf, C.M., 147, 148
Wolf, S., 147, 148
Wolpe, J., 9, 13, 16, 17, 20, 27, 28, 30, 31, 36-44 *passim*, 51, 55, 73-76 *passim*, 83, 84, 93, 141, 187, 209
Woods, S.M., 182
Woodworth, R.S., 84
Woody, R.H., 63
Woolfolk, R.L., 188, 224

Yates, A.J., 37
Young, W.T., 153, 209

Zajonc, R.B., 206-208 *passim*
Zener, K., 84
Zilbergeld, B., 30, 122, 161-163 *passim*, 173, 175

Subject Index

addiction
   cigarette, 91
   see also alcoholism
affect, *see* BASIC I.D., emotions
agoraphobia, 188
   clinical case study, 193-204 *passim*
Alcoholics Anonymous, 7
alcoholism, 1-7
   defined, 2-4
   therapy for, 5-7
antidepressants, 57, 188
anxiety
   vs depression, 55-56
   multimodal view of, 210
   see also phobic disorders
assessment
   of depression, 56-57
   multimodal, 66-68, 115-118 *passim*,
      122-132 *passim*, 195-199
   sex therapy, 163-166, 171-172
   tracking in multimodal, 199
   see also BASIC I.D.
avoidance, 130
   see also resistance

'bad therapy', 146-148
BASIC I.D., 65, 120-121, 124, 129, 163,
      210-213 *passim*
   modality firing order, 148-149, 199
   second-order assessments, 131-132
   in sex therapy, 163-166
behavior rehearsal, 38, 39, 136, 152
   defined, 44
   vs other approaches, 46-48
behavior therapy, 9-10, 36-42 *passim*
   vs behaviorism, 80
   clinical material, 10-15, 38-39
   critique of, 80-86
   emotion and, 209
   multimodal, 62-71, 132-138
   outcome superiority of, 187-188
   in treating depression, 57-61

   see also behavior rehearsal;
      cognitive-behavior therapy;
      conditioning; learning theory
behaviorism, 80, 82
   see also behavior therapy; conditioning
bibliotherapy, 140
   in sex therapy, 173, 175
bridging, 130-131
bulimia nervosa, 188

case histories, *see* clinical material
change, *see* therapeutic change
client-centered therapy, 94
   see also non-directive therapy
clinical material
   assessment of depression, 56-57
   behavior rehearsal, 45
   behavior therapy, 10-15, 38-39
   bridging, 130-131
   case of George, 193-204
   client cooperation, 134-136
   client resistance, 150-151
   cognitive restructuring, 77-78
   cognitive therapy, 139-140
   depression, 58-59
   emotive imagery for phobias, 32-34
   homework assignments, 136-138
   multimodal assessment, 115-116
   multimodal behavior therapy, 68-70,
      134-138
   multimodal sex therapy, 169-179
   obsessive-compulsive disorders, 40-41
   paradoxical procedure, 107-108
   problem identification, 67-68
   resistance, 105, 107-110 *passim*
   time projection, 142-143
cognition, 124-125
   behavior therapy and, 83-84
   -emotion debate, 206-208
   and sexual dysfunction, 164
cognitive restructuring
   desensitization and, 73-79 *passim*

cognitive therapy
  for depression, 188
  multimodal, 138-141
  see also cognitive-behavior therapy;
      cognitive restructuring
cognitive-behavior therapy, 80, 138
  for bulimia nervosa, 188
  technical eclecticism in, 187
  see also behavior therapy; cognitive
      restructuring; cognitive therapy
conditioning, 73-76 *passim*
  in alcoholism, 3
  critique of, 82-84 *passim*
  see also behavior therapy; behaviorism

depression
  affective expression and, 59-60
  vs anxiety, 55-56
  clinical assessment of, 56-57
  cognitive therapy for, 188
  definitional issues, 53-55
  learning theory in treating, 53-61 *passim*
  modality profile of, 212-213
  time-projection technique, 58-59
desensitization
  and cognitive restructuring, 73-79 *passim*
  resistance to, 108
  see also systematic desensitization
deserted island fantasy, 143-144
drug treatment, 125, 126, 141
  effects on sexual desire, 162, 164
  for panic disorders, 188
dysfunctional beliefs, 140-141

eclecticism
  vs fusionism, 182
  Lazarus's, 181-192, 225
  see also technical eclecticism
electroconvulsive therapy (ECT), 56
emotions, 205-217
  cognition-emotion debate, 206-208
  definitions of, 205
  modifying affect, 214-215
  and psychotherapy, 208-209
emotive imagery
  for children's phobias, 30-35
  defined, 31

fusionism, 182

generalization fallacy, 114
gestalt therapy, 66
grief, vs depression, 55
group therapy
  of phobic disorders, 17-29 *passim*

homework assignments, 152
  client compliance with, 136-138
  resistance to, 101-102
hypnotic procedures, 15-16
  for depression, 58-59

imagery, 124
  clinical material, 173-174
  coping, 152-153, 198
  projected, 153
  and sexual dysfunctions, 164
  see also emotive imagery
incomplete treatment, 37
integrationism, 181-183
  equality-of-outcomes myth, 187-188
  ill-defined labeling and, 186-187
  objections to (Lazarus), 183-184
interpretation
  group, 22-23, 24-29 *passim*

learning, 9
  behavior disorders and, 121
  implicit, 207
  see also learning theory; social learning
      theory
learning theory
  and treating depression, 53-61
  see also social learning theory

medication, *see* drug treatment
meta-analysis, 187
metacommunication, 121
Morita therapy, 60
multimodal (behavior) therapy, 62-71, 86,
      120-158, 189
  assessment in, 115-118 *passim*, 122-132
      passim, 195-199
  behavioral strategies, 132-138
  clinical case study, 193-204
  cognitive therapy in, 138-141
  emotions and, 209-217
  fostering generalization, 152-153
  modality profile, 124-125, 196-197,
      212-213
  Multimodal Life History Questionnaire,
      123-124, 171
  non-behavioral/cognitive strategies, 141-144
  overall effectiveness of, 154-155
  preventing resistance, 148-151
  problem identification, 67-68
  for schizophrenia, 213-214
  session structure, 129-131
  for sexual desire problems, 163-180
  structural profile, 125-126
  theory of disorders in, 120-122
  tracking in, 199
  treatment of affect in, 141
  treatment stages in, 127-129
  see also BASIC I.D.

narcosis, 60
non-compliance, *see* resistance
non-conscious processes, 121, 185
non-directive therapy
  vs behavior rehearsal, 46-48 *passim*
  see also client-centered therapy
nymphomania, 160

obsessive–compulsive disorders, 40–42,
    90–91, 188
  clinical material, 40–41
  specificity factor in, 116–117

panic disorders, 188
  see also agoraphobia
paradoxical procedures, 84, 104
  clinical material, 107–108
pessimism, 211
phobic disorders, 36–37, 84, 91, 188
  clinical material, 32–34
  cognitive restructuring and, 76–77
  conditioning and, 73–75 passim
  emotive imagery in children's, 30–35
  systematic desensitization for, 17–29
psychoanalysis, 40, 66, 82, 121
  emotion and, 208–209
  the unconscious in, 184
psychotherapy, 8–16
  for alcoholism, 5–6
  as an art, 95–96
  boundaries in, 220
  causes of change in, 89–96
  and emotion, 208–209
  equality of outcomes in, 187–188
  ill-defined labels in, 186–187
  limits of, 111–112
  meta-analysis of, 187
  schools of, 221–223
  specificity factor in, 114–119
  systems approach to, 109
  termination of, 128–129
  training, 219–220
  treatment errors in, 146–148
  treatment impasse in, 151
  see also behavior therapy; client-centered
      therapy; cognitive therapy; gestalt
      therapy; group therapy; Morita therapy;
      non-directive therapy; psychoanalysis;
      rational–emotive therapy; reciprocal
      inhibition therapy; sex therapy

rational–emotive therapy, 78
  emotion and, 209
reciprocal inhibition (therapy), 17, 27, 30–31,
    83
relaxation training, 224
  see also systematic desensitization
resistance, 98–112 passim
  clinical material, 105–110 passim
  (counter)control, 102–105
  to homework assignments, 101–102
  individual characteristics and, 106–108
  interpersonal relationships and, 108–109
  limits of therapy and, 111–112
  multimodal prevention of, 148–151
  as psychodynamic mechanism, 100
  to the therapist, 109–111
  see also avoidance

role-play, 44–46 passim

satyriasis, 160
schizophrenia, 213–214
self-disclosure, 147
self-efficacy, 95
sex therapy, 66, 91, 145
  assessment in, 163–166, 171–172
  clinical material, 169–179
  desire discrepancies, 162, 166–169
  hyperactive desire, 159–160
  hypoactive desire, 160–163
  multimodal approach, 159–180
sleep therapy, 60
social learning theory, 37, 66
  see also learning theory
specificity factor, 114–119
  and multimodal assessment, 115–116
  and obsession–compulsion, 116–117
symptom substitution, 36–37, 41–42
systematic desensitization, 17–29 passim, 31
  effectiveness of, 187–188
  group, 20–22

technical eclecticism, 50–52, 70, 182–186
    passim
  vs theoretical, 132–139
techniques
  deserted island fantasy, 143–144
  empty chair, 144
  Rogerian reflection, 144
  time projection, 58–59, 142–143
  see also technical eclecticism
therapeutic change, 64, 133
  causes of, 89–96
  faith/hope in, 95
  non-specific factors in, 94
  self-efficacy in, 95
  theory of multimodal, 122–132
  therapist expectancy and, 94–95
therapeutic relationship, 17, 128, 145
  and techniques, 183, 204
therapist
  expectancies, 94–95
  intuition, 156
  note-taking, 129–130
  resistance to, 109–111
  role in multimodal therapy, 145–148
  self-disclosure, 147
  see also therapeutic relationship
thresholds, 121
time projection technique, 58–59, 142–143
treatment sequence, 127–129

vitamin therapy (alcoholism), 5–6

weight reduction, 91

WM420 BR4